# LIBRARY
# OF
# WALLS

# LIBRARY OF WALLS

THE LIBRARY OF CONGRESS
AND THE CONTRADICTIONS
OF INFORMATION SOCIETY

by

Samuel Gerald Collins

Litwin Books, LLC
Duluth, Minnesota

Published in 2009 by Litwin Books
P.O. Box 3320
Duluth, MN 55803
http://litwinbooks.com/

This book is printed on acid-free paper meeting present ANSI standards
for archival preservation.

Cover designed by Topher McCulloch
Interior designed by Gwendolyn Prellwitz

Library of Congress Cataloging-in-Publication Data

Collins, Samuel Gerald.
    Library of walls : the Library of Congress and the contradictions of infor-
mation society / by Samuel Gerald Collins.
        p. cm.
    Includes bibliographical references and index.
    ISBN 978-0-9802004-2-3 (alk. paper)
    1. Library of Congress. 2. Library of Congress. National Digital Library
Program. 3. Information society--United States. 4. Library of Congress--In-
formation technology. 5. National libraries--United States. 6. Digital librar-
ies--United States.
I. Title.
Z733.U6C593 2009
025.1'97573--dc22                                                    2008042285

# TABLE OF CONTENTS

# FOREWORD

My first experience of what would become Samuel Gerald Collins' *Library of Walls* came several years back, when I was an editor for the journal *Reconstruction* <reconstruction.eserver.org>. My editorial curiosity was piqued by the title of an article that Collins submitted for consideration in a special issue of the journal on "Technology and Historiography," guest-edited by Haidee Wasson. The title: "Reading Over the Shoulder of the Future at the Library of Congress." In one phrase, the writer had managed to tie my scholarly interest in "futurism" and "information" to my post-9/11 concerns about "surveillance" and "democracy" and to ground it in the unsexy Library of Congress. At a time when I was reading submissions on video games, TV, and comics (all things that I write about, by the way), I was stunned by Collin's willingness to take on such a daunting subject. In those few words, I had been taken in by his ability to find a node where disparate discursive lines converge to form a site of meaning that could provide insights into the larger cultural landscape. After wading into the first few paragraphs I was blown away.

When I got the chance to read an early draft of Collins' completed manuscript, I leapt at the opportunity, expecting a more fully-fleshed out discussion of the ideas explored in the article. Instead, it was much, much more. The experience was something akin to watching a reality show featuring Jorge Luis Borges, Marshall McLuhan, Michel Foucault, Lewis Mumford, and Paul Virilio in the Library of Congress—surreal twists of perspective, profound insights into mass media, piercing critiques of power, solid sociocultural observations, and dire warnings about the future—twisting through a maze of stacks and fiber optic cables at the heart of the American political establishment. This is no mere book about libraries (though it is that, too), it is an ambitious investigation of the Information Society itself—its mythology, economics, and politics.

Ultimately, the strength of *Library of Walls* rests in the utter appropriateness of its topic. The temporal situation of the archive, both as an attempt to account for a history of the present as required by a future that does not exist yet and as a fragmented account of the past, offers a compelling account of the process of culture as both historically rooted and up for grabs. It is culture in the "future perfect," determined but not overly so, free but not without limit. And the Library of Congress is the archive par excellence. It tells a valuable story of American history, but, more importantly, it maps traces of the new world order, the neoliberal priorities of an emerging global marketplace, and the practices of the new economy. Fortunately, Collins is able to connect these dots with creativity, skill, and originality.

Collins maps sweeping changes in the Library's vision and management against changing attitudes towards knowledge and public life and technical innovations. Each period of expansion of the Library of Congress is characterized by an attempt to anticipate its place in society against succeeding information revolutions. In each case, Collins is careful to ground the potentially mystifying field of information in material practices that make such revolutions possible. Budgets, building construction, library use, and human labor all factor into Collins' analysis of the ideologically-loaded idea of "information." Coupled with his predilection for critical theory, science fiction, and new media, Collins' training as an anthropologist and his hours of careful ethnography provide a perspective that subverts the naive utopianism propagated by commercial interests, reminding readers that information is not a simple product detached from the people that create, organize, consume, and reproduce it. In Collins' formulation, information is intimately linked to human subjects, a point which is too often lost in our current fascination with the many dazzling new media technologies.

Especially telling is the attention Collins devotes to the dramatic changes afoot in the Library since the 1980s—both in terms of the rapid rate of technological change and its impact on archiving, organization, and distribution and shifts in the political landscape which began in the Reagan era. Against the rise of technology, Collins maps the minimization of labor. Consistent with industrial trends like outsourcing, downsizing, and deskilling, the Information Society ethos of the Library's management seeks to free information from the human hands that build the archives, the eyes that interpret its meaning, and the minds that will subsist on the symbolic order of its future. In its place, this new order offers information detached from any democratic purpose or historical context, information as a consumer good. Collins notes that this Information Society, though it seems swathed in the postmodern notion of relativistic, post-political egalitarianism, is heavily laden with ideological assumptions and real consequences for working people. In *Library of Walls* Collins obliterates the neoliberal fairytale of liberty through consumerism, and illustrates its contradictions through the definitive record of American culture.

Thankfully, Collins is not the only scholar who has identified the cracks in the edifice of power. But with his awareness of his discipline's troubling imperial legacy alongside its invaluable ethnographic tools, Collins the anthropologist provides a unique perspective on the cracks in the edifice. And through his topic, "a library of walls," Collins succeeds in identifying the edifice itself with staggering accuracy.

Adrian, Michigan                                                    Davin Heckman

# ACKNOWLEDGEMENTS

This book is based on my dissertation, "'Knowledge Will Forever Govern Ignorance'" (American University, 1998). Chapter 6 has been published in a special, conference proceedings issue of the *Journal of American Studies* (Korea), as "Corporeal Labor at the Virtual Library" (1998). Small parts of several, other chapters were published as "Reading Over the Shoulder of the Future at the Library of Congress" in *Reconstruction* 4(1).

Revising this manuscript for publication has reminded me of the many people who helped me through this process, and I want to reiterate my thanks to people at the Library of Congress, to my faculty advisor, Professor Brett Williams, and to my dissertation committee. The final stage of this research was underwritten by the Harvey and Sara Moore Fellowship; my thanks to American University's anthropology department for the award.

## CHAPTER 1

# Introduction:
# If On A Winter's Night A Reader

You would like to begin reading Samuel Collins's book, *Library of Walls: the Library of Congress and the Contradictions of Information Society.*[1] But there is some distance, Other Reader, between a desire to read, the imagination of reading and the enactment of reading. You'd like to relax. You'd like to: "Concentrate. Dispel every other thought," pick up the book and go sit at your desk, recline on your chair, lie on your bed, flip through the ponderous tome, pick out what you want and be *done* (Calvino 1981:3). But it's not really that simple, is it?

When you saw the book listed on the Litwin Books website (www.litwin-books.com), it piqued your interest, but only piqued! There might be something there useful to your own research, your own dissertation, that article you've been working on for six months. But, again, there might not be! In any case, however Samuel Collins's monograph might pan out, you are unlikely to spend the money for a copy of the thing. I mean, the halcyon days when your university or your job would pay for anything are long gone, aren't they?

But perhaps you don't need to shell out the cash for the book, after all. With a twitch of your mouse, you click on to a search engine. And chances are (and whether you like it or not), it will be Google. You type

---

1 This introduction shadows Italo Calvino's novel of intertextuality and metonymy, *if on a winter's night a traveler* (Calvino 1981). More than a novel about reading, the novel connects a train of vignettes about readers. Calvino's work strikes me as a good place to begin: in the interstices between reading, "between the book and the lamp," as Foucault has said of Flaubert's The Temptation (Foucault 1977:90).

What the following attempts to do is to, in some ways, slip behind the egoism of the page into the systems, social relations and institutions that make it possible in the first place. It is a tall order in a time infatuated with the book —and its electronic, textualized fetches—but unconcerned with the table that props it up. To look behind the curtain of our end-of-millennium graphophilia/bibliomania is to look into the corona of "information society," that place where our dreams of knowledge and enlightened, empowered politics are recombined into the commodity of information.

---

in "Library of Walls" and, within .15 seconds, the results flash onto your monitor.

Well, that didn't work. Or, rather, it worked, but too well. Out of the 1,000,000 hits (including the "Library Without Walls" project at Los Alamos Laboratories), Samuel Collins's book, *Library Of Walls*, is conspicuous by its absence. Or, rather, in this era of attention deficit, you no longer have the wherewithal to scroll down much past the first page. Is there another place?

"Books.google.com" coughs up rather fewer hits: just 1400. Several entries down the page, success: Samuel Collins's *Library of Walls*, complete with cover facsimile *and* there's full text! Or, wait: "some pages are omitted"; it's a copyrighted work, after all, and the pages you'd like, Other Reader, are not available. Of course, there are links to online book vendors. Oh, well, this isn't a library, you know; somebody's got to make money. But, after the online vendors have been given their due, there's another link: "Find This Book in a Library." Maybe you could find it at your own university library? Using seamless protocols integrating WorldCat into Google, the closest libraries with the text in question pop up.

But that's no good either. Your university library is a no-show on this list, and you're sorely tempted to give up this scholarly micro-enterprise. But let's say that you pick up the telephone.

"Hello," you say to the librarian at the other end of the telephone, "I'm looking for a book." "Yes, I know that the our library doesn't have it. I just want to know where I can find it." "Interlibrary loan?" "Up to 2 weeks?" Although there are those scholars who would persevere here, you, Other Reader, are not one of them. But what if you were going to be at a library with larger collections? What if you were going to the Library of Congress?

Of course, as the Library repeatedly cautions researchers, they *do not* have every book that's been published. But let's say, for argument's sake, that you go to www. loc.gov, consult their online catalog, and find the catalog record for this book.

And maybe you have a conference to attend, a paper to give, some family to see, an acquaintance to renew, a job to interview for or, perhaps, you're going there with the family to see the Smithsonian museums, the Corcoran Gallery, an opera at the Kennedy Center or jazz at the Lincoln Theater. So: amidst all of the other foofaraw in your life, you *might* have some time to stop there, at the Library of Congress, and give the thing a look.

You're in Washington, D.C., Other Reader. Maybe you've driven in for the weekend down Interstate 95, maybe you've taken a train up from Atlanta, Georgia or flown into National Airport from parts unknown. However you've gotten here and for whatever reason, the city opens up for you: its stentorian traffic, its grand, though pockmarked, boulevards, the full kaleidoscope of gardens that embroider the yards of even the most modest homes. It all stirs some excitement for you, even if you are a bit of a jaded *flaneur*.

You've checked into your hotel at Dupont Circle now, or on New York Avenue, or at Metro Center. Or perhaps you're staying with friends you met in school, or in the Peace Corps or the Army. Or maybe you're with relatives that left your small, Southern town sixty years ago. It's great to keep up these ties with people, however distant they are from your life right now.

You tell the cab driver to let you off at the Mall and, after lots of traffic lights and a little commotion, you're standing on its broad, grassy expanse, circumferenced by a gravel path rife with joggers and tourists. The Smithsonian Castle, an architectural malapropism with its ambitious, Gothic spires, squats in front of you. It's tempting to go to the museums now, but there will be time for that later. There's a man with a backpack wearing a dress shirt walking past you. He doesn't look like a tourist.

"Where's the Library of Congress?" you ask.

"Well," he answers, "There's three main buildings to the Library of Congress, plus a score of subsidiary branches housing different collections. What are you looking for?"

You're taken aback by his annoying pedantry and his ingratiating manner, but you answer anyway. "A book about the Library of Congress."

"Ah," he continues, "Then you want the Jefferson Building; it's right at the top of the hill. You can see the dome rising behind the Capitol."

There it is. The oxidized copper-green dome shadows the slightly menacing white of the Capitol Dome. It doesn't look that far off, and you turn and walk down a gravel walk towards the rising Capitol, past the Botanic Garden Conservatory and up Independence Avenue.

The Jefferson Building is a huge pile of granite with massive keystone arches surrounded by a gently landscaped garden. It is, you decide, somewhat in the "Renaissance style," particularly if you don't look too closely. Its front overlooks the Capitol Building and you enter under the stairs of the Main Entrance. Inside, you pause to remove metal objects from your pockets and you run your backpack through the x-ray machine. Inside, finally, you can't help but gasp at the vaulted arcade of the Great Hall, bounded by a labyrinth of arches and countless, decorative flourishes. But a guard informs you that this, in fact, is not the *reader's* entrance to the Library, but the *tourist's* entrance. You'll have to walk around to the other side.

A little abashed, you walk back out into the afternoon. At the back of the Library, on 2nd Street, it's a little more business-like; the parking lot's full of cars and there's a catering company unloading folding tables into a large garage. On the far side of the garage, near some picnic tables, you see an entrance, but it doesn't look like much.

"This entrance for staff, researchers, and persons on official business only." Well, you aren't staff and you aren't here on official business. You're definitely a *reader*, but do you rank as a bonafide *researcher*? I mean, you're here to read a book, not write one! Perhaps there's another, semi-official, entrance for the likes of you? One that looks less like a loading dock?

Well, there isn't, and you certainly feel stupid for walking around the building again. You go into the forbidding back entrance and, at the end of the short hallway past the vestibule, you again deposit your cell phone and change into a plastic bowl and allow your backpack to be scanned.

"Where can I find the Main Reading Room?" you ask, a little anxious now that it seems like you're actually getting somewhere.

"Hold on. If you want to check out materials, you have to register first. Go downstairs and take the hallway over the Madison Building. On the first floor of the Madison Building, look for Room 140, Reader Registration Services."

Not really sure what to do, you reluctantly walk down the stairwell to the basement. But it can't be right—it looks like the inside of a factory, not a library; there's machinery clattering overhead and you can even hear a buzz saw off in the distance. But, sure enough, there's a sign pointing in the direction of the Madison Building, and you follow the tunnel past library staff wheeling book trucks into the Madison Building, up the stairs again, and, after a couple of false starts, to Reader Registration Services in Room 140. In this spartan office, you present ID and a staff member sits you down at a computer terminal. Where do you live, Other Reader? How much education have you had? What are your primary research interests? What materials do you think you'll use most often: photographs, monographs, microfiche or sound recordings? Do you really have to divulge all these details of your life? You scroll through all the possibilities and click onto some for good measure. You're here for a book now, but, who knows? Maybe you'll undertake some vast, genealogical project later. Next, you "sign" on a digitized writing pad and a young man takes your picture. Smiling, the young man gives you your completed "Reader Identification Card." You'll be pleased to know you have been verified!

You trudge back down through the tunnel to the Jefferson Building, ascend the stairs and stop, again, to check your backpack in at the Cloak Room before going upstairs to Room 100, the Main Reading Room, where you present your reader card and sign the visitor's book. Sitting at one of the simple carrels, you lean back to take in the soaring dome, the art, and the warm, yellow light glancing off the room's brown marble. But what about the books? Back to the entrance, where one of the reference librarians helps you fill out a call slip with the title of the book, the author and the call number. Back in the center of the room, deck attendants accept and stamp your request, where they shoot it off in a pneumatic tube where it's picked up by another deck attendant.

"We should have it up here in about forty-five minutes," she says, "We'll bring it to your desk."

Forty-five minutes? Well, you can wait in the Main Reading Room or even walk back around the building to the tourist's entrance to see the exhibits.

But, whatever you do, Other Reader, when those forty-five minutes are up you're back in the Main Reading Room looking for your book.

But, instead of a book, someone has placed a small slip of paper on your desk. Someone has printed "N.O.S" across the slip. What does "N.O.S" mean?

"Not on shelf," says the woman behind the desk.

Hmm![2]

Italo Calvino's *if on a winter's night a traveler* is a romance of the postmodern reader, the "Reader" who occupies the second person position in Calvino's mystery/romance/*bildungsroman* and is swept along by successive waves of vertiginous desire for the book. In the story, a Reader (male, middle class, vaguely intellectual) searches for an illusive, originary text: the authentic Calvino. Events are set into motion when "You," the Reader, purchase Italo Calvino's new novel, *if on a winter's night a traveler*, begin to read it and discover that, through a printer's mistake, Calvino's novel has been replaced with "the Polish novel *Outside the Town of Malbork* by Tazio Bazakbal" (Calvino 1981:28). However, tracking down Bazakbal's novel only leads to another, *leaning from the steep slope*, and so on, each story opening into the next in a dizzy, dreamlike train of desire for narrative closure. Its moral lesson stems from an almost anti-*bildungsroman*: the accretion of experiences (readings) leads not to the formation of the subject, but to the dissolution of the subject. In the end, there is no "originary" text to return to.

Predictably, perhaps, the hierarchy of subject and object is preserved in the gendered relations of readings, for Calvino's "meta-novel" is also the romance of the Reader (male, middle class, vaguely intellectual) for the "Other Reader" (female, middle class, vaguely intellectual) and the desire for the (elusive) *body* of the text is also the desire for the (acquiescent) body of Ludmilla, the Other Reader, a lover of books and the narrative foil to the Reader's bibliophilia. As Teresa de Lauretis points out, the Other Reader wants only to *read* (de Lauretis 1987).

> She won't even go to the publishing company's office in order not to cross the boundary between those who make books and those who read them. She wants to remain a reader, "on principle." (Calvino 1981:79)

Ludmilla is the ultimate, postmodern partner to the Reader, fascinated with the text, eager to chase down the metonymic chains of signification and prisoner of that somewhat witless Barthean adage that "Every text, being itself the intertext of another text, belongs to the intertextual" (Roland Barthes, quoted in Conquergood 1992:109). The Reader and his phallic projection—Woman Reader—are, ultimately, the postmodern *topoi* for an age that elevates reading over knowing and the quotation of surfaces over the comprehension of structure (Jameson 1991). It is this willingness to continue reading against hope, against criticism and against, ultimately, understanding, that brings together these two readers; it is their purposeful surrender to the world of intertextuality that structures their relationship.

Calvino's novel certainly confirms the conservative, reactionary proclivities of some strains of postmodern thought: is this a brave, new world beyond history,

---

2　The unfortunate truth, as Micaela di Leonardo has written of the work of Michael Taussig, is that bad storytelling is never a substitute for good ethnography (di Leonardo 1997).

beyond identity, or just literary formalism carried on by *other means* (Erkkila 1995)? However, there is an alternative ending to Calvino's novel, one centering on the Other Reader's much-maligned sister, Lortaria, the political feminist who refuses to keep her place in the *salon* of formalist literary interpretation.

> If you start arguing, she'll never let you go. Now she is inviting you to a seminar at the university where books are analyzed according to all Codes, Conscious Unconscious, and in which all Taboos are eliminated, the ones imposed by the dominant Sex, Class, and Culture. (Calvino 1981:45)

It is the figure of Lortaria who offers us a way out of the smoke and mirrors of the postmodern signified into the world of historical, institutional literary practice (de Lauretis 1987). By re-reading *if on a winter's night a traveler* through the (unjustly) maligned Lortaria, we begin to notice that this interminable desire for reading and readers is imbricated at every turn by sociohistorical forces: publishing housing, universities, nationalisms, ethnicities and imperialism. All of these fuel Calvino's metonymic engine, even as he consigns them to the *deus ex machina* of his narrative proscenium. Only in the last instance, is this a romance of reading and readers!

## Where Once Were Readers: The End Of The Gutenberg Age

My fascination with the Library of Congress begins with an apparent paradox. The twenty-first century seems to spell—if we believe all of the paeans to the lost art of the book and the death of the classics—the end of reading and the superimposition of glossy and shallow multimedia over the archetype of reader and book. As biblical scholar Robert Alter perorates:

> The neo-Marxist critic Terry Eagleton shows admirable candor and consistency in proposing that a curricular move be made from literature to "discourse studies," so that instructors would be free to teach Shakespeare, television scripts, government memoranda, comic books, and advertising copy in a single program as instances of the language of power. What is regrettable, though also characteristic of a certain ideological coerciveness, is that Eagleton also proposes the abolition of departments of literature, having demonstrated, at least to his own satisfaction, that there is no coherent phenomena that can be called literature. (Alter 1989:13-14)

The "classics," according to these essayists, have been deposed in favor of fleeting, if more inclusive, works while the silvered thread of Western civilization has been fragmented into insouciant eddies of identity politics. Indeed, both postmodernism's jocular nihilists and embittered conservatives seem convinced of the dissolution of Western knowledge into the anomie of schizophrenic information. As James Billington, Head Librarian of the Library of Congress, confessed:

> I am haunted by the thought that all the miscellaneous, unsorted, unverified, constantly changing information on the Internet may inundate knowledge, may move us back down the evolutionary chain from knowledge to information, from information to raw data. (Billington 1996:38)

Billington's and Alter's concerns both echo a common postmodernist insight that twenty-first century knowledge has been shorn of its semantic content under the detritus of undifferentiated information flows, that endless profusion of signs (Baudrillard 1983).

On the other hand, it seems to me, *reading* has never been so widespread as it is now. This is not the triumph of the computer over the book, it is the triumph of *reading* over other instanciations of social and political life. The computer is the *reading machine par excellence*. The only reason the E.D. Hirsches, Alan Blooms and Robert Alters of the world complain over the demise of reading is because the act has become universalized in an age obsessed with the interpretation of textual orders. No longer the special province of litterateurs and critics, "reading" has been *popularized*, with all the attendant inequalities that it implies.[3] Almost all aspects of life have been penetrated by the logic of the readerly; even wars and executions become somehow diaphanous in the age of information, the flesh falling away to reveal the "message" beneath. Our relationships and the practice of our everyday lives seem less important than the auto-referentiality of the messages we send. "Today, the President sent a message to Congress," drones National Public Radio, cutting to the chase of interpretation and neatly eliding the tragedy of world events for the semiotic gems hidden just beneath their tortured flesh.

> From TV to newspapers, from advertising to all sorts of mercantile epiphanies, our society is characterized by a cancerous growth of vision, measuring everything by its ability to show or be shown and transmuting communication into a visual journey. It is a sort of *epic* of the eye and of the impulse to read. The economy itself, transformed into a "semeiocracy" (26), encourages a hypertrophic development of reading. (de Certeau 1984:xxi)

Is it possible to elegize the Gutenberg Age even as we blast off into the Gutenberg Galaxy? How can our society be reading less even as it reads more? Better yet, how do we theorize a society where *semiology* has replaced *bibliology* and where it may be more important to read one's t-shirt and blue jeans than Richardson's *Clarissa* or Eliot's *The Mill On the Floss* (Eco 1986; Fiske 1989)?

These (apparent) contradictions and (feeble) ironies have become a familiar part of the rocky topography of "information society," those revolutionary changes in the way we live, work and exist that are, for some, a bygone conclusion and, for others, still a site of shadowy emergence. Sometimes linked to greater *quantities* of information technologies, information workers or infor-

---

3    This erstwhile "reading" is itself a recent development in our social lives. As Elizabeth Long, Jonathan Boyarin and others have pointed out, *reading* is thoroughly social and historical, changing throughout history and across culture and identity (Boyarin 1993).

7

mation production and, at other times, to the logarithmic growth of images steadily approaching an asymptote of oblivion, "information society" is at once solid *and* indistinct. In a 1995 book, sociologist Frank Webster sketches the theories of "information society" and finds them all lacking convincing, evidential force.

> One can scarcely have confidence in a concept when its defenders diagnose it in quite different ways. Moreover, these criteria, ranging from technology to occupational features to spatial features, though they appear at first glance robust, are in truth vague and imprecise, incapable on their own of establishing whether or not an 'information society' has arrived or will arrive at some time in the future. (Webster 1995: 29)

This is doubly ironic given information society pundits' predilection for *quantifiers* of social change and their insistence on marking the arrival of an entirely new era.[4] Can we truly distinguish a new epoch of life and work from what went before? What measure do we use? Is "information society" a matter of value? Of labor? Of power?

It is my belief that "information society" is none (or all) of these things or, at least, that whether or not the "information age" is *here* or *on its way* is not the most interesting question we could be asking. After all, when we find it reasonable or even desirable to compare the "rate" of knowledge production today to that of tenth century Europe, we are already in the midst of "information society." Rather, what seems to most distinguish the past, say, fifty years from the century or so preceding them is the insistence on using ideas of "information" as benchmarks of change, harbingers of the future and messengers from the past. In an "information age," "information" becomes a measurement of *worth*, of *productivity* and *efficiency*, as well as an index of *control* and *oppression*. In short, "information" telescopes all of the contradictions and tensions of modernity.

This book is an ethnography of something called "information society" at the Library of Congress (LC), the *de facto* national library for the United States located (mostly) in Washington, D.C.[5] My work there began in Summer of 1992, when I interned at the American Folklife Center in the LC's "Cultural Affairs" division. That summer, I did some archival work, a little filing and writing, but I was, I think, a rather lackadaisical intern. My real fascination was

---

4    A balance sheet of theorists who interpret "information society" as a definitive break with the past versus those that see today's society as an (accelerated) continuation of the past shows an instructive, if predictable, split between postmodernists and political economists (Webster 1995:25).

5    The Library began in 1800 as a legislative collection for Congress housed in the Capitol building. Over the intervening two centuries, the LC has grown into a complex of buildings housing over 110 million items, making it the largest library in the world. There are several excellent histories of the Library of Congress, notably Salamanca (1942), Mearns (1947) and Cole (1993).

the Library itself: its discombobulating procedures shifting in a heartbeat from stunning displays of organized knowledge to low comedies of loquacious waste and suffocating inertia. The parts of my summer I enjoyed the most—repatriating collections of books between departments, researching steam threshers for some Congressperson misusing legislative authority (was there a steam thresher bill I haven't heard of?), delivering memoranda to other departments in other buildings—seemed, to my co-interns, a trifle bizarre, considering the wealth of fascinating ethnographic and ethnomusicological collections housed in the AFC. From fall of 1994 until summer of 1996, I returned to do field research on this, the LC's "information society." Over those twenty months, my roles shifted continuously. Although I was, much of the time, an ethnographer plying my interlocutors with questions, I also had the opportunity to wear other hats: a contract researcher ransacking the Library's catalogs, a historian engaged in the work of social history and even a tourist wandering the LC's exhibits and sitting through its (self) promotional films. But the most interesting, entertaining and engaging parts of this "information society" of almost five thousand employees (at its height in the 1970s and early 80s) and over 134 million items lay (for me) in its *society* rather than its *information*. As a cataloger told me later, "You can catalog a sandwich if you know the cataloging rules." In other words, the most noteworthy dimensions to the Library are those social conditions that make its work possible in the first place.

In what follows below, I argue that, during a period of fiscal and social crisis in the 1990s, the Library of Congress, reeling from calumnious budget cuts in the 1980s, fastened onto a particular image of "information society" grounded in technological determinism (the development of a digital library) and appropriating a powerful discourse of democratic access referring to the (mythical) past as well as a (utopian) future. In doing so, I believe that the Head Librarian and LC Management hoped to counter one image of information society as progressive and future-oriented to another, equally probable version rooted in the chaos and noise of an "information explosion." But while that vision proves somewhat salutary in Congressional appropriations hearings, it is also disingenuous, reducing powerful contradictions in space, social relations, power and access to smooth, techno-fetishist homogeneities. And while the "virtual world" manages to conceal possibly damning racial, labor-management and organizational problems, it does so at the cost of at least some of the Library's legitimation as a repository for the "national memory."

What emerges is an idea of "information society" less rooted in the multiplication of processors, networks, routers and backbones and less a matter of "Post Fordism" and "Advanced Capitalism" than the raw stuff of *culture* and *hegemony*. To the people in this book—Deck Attendants, Catalogers, Scholars, Head Librarians, Contractors and Congress—"information society" condenses both a hope for the future and a nostalgia for the past, both a critique of power and a desire for more of it.

## Ideology In The Age Of Reading

I use "information society" guardedly; it's ultimate *telos* remains to be seen. More than the adoption of this or that technology, information society includes sweeping changes in areas of life far removed from computers and software: not only in the way we interact with each other, but in the ways we think about our past and plan for our future. That is, "information society" signals profound *social* and *cultural* changes that only incidentally involve technologies (Castells 1989). As Sherry Turkle has pointed out, we make our machines to reflect something of the way we would like to live and interact; the computer is only the latest condensation in our long history of technological fetishization.

> But here the computer experience was used to think about more than oneself. It was used to think about society, politics, and education. A particular experience of the machine—only one of the experiences that the machine offers—became a building block for a culture whose values centered around clarity, transparency, and involvement with the whole. Images of computational transparency were used to suggest political worlds where relations of power would not be veiled, where people might control their own destinies, where work would facilitate a rich intellectual life. Relationships with a computer became the depository of longings for a better, simpler, and more coherent life. (Turkle 1984: 173-174)

It's worth asking, however, if it's most useful to think of these artifacts of information society as primarily *symbolic* or *mimetic* in their effects. Computers may communicate, but is that their only purpose? Are computers just another bundle of discourse on identity and the self? To me, the propensity to see our technologies as mirrors of identity means a transformation has already taken place: the apotheosis of reading in the Age of Information, the capacity of the world to *inform*. In short, to discourse on self and information society is to already beg the question of social change and cultural history.

Unfortunately, locating "information society" in some vision of *culture change* does not really solve the puzzle, particularly in the late-1990s when it appeared as appropriate to write of "Maori culture" as a "culture of poverty." Much of this confusion has to do with the disciplinary fracas over the *idea* of culture. There has been, from the 1980s, a perceived passage of disciplinary control of ideas and theories of culture and behavior from anthropology to cultural studies, an 'epicycle' of crisis in a decade beset by an entire bestiary of crises (Roseberry 1992; Turner 1993). Whether or not anthropology ever exercised, in its "halcyon" days, *de jure* rights over theories of culture is a matter open to debate, but the relative ability to theorize culture and society seems to have indeed shifted to the smoke and mirrors of rhetorically florid essays whose patented "look and feel" draw more from theater and film criticism than from the studied ethnographies of yore. The experiential, always naive, but never so suspect as in this media-tized age where first impressions are never justified and where the phenomenological is another production to be bought and sold, seems inadequate to new generations of anthropologists who seem to speak from everywhere and nowhere at once.

As an idea or a "unit of analysis," *culture* displays considerable—even exasperating—ambiguity, as Raymond Williams has amply demonstrated in his *Culture* (1981). The usage of "culture" in cultural anthropology derives from two of the traditions Williams traces. The first "tradition" originates with Matthew Arnold's *Culture and Anarchy* (1869), where "culture" appears as a canon of works and ideas: a typology of textual knowledge differentiating the "civilized" from the "rabble." This notion of culture crested with the work of J.G. Frazer, Lewis Henry Morgan, General Pitt Rivers and schools of ethnology stressing the dissemination of material artifact, ritual and myth across "culture areas." Preserving Arnold's distinctions between "high" and "low" culture, these classificatory or typological models of culture frequently supported racist ideas of "cultural evolution" and Social Darwinism prevalent in Western science throughout the nineteenth and much of the twentieth centuries.

The other strand of "culture" in anthropology begins, at least in part, with the work of E.B. Tylor, particularly in his 1871 *Primitive Culture*. It was there that he elaborated on culture as "that complex whole which includes knowledge, belief, law, morals, custom, and any other capabilities acquired by man as a member of society" (Tylor 1871). Although, as Stocking (1992:284) has pointed out, Tylor had hardly transcended a more typological approach, his definition opened up possibilities for notions of culture less overtly "yoked" to civilization, ideas that were to reach florescence in the Boasian school of the early twentieth century (Harris 1968).

While many textbooks introducing cultural anthropology stress the triumph of the ideational model over the material model of culture, it seems clear that anthropology still struggles with both traditions and the dialectical movement between "culture as an idea" and "culture as an object" forms a *leitmotif* in cultural anthropology right up to the present. That movement is, perhaps, an inevitable by-product of analysis. While anthropologists tend to think of "culture" as an inchoate idea or widespread practice, their *study* of culture more often than not devolves upon the analysis of a key text, an interview, a ritual or an image: in short, an *object*. That movement between "subject" and "object"—as analytical artifacts—could be said to characterize anthropological fieldwork, considered by many as a defining synecdoche of anthropology as a discipline.

This becomes all the more important with "information society." Fuzzy and ill-defined even to the technocrats charged with its legitimation and reproduction, "information society" has, paradoxically, never seemed more ubiquitous. Like the "Magic Eye," that mid-1990s novelty toy, information society seems part of the wallpaper until you discover that one, special angle to look at it. Even then, it's an optical illusion, losing coherence when you shift your gaze. Even so, much of its "wisdom"—those bumpersticker credos apotheosizing efficiency, innovation and flexibility—have passed into the dense, undifferentiated verdure of everyday life. But where is information society's "outside"?

Where does it begin and where does it end? Do we "debate" information society in a "public sphere" or have we already acquiesced to its mass-produced imperatives? Who runs things, anyway?

## Studying Information When Society Already Knows

Can we study information society as a "zone of cultural debate"? It depends, of course, on what we mean by that loose rubric, "information society," for, by invoking it, we're already prescribing a certain sort of *episteme*, a way of differentiating the present from the world that went before. To the journalists, scholars and politicians who have been the commentators, critics and celebrants of the information age, "information society" *means* many things: a characteristic mode of production different from the Fordism that went before, a sector of the economy engaged in the production of knowledge, the myriad effects of information technology on public and private life, or even the defracting selves and splintered identities of a "digitized" and "mediatized" people forced through the sieve of networks, routers and gateways. In the following essay, "information society" is all and none of these things. Without broaching the question of causation, I want to suggest that information society refers to characteristic shifts in the way people understand themselves, their world, and their *future* as much as it involves the impositions of new technologies and new organizations. Consider the following:

> So, today's defining question is: What to do about the future? Do we search for the stasis—a constrained, regulated, engineered future? Or embrace dynamism—the open-ended, evolving future? Do we demand rules to govern each new situation and keep things under control? Or do we limit rule making to broad and rarely changed principles, within which people can craft an unpredictable future? These two poles—stasis and dynamism—will increasingly define our political, intellectual, and cultural landscape. (Postrel 1998:54)

"Information society" describes a place where it is possible (and, indeed, profitable) to contrast a "static" past to a "dynamic" future, where the language of living, working, and knowing dovetails with managerial jargon and, finally, where untrammeled capitalism represents "freedom" and Statist intervention "oppression." "Information society" is that which not only does not recognize alternatives to the "post-Fordist" present, but which works to colonize the future and subtend the past into its image, so that "information society" becomes not only the undisputed present, but also the controverted past and the subverted future.

## Towards A Genealogy Of Information Society

In order to understand information in all its discursive and institutional com-

12

plexity, I analyze the Library of Congress as it works towards its millenarian vision of a "National Digital Library," an archive of books, photographs, manuscripts, sound recordings and motion pictures available online. This may strike some readers as an idiosyncratic choice. The Library of Congress (LC), as the *de facto* national library for the United States and the largest library in the world, is definitely a center of information services and even "knowledge."[6] But it seems doubtful that the LC represents the absolute vanguard of the coming information society (although librarians have long-occupied a prominent place in lists of "knowledge workers" propounded by social theorists). That honor, perhaps, should go to Apple, Microsoft, or—better yet—venture capital software and hardware companies, industry upstarts that form the dubious protagonists of heroic narratives in *Wired* magazine and cyberpunk fiction. Even insider accounts of the Library stress its conservative character and its sometimes stultifying inertia:

> For the past hundred years, one of the standard dialogues at Library conventions has started with the question: Why is it so hard to get the Library to do something new? The profession has always been ahead of the Library [ . . .] Again and again throughout the Library's history, the Librarians of Congress and the department heads have been selected because of their imagination and because of the aggressive, innovative ideas they have demonstrated in their home libraries— only to have these qualities evaporate when they reach the great grey building on Capitol Hill. (Goodrum 1974: 233-34)[7]

The Library of Congress has sometimes been portrayed as an information dinosaur with more in common with the earlier "Gutenberg" age than the "digital revolution" purportedly transforming our lives. For example, "The Library of Congress is a dumpster full of atoms. Books check in but they almost never check out" ("A Bill of Writes" 1995:224). So why not spend eighteen months with a roomful of software developers and "Net-Heads."?[8]

There are three reasons to pursue information society at the Library. First of all—whatever its conservative proclivities—the LC has devoted considerable resources to online activities in archiving, cataloging, exhibits and collections. Like many government agencies in the 1980s and 90s, the Library tried to approximate the flexibility and "total quality management" associated with the Deming-style corporation. In the language of Albert Gore's National Performance Review, the LC developed new "products" and "services" targeted at its "consumers" (Drucker 1993). Second, although the "Information super-

---

6    Despite periodic memos from Head Librarians and votes in Congress, the Library of Congress has never been *officially* designated the "national library" of the United States: this, despite the centralization of copyright and cataloging at the LC.

7    I will take up this interesting (and no less mythological) theme of the earnest, energetic manager and the sluggish, inertial bureaucrat towards the end of this book.

8    Many anthropologists have, in fact, done research in those areas (Cf. Harvey 1995; Batteau 1995; Sutton 1995).

highway" is usually portrayed as a revolutionary force, that "information" has overwhelmingly involved the stuff of corporations and military: credit reports, stock trading, shipping logs and LANDSAT images. It has yet to be demonstrated whether or not "information" in the public sphere (health care, community services, public education) has undergone a similar expansion; I think it likely that, in practice, these areas have experienced a *diminution* in publicly available knowledge (Schiller 1981). Whatever the budgetary shortfalls of libraries in the twenty-first century (and they are many), they are still the symbol, if not the source, of publicly available knowledge; information pundits, therefore, draw some legitimacy from their image (NRENAISSANCE Committee 1994:135). Representing Internet services as extensions of libraries focuses attention away from the commercial character of recent developments and towards mythopoetic evocations of the Internet's "democratic" and "empowering" potentials.

Finally, anthropologists frequently find more answers to their questions on the margins of movements, trends, cultures and institutions, than at their center (Tsing 1993). People at the center often have little reason to question the way things work, the distribution of power and decision-making, or the different forces invigilating their lives (Bottomore 1993). This is not to say that these elites form a homogeneous block or even that the "center" expresses a coherent, contradiction-free worldview (Kellner 1990). Nevertheless, many anthropologists have found that the different processes associated with *modernity*, for instance, are best illuminated on the edges of modernity's expanding, tumultuous ambit (Hess 1994). It is as important to track appropriations, re-appropriations, subversions and elisions of "official knowledge" as it is to elucidate that official knowledge in the first place.

Importantly, the Library of Congress is not exactly at the margins of information society. Rather, it forms an important scaffolding for the more mobile, more capitalized organizations that typify our information age. The LC is charged with the production of crucial, state-sanctioned orders that frame information—e.g., copyright, cataloging, LC Classification and Dewey Decimal numbers, ISBN and ISSN numbers—and allow it to be bought, sold, copied, loaned, codified, shelved, filed, stacked, ordered and indexed. Without the Library's explicit *productions* of information, there would not be "information" or "knowledge" to speak of. Nevertheless, the Library has little to do directly with the development of new information technologies or the buying and selling of "information" characterized by "flexible accumulation" (Harvey 1989).[9] Insofar as it develops cutting-edge programs like the National Digital Library, it does so with only a tiny amount of its total resources, leaving the vast majority of its infrastructure behind.[10] The LC acts as an *archive* of

---

9    The Library used to develop some software applications "in house" but has since discontinued these programs. Today, the LC is as much a *consumer* of information as anyone else.

10    This problem of "integration" has plagued the Library since it began experimenting with automated cataloging in the 1960s and has been particularly evident with the development of the

information rather than an agent of information society. I mean this in two ways: first, in the literal sense of a palimpsest of ratios, practices and orders of "information" drawn from different epochs: dictionary lists, card catalogs, bibliographies, optical disks, computer tapes and World Wide Web servers, a trail of information's past all still actively in use. Second, the LC's "information archive" is a register of different imaginary relations to the world of knowledge and to the different way people have set about—or imagined they were setting out—to understand the world (Richards 1993).

## Methodological Notes And An Anarchistic Theory Of Knowledge

Like many ethnographies today, my fieldwork at the Library can best be described as opportunistic: diverse materials, informants and events worked their way into my anthropology. There were two reasons for this. First, an anthropology of modern life (however construed) presents a researcher trained in anthropology's more holistic traditions with a bewildering *surfeit* of cultural knowledge and insights from media and material culture as well as from people. Although anthropologists—as practitioners of a field historically premised on the study of pre-literate and non-literate people—privilege face-to-face interaction, it would be an epistemological misstep to ignore the many texts that enfold the lives of people. "Texts"—books, television, film, reports, memoranda, letters, e-mails and so on—are tools that (literally) enable modern life. From birth certificate to credit reports to hospital records to obituaries: each moment in the life of a person is authorized by countless texts that are more than mere memorials. Like J.L. Austin's speech acts, they are "illocutionary," texts and lives woven together; the modern is ineluctably a graphophile. Additionally, texts *are* the life of the institution, enframing and legitimating every act. This is particularly the case at the Library of Congress, which LC historian David Mearns has characterized as the most "fenestrated" institution on Capitol Hill. So: along with many "human" informants, I also include here many "textual" informants, including the artifacts of information society: cataloging programs and architecture.

Secondly, I needed an "in" at the Library. Anthropologists often research places where their role is—to say the least—ambiguous. Even today, there are comparatively few situations where anthropologists can step into a predetermined position as an ethnographer. In order to accomplish the work of ethnography, then, anthropologists adopt other roles—advocates for indigenous rights, surveyors of pre-natal care, distributors of free needles at health clinics—that allow them some freedom to pursue their fieldwork. However: this "non-fieldwork," far from being extraneous to anthropological knowledge, winds its way in and out of interviews and participant observation becoming, in the end, part of an ethnography. Such is the case at the Library of Congress, where an *anthropologist* would not be welcome, but a *researcher* always is. I had

---

National Digital Library (NDL).

already established an identity as a researcher in 1992, when I interned at the Archives of Folk Culture, and I found it easy and even pleasurable to resume archival work.

When I entered the field in 1994, I began *historical* research on the LC, looking to primary and secondary sources for the history of the LC's systems, organization and spaces. That work led me to consult the different divisions within and without the LC: the Library's general stacks, Manuscript Division, Prints and Photographs Division, Rare Books Division and Motion Picture Division, but also the National Archives in College Park, Maryland, the Archives of the Architect of the Capitol and countless college and public libraries in and around the Washington, D.C. metropolitan area.

In the 1995-1996 period of fieldwork, my role of anthropological fieldworker shifted again, this time as my money began to run out and I contemplated part-time employment to underwrite my dissertation work. I experienced almost a full month of excruciating indecision. Was it better to get a job inside or outside the Library? Was I compromising the integrity of my discipline? Did I really want to do restaurant work again? In the end, predictably, monetary considerations won out over the tendentious voice of anthropological ethics, and I began to take small jobs in contract research for a variety of clients. Contract research gave me an entirely different perspective on the Library of Congress; removed from the ivory tower of scholarship and cataloging, I began to see the LC's collections and information systems as sources of value to the less information-savvy of the world. Even though I only worked for non-profits that were not politically repugnant to me, I was still paid handsomely for what were, after all, readily available resources. Through contract research, I met not only clients, but a whole, shadowy network of scholars/contractors who were, like me, ambiguous liaisons between a world of public, free knowledge and one of private, valued information.

The Library of Congress brings together a Dickensian gallery of people, and I tried to interview people in as many different areas as possible. Nevertheless, I soon found myself concentrating on certain parts and people in the LC to the exclusion of others. Two areas that I've more-or-less ignored in this study are extremely important to an understanding of the cultural shifts subsumed under the ideas of an "information age": the Copyright Division and the Congressional Research Service. Unfortunately, research at those divisions proved logistically difficult. Intellectual property and copyright are abstruse areas of law in the United States. Lawyers specializing in these areas are widely considered the most academic of the legal profession and changes in the "container type" of copyrights—from print to CDs and online files—have stimulated an incredible intellectual foment. I was, I confess, not up to the task and, realistically, was not able to acquire enough legal knowledge to effectively interview Copyright Division staff and users. The Congressional Research Service, on the other hand, engages in research of all kinds: education, social policy, economics, politics. In short, CRS researches any subject that is or may become of interest to Congress. There are, I believe, even a couple of anthropologists on CRS's staff! However: much of the research and work at CRS is necessarily proprietary. Topics developing in Congressional subcommittees for eventual legislation are, of course, classified. Although it's quite easy to access CRS briefs and reports after the fact, as it were, the research CRS does for Congress is (necessarily?) a secret. And although I had the fortune to interview several staffers at CRS, I was not able to follow through on my research to my satisfaction; there was too much *unsaid* between the texts of my interlocutors. In my defense, the Copyright Division and the Congressional Research Service—while vital to the LC's continued existence—are widely perceived as self-contained institutions-within-an-institutions whose inclusion in the LC's organization was more-or-less a historical accident. Over the years, various Congressional Committees have broached the possibility of removing them from the Library's purview, a suggestion that Head Librarians have fiercely countered.

Over all, I conducted 130 interviews with researchers and staff from all over the LC. Who were they? Roughly half were Library of Congress employees (some were both employees *and* researchers, while others were *former* LC employees). Of those, perhaps one-quarter could be unproblematically labeled LC *management*, the rest falling into a spectrum of technical and professional work that I explore in more detail in Chapter 6. Most of my older, managerial respondents were men, although I also interviewed women in management positions. Most of my technical and professional respondents were women and many might identify as African American. Most of the scholars I interviewed were men, while most of the contract researchers were women. Their ages varied widely: scholars were older and some were retired from academics or government while contract researchers were (generally) younger, although there are many older people who undertake contract research well into retirement.

The topics of our discussions sometimes wandered far afield, but always wound back to the question of "change" and "information society" at the LC, ideas that I purposely kept vague in interviews, allowing my interlocutors to make sense of them in their narratives of life, work and scholarship. During the first two months of my research, I relied on a small, tape recorder and subsequent transcripts. However: it became clear that the tape recorder was making everyone nervous, particularly Library staffers who were afraid of reprisals from their superiors. Also, far from contributing a nimbus of authenticity and professionalism to my novice fieldwork, the recorder reminded people too much of journalism which, a la Watergate, most civil servants have a healthy fear of. So: thrust back onto taking notes, I developed a shorthand that allowed me to transcribe much of the interviews I conducted.

Issues of security and confidentiality were vitally important to me throughout my fieldwork tenure. In a relatively small institution with a nasty history of punishing whistle-blowers (Cf. Gleick 1995), there's a very real risk that employees will be identified and summarily punished for "taking their problems to outsiders."[11] In order to reduce that risk, I have excerpted quotations that do not specify work details and personal names and that do not evidence easily identifiable rhetorical flourishes. Where these things do occur, I have altered the transcription. Attentive readers will notice that I prefer small excerpts to larger, more narrative blocks of transcripted material. I also make oblique reference to unexcerpted interviews, indirectly citing informants in the body of the text rather than in offset quotations. Finally, when possible, I used *published* sources over my interviews. Appropriations hearings, for example, are extraordinarily revealing public documents that, were they more closely studied by the electorate, would say much more than many people in government would probably be comfortable with. It is as fortunate for them as it is unlucky for us that journalists and the plebiscitary largely ignore the transcripts of these otherwise routine committee hearings! But even when I substituted public sources for my interviews, readers should understand that my interlocutors shaped both my understanding of LC history and policy and profoundly influenced the questions I asked of the archival record.

## Explanation Of Chapters

In the following chapters, I attempt to trace information society beyond its apparent homogeneity and hegemony in the apotheosis of the reading machine by following "information" into a zone of cultural debate. In doing so, I utilize a shop-worn tactic of anthropologists and social critics everywhere: unraveling the object into its constituent social relations and cultural ideas. It is through this exploration of subfuscous meaning and submerged debate that I reveal information society as only incidentally concerned with computers, networks and the "virtual life" of a digitized, mediatized elite, instead exploring the Library of Congress as part of a politics, a social life and a cultural understanding of work, freedom, debate and knowledge.

The following chapters follow that movement from text and material culture to the ideas and social relations both instantiated and concealed by them. The chapters are structured by a metonymic chain of desire whose engine is the inadequacy of the text to account for social life. Like Calvino's *if on a winter's night a traveler*, each chapter builds on the absences of what came before; each attempts to wrest the "authentic" Library, to describe the "real" information society. That is, each chapter introduces ideas and artifacts whose meaning is never exhausted by bounded, self-description but whose ultimate *telos* lies beyond them in widening ambits of society of culture. This movement begins in the Introduction with the drama of the Reader, that postmodern figure of fleeting subjectivity and distorted communication whose Self seems like a shadow cast by the reality of the text, digital or otherwise. That character is, I suggest,

---

11 In fact, Head Librarian James Billington admonished his employees for just that in a 1995 memo.

in many ways the belated afterglow of capitalist triumph, concealing much beneath a panoply of identity and difference. In Chapter One, I turn away from the "jouissance" of deferred reading and errant textuality to the emergent discipline of science and technology studies (STS) as a way of uprooting the complex of power, knowledge and inequality beneath the seamless "objectivity" of information society and knowledge production in the same way science and technology studies look beyond the incontrovertible facts of science to the social truths that make science possible: those gender, class, racial and national inequalities that are the precondition of corporate science at the end of the twentieth century. The emergent discipline of STS is, in a sense, a precondition for work on the information age since that is where anthropology excels in illuminating the dynamics of power, knowledge and social organization at the heart of advanced capitalism. More than many other anthropologists, those scholars studying the opacity (and transparency) have become adroit at studying "cultures of no culture" (Sharon Traweek, quoted in Martin 1997:134). In particular, I suggest that science and technology studies allows me to illuminate the "future work" implicit in information society and the extent to which the reorganization of the present is, in the logic of advanced capitalism, indistinguishable from the descriptions (or prescriptions) of the future. The work of "reproduction" has never been so important and much of the knowledge work done today is embroiled in the careful enframing of the future. Chapter Three moves beyond the textual realm altogether, focusing instead on the spaces hemmed and limned by readers and their reading (both in this world and the digital world beyond). It is there that I begin to suggest that aspects of cultural life ordinarily thought removed from the telematic world are equally a part of the "information society" and make up key ingredients in its imaginings. Chapters Four and Five, therefore, put the theoretical and methodological program outlined in Chapter One and the "space" opened up between the seams of an ideologically seamless "information society" into practice by contrasting the container to the "thing contained," turning to what Foucault has called the "interval between books," the varied artifacts that make the bibliomantic world possible in addition to the digitizations of knowledge and knowing that purport to re-make that textual scape altogether (Foucault 1977:91). But the Library's information systems—its books, its cataloging, its computers, just as with its spaces—can only tell us some things about information society. They are, after all, reflections of each other, one knowledge-machine presaging another. As such, those artifacts can confirm what we think we know but rarely can they *contest*. Chapter Six, therefore, moves to the Library's *people*, its staff and users who, through their knowledge practices in their work and scholarship, their debates over Library policy, their worries over their jobs and careers, take "information society" well beyond the technological fetishes of faster co-processors to the stuff of "culture."

CHAPTER 2

# Anthropology and the Imperial Archive

Visitors to the Great Hall of the LC's Jefferson Building climb a series of stairs to three bronze doors leading to the entrance pavilion. Set into the exterior walls at the entrance and in subsequent pavilions around the perimeter of the building are mounted 33 ethnographic heads derived from studies done by Otis T. Mason at the Smithsonian, each an ideal "racial type" ranging from "Blonde European" and "Brunette European" in the front to "Australian" and "Negrito" in the back.

> The list of races, beginning at the north end of the Entrance Pavilion, and thence continuing south and round the building to the Northwest Pavilion, is as follows, each head being numbered in following the order in which they occur: 1, Russian Slav; 2, Blonde European; 4, Modern Greek; 5, Persian (Iranian); 6, Circassian; 7, Hindoo; 8, Hungarian (Magyar); 9, Semite, or Jew; 10, Arab (Bedouin); 11, Turk; 12, Modern Egyptian (Hamite); 13, Absynnian; 14, Malay; 15, Polynesian; 16, Australian; 17, Negrito (from Indian Archipeligo); 18, Zulu (Bantu); 19, Papuan (New Guinea); 20, Soudan Negro; 21, Akka (Dwarf African Negro); 22, Fuegian; 23, Botocudo (from South America); 24, Pueblo Indian (as the Zunis of New Mexico); 25, Esquimaux; 26, Plains Indian (Sioux, Cheyenne, Comanche); 27, Samoyede (Finnish inhabitant of Northern Russia); 28, Corean; 29, Japanese; 30, Aino (from Northern Japan); 31, Burmese; 32, Thibetan; 33, Chinese. (Small 1901:15)

Mixing linguistic groups and cultural traits with so-called "physical types," the ethnographic heads translate the rampant Social Darwinism of the time into a vivid, sculptural display, marking an entrance into a nexus of imperial power and productive knowledge. They are the brutal trophies of nineteenth century imperialism and reveal the collusion of nineteenth century anthropology with State power; they encapsulate a *moral order*, an attitude to the world grounded in the (a)morality of imperialism and the manifest destiny of capitalist expansion.

Otis T. Mason's heads are more than just an atavistic reminder of anthropology's guilty past. They are, after all, still *there*, just as vivid and clear today as they were at the building's unveiling in 1897. To me, they are indicative of a persistence of anthropology's vision, anthropology's *readings*. Just as we are—as readers—locked into an order of books that lie to the margins of the text, so anthropology is hemmed by its past readings of the world's marginal peoples. To engage an anthropology of a knowledge-institution like the Library of Congress is to face anthropology's own pernicious entextualizations, for we are as much a part of the "imperial archive" as any map, census or museum (Richards 1993). In other words, it may be more accurate to site anthropology in the Library of Congress than in the putatively small societies with which it is ordinarily associated.

Additionally, undertaking an anthropology of "information society" begs the question of *location*. The preceding introduction raised serious questions about the wisdom of reifying "information society" to some bounded locus of institutions, demographics and ideas. Can we finger "knowledge workers"? Can we differentiate the production of information from the production of, say, tractors? When do we exist in an "information society"? By some definitions, "information society" is everywhere and nowhere, a flexible, shifting and recombinant amalgam of productions, social relations and identities just as present on the factory floor as on the Senate floor and as much "Western" and as much a part of the "Self" as an attribute of the "Other." As Appadurai suggests, "The task of ethnography now becomes the unraveling of a conundrum: what is the nature of locality, as a lived experience, in a globalized, deterritorialized world?" (Appadurai 1991:196). As Marcus (1995) and others have pointed out, anthropologists need to adopt a method and an object respectful of both local and global, respectful of both the lives of people they study as well as the twisted etiologies of increasingly interpenetrated global cultures.

## Studying Dangerous Fictions: Researching The Present When All Around Is Future Shock

Consider the following evocation of a twenty-first century public sphere, typical enough in bygone, dot.com days when buying a personal and cell phone was adduced as a cure for all manner of societal problems:

> This democratic political transformation is being propelled largely by two developments—the two- hundred-year-long march toward political equality for all citizens and the explosive growth of new telecommunications media, the remarkable convergence of television, telephone, satellites, cable, and personal computers. This is the first generation of citizens who can see, hear, and judge their own political leaders simultaneously and instantaneously. It is also the first generation of political leaders who can address the entire population and receive instant feedback about what the people think and want. Interactive telecom-

munications increasingly give ordinary citizens immediate access to the major political decisions that affect their lives and property. (Grossman 1995:4)

What polity is Grossman writing about? If it's the United States, I can't disagree with him more. By all accounts, the 1980s and 1990s witnessed a profound denudation of "empowerment," not their florescence. Wealth and its corollary under a capitalist economy, political power, are concentrated in fewer hands today than in the late 1960s, with sixty percent of the population controlling only thirty-three percent of the GDP (World Bank 1990:237). But this is, for pundits of twenty-first century American life, quite immaterial. It all has to do, of course, with the etiology of *progress*, that limitless, mythopoetic engine of American mercantilism. Whatever the economic or political climate of the nation, however bad the class and race wars of the late-twentieth century grow, "inexorable progress" is the postulate that underlies every facet of life in the United States. As a powerful myth, it is also a time machine, figuring a curiously ahistorical past where Americans can return to the nostalgia of patriarchy, the enlightened despotism of Victorian philanthropists or to the Edenic community of a racially pure United States before the "Fall" of urban minorities and undocumented immigrants. It doesn't matter, of course, that these rosy times never actually existed, progress is a bit of pernicious sophistry that *rhetorically* figures the past; in other words, it has nothing to do with the truth of history, and everything to do with the myth of the pastoral (Marx 1964).

## Theorizing The Nation: Frontiers And Limits

One of the pre-eminent, utopian figures of modernity has been the *nation*, at once a dramatic synthesis of various localisms and a production of difference consigning aliens, ethnic and racial minorities and Others to a defined limit outside the ambit of national belonging. The success of what Anderson calls the "imagined community" rests precisely on the nineteenth century aptitude for subsuming certain differences (e.g. class and gender differences) under the figure of "citizen" while accentuating other differences to the exclusion of the "alien." That is, the efficacy of nation lies both in its capacity to include *and* exclude; nations can only exist rimed by dangerous others contained in varied allochronies and allotopoi.

We are now well familiar with the different forms this "official nationalism" takes, from historical pageants, patriotic songs, approved histories, television programs, clothing and so on (Handler 1988; Hobsbawm 1984; Gellner 1983). It is certainly these forms that are manipulated most in the oftentimes violent resurgences of ethnic nationalisms (Denich 1994). However, exclusive concentration on these more performative aspects of nationalism may obscure certain practices and techniques that, while more quotidian (or perhaps *because* more quotidian), nevertheless profoundly shape the apperception of the nation and the nation's citizenry. As Herzfeld points out:

> It is as though we confronted two different worlds: symbolic analysis is appropriate for the soft definitions of religion and ritual, but the real world of government organization calls for sterner approaches. (Herzfeld 1992:17)

Whatever those "sterner approaches" may turn out to be, they should not ignore the manifest symbolic world, i.e., the *grammar* of nationalism, the syntax of inclusion and exclusion that delimits the national imagination.

> Few things bring this grammar into more visible relief than three institutions of power which, although invented before the mid-nineteenth century, changed their form and function as the colonized zones entered the age of mechanical reproduction. These three institutions were the census, the map, and the museum: together, they profoundly shaped the way in which the colonial state imagined its dominion—the nature of the human being it ruled, the geography of its domain, and the legitimacy of its ancestry. (Anderson 1991:164)

That is, nationalism involves the location of people and places along a classificatory grid; it's all about *objectification*—the assignation of people and places to slots in a power-full hierarchy—and *interpellation* (in the Althusserian sense)—the specification of a relationship between self and State. The elaborate symboling of nineteenth-century nationalisms is only one part of a vastly productive nationalist machine and Anderson's recourse to a "grammar" of nation suggests the extent to which the operations and techniques that condition the possibility for historical nationalisms are at least as important as the rituals they produce. In other words, nationalism implies a practice; it inculcates a *habitus* in its most invidious sense as an organized locus of practices reproductive of a status quo (Bourdieu 1977:78). Sometimes, that classificatory grid is relatively benign, as with the adoption of a formalized system of Breton language schools in Brittany (McDonald 1989). Or, it can mean disaster, as years of horrible violence in the former Republic of Yugoslavia have borne out. As Robert Hayden has argued, at least part of the violence in the former Easter bloc nation can be traced to the imposition of a prescriptive notion of culture over one based on the lived experiences of people (Hayden 1996). That is, nationalism can be thought of as a content, but it is also an *order*, a way of imaginatively incorporating part of the world into the scape of the nation while derogating other parts to varying degrees of "otherness." Nationalism's many potent and mobilizing symbols are, in the end, ancillary effects of nationalism's vast, productive machine, a machine literally charged with producing the subjects as well as the objects of empire.

Like the census, the map and the museum, the library (and particularly the national library) is another technique of the nation, a way of producing the "grammar" upon which the imagined community can be built. It is surely no accident that the Library of Congress comes of age in the United States during the heyday of nineteenth-century nationalism and coincides with the rise of indigenous intellectual institutions such as the Smithsonian Institution

24

(1846) and John Hopkins University (1876). Although the LC is less spectacular (and *specular*) than other institutions originating in the "museum age" (e.g. the Philadelphia Exposition of 1876), it is no less germane to the development of nineteenth-century nationalism and its characteristic combination of imperialism, racist paternalism, Protestant capitalism and sublimated class conflict (Jacob 1994; Ripley 1970).

Whatever *sociotechnical systems* nationalism may derive from, it is a mistake to impart a monolithic homogeneity to structures that could be said to be hegemonic only in the most fleeting sense (Hughes 1989). The only thing durable about modern nationalism, in my mind, at least, is its near-constant state of crisis and its concomitant need to re-invent itself or work towards alternative sources of legitimation. Anthropologists utilizing *hegemony* in their analyses of "domination" and "resistance" have often emphasized the power of people to "appropriate" hegemonic configurations for their own uses; but this overestimation of "counter-hegemony" both minimizes the power of hegemony to structure what will count as "common sense" while over-exaggerating hegemony's cohesion. Since they literally come from everywhere and everything at once, hegemonic ideas are particularly vulnerable over time, even if relations of production remain unchanged. As Kellner has pointed out with regards to American television,

> While I admit that full-fledged democracy does not really exist in the United States, I shall argue in this book that conflicts between capitalism and democracy have persisted throughout U.S. history, and that the system of commercial broadcasting in the United States has been produced by a synthesis of capitalist and democratic structures and imperatives and is therefore full of structural conflicts and tensions. (Kellner 1990:15)

As the *nation* coalesces into a characteristic way of imagining the world in the late nineteenth-century, it incorporates a wide range of institutions, "grammars" and subjects; this is both its strength and its weakness.

> Imperialism was more than a set of economic, political, and military phenomena. It was a habit of mind, a dominant idea in the era of Europe's world. (Greenhalgh 1988:ix)

Clearly, by the turn-of-the-century, the nation—as an idea—was coming from all spheres of society and many conservatives, liberals and leftists alike seem to support explicitly colonial campaigns in Cuba and the Philippines in what can be thought of as a surfeit of nationalist zeal (Zinn 1995). But that seeming consensus was, at the same time, riddled with weakness. In turn, those fractious ideas became part of the Library of Congress's day-to-day operations, its production of *information*.

## Library And The Nation

> A popular government, without popular information, or the means of acquiring it, is but a Prologue to a Farce or a Tragedy; or, perhaps both. Knowledge will forever govern ignorance: And a people who mean to be their own Governors, must arm themselves with the power which knowledge gives. (Madison to Barry, in Hunt 103)

The United States is one of the first nations to ground its legitimation in an ideal relation between its citizenry and knowledge. That is to say, the ideology of representative democracy depends upon at least a theoretical transparency of government and governance. Even if citizens do not know their elected officials' names or the bills before their Congress, there is—in this system—the assumption that they could find out. Likewise, even if constituents never contact their elect representatives to register their complaints or their support there is the assumption that they could. This is an important (if often unacknowledged) part of what Jurgen Habermas terms "civil privatism," the "uncoerced obedience" that allows ruling elites to maintain control over a society theoretically ruled by the *demos* (Habermas 1973:76-77). Yet, this ideology has come unraveled over and over again throughout the life of the Republic, from the secrecy surrounding barbaric acts of Indian Removal to the October Surprise and, more recently, the Executive manipulation of the citizenry. The gap in the rank-and-file's knowledge of governance and policy is made even more dramatic because the legitimation of government depends—ostensibly—on the "people's" (potentially) perfect knowledge (hence accountability) of government. All of the great knowledge-institutions that burgeoned in the nineteenth century—public libraries, public schools, museums, etc.—must be seen as at least in part involved in the work of legitimation: that is, in the projection of an ideal relationship between governing and governed based on the hypothetical exchange of one for the other and mediated by flows of knowledge. This "information utopia" has been utilized since the nineteenth century to bolster the ideology of "liberal democracy" in the face of manifest inequalities in race, class and gender and part of understanding the role of *knowledge* in the information age involves tracing its ideological work (Smith 1993).

> Libraries, especially national libraries, constitute what are known in the sciences as "reduced models" of their country's social reality and ideological complexity. A few years back, Peru's national library was closed because it was discovered that it had become a hideout for members of the Shining Path guerilla movement. France's Très Grande Bibliothèque is both a reflection of the Mitterand administration's cultural agenda and the cultural heritage of a people who have long maintained a literary and bookish relationship with reality. The US Library of Congress, already housing some eighty million items and placing yet another seven thousand on its shelves daily, is the product of a culture that has dominated the world this century. (de Sant'Anna 1996:267)

That is, the information age is not only a cache of certain ideas about the way organizations and economies should work, but also a disquisition on the organization of society, authority and politics. In other words, the work of the Library in the "information age" is not only a matter of arranging and classifying "information," but about positioning "citizen-readers" in relation to it and, by synecdochic extension, to the reigns of government and the power of the State. It is no mistake, I think, that the design and construction of the LC's three buildings in the 1890s, 1930s and 1970s, respectively, coincided with periods of high unemployment and social unrest and while we might argue that the Library is not as key to the maintenance of nationalism as, say, the armed services or the State Department, we would nevertheless be missing a key dynamic of information society by not considering the *symbolic* dimensions of its operations.

Since the beginning of the twentieth century, the Library has, to a certain degree, struggled to reconcile these different mandates: the production and maintenance of classificatory orders (cataloging, copyright, ISBNs, ISSNs, etc.) and the production and maintenance of *national* orders. This shifting between what some might perceive as mutually exclusive goals is a frequent source of consternation for employees and users alike. As one former section head said, "The LC was more government than Library . . .it doesn't work like a library." And researchers were often bewildered by cutbacks in cataloging and library hours that followed on the heels of expensive renovations, as with renovations to the Adams and Jefferson Buildings and the ongoing construction of a massive, underground "Capitol Visitor's Center." As one researcher commented, "How much of that renovation was structurally required? Who was that important to? The touring public!" Scholars, users and staff tend to de-value the role of the Library in producing national sentiment and seem continuously surprised when these largely *symboling* functions are funded over more bureaucratic and scholarly projects.

But this is not surprising, given the core activities initiated by Librarians of Congress from the late-nineteenth century to the present. In 1891, six years before the completion of what is now known as the Jefferson Building, Head Librarian Ainsworth Spofford suggested what was, perhaps, the first large emendation to the *role* of the national library.

> We ought to have one comprehensive library in the country, and that belonging to the nation, whose aim it should be to preserve the books which other libraries have not the room or the means to procure. (quoted in Cole 1979:380)

As Jane Rosenberg has pointed out, Spofford's conception was broader than that pursued by national libraries in France, Ireland and elsewhere whose purposes were tied to the pragmatics of copyright storage (Rosenberg 1993). As head librarians since Spofford often repeat, the Library of Congress—unlike many other national libraries—endeavors to build "universal" collections embracing the intellectual productions of all nations, a goal which can be traced back to Spofford.[12] By 1939, Head Librarian Putnam had extended the Library into even more wide-ranging directions, incorporating the Legislative Reference Service (now the Congressional Research Service), the National Library Service for the Blind and Physically Handicapped, and adding a number of "consultants" to the Library's staff who functioned as an academic faculty (Rosenberg 1993:103). By Luther Evans's tenure as Librarian, the widening ambit of Library activities, products and staff had been codified into what we would now call a "mission."

> For the Congress had extended the privileges of its Library to co-ordinate branches of Government, to international bodies seeking the security and betterment of the whole family of man, to the world of learning as represented by academies and universities and galleries and museums, to private scholars engaged for their fellows in discovering new or recovering old knowledge, to the great industries and little businesses and the organizations of labor which together are the American community, and to the citizens of the free Republic who find their answers in the reading rooms. (Library of Congress 1951:12)

More than a universal scope of collections, the Library cultivated what it considered were a *universal constituency* encompassing, seemingly, all nations, institutions and peoples.

Shortly after his accession to Head Librarian in 1987, James Billington had codified—following on the tails of corporate drives to instill homogeneous "cultures" into their organizations—all of these diverse constituencies and activities into a three-fold "mission" towards Congress, the *nation* and scholars, in that order (Gordon 1995). The frequency of this mission's recitation may be, perhaps, an indication of both its power and its incoherence:

> I. THE FIRST PRIORITY of the Library of Congress is to make knowledge and creativity available to the United States Congress. [ . . .]

> II. THE SECOND PRIORITY of the Library of Congress is to *preserve, secure, and sustain* for the present and future use of the Congress and the nation
> (A) a comprehensive record of American history and creativity; [ . . .]
> (B) a universal collection of human knowledge. [ . . .]

> III. THE THIRD PRIORITY of the Library of Congress is to make its collections maximally *accessible* to (in order of priority)
> (A) the Congress,
> (B) the U.S. government more broadly,

---

12  Cole (1975, 1993) traces the valuation of "universal" collections to the beneficent influence of Thomas Jefferson who introduced a certain encyclopaedism into the more parochial interests of the legislature by selling the Congress his wide-ranging library of 5000 books in 1815.

(C) the thinking and creative public.

IV. THE FOURTH PRIORITY is to add interpretive and educational value to the basic resources of the Library in order to enhance the quality of the creative work and intellectual activity derived from these resources, and to highlight the importance of the Library to the nation's well-being and future progress. (Billington 1995a:7-8)

While the Library's fealty to the Congress is not surprising, its more symbolic functions of compiling a "comprehensive record of American history and creativity" and highlighting the "importance of the Library to the nation's well-being and future progress" may seem slightly beyond the scope of a bureaucratic institution. What does it mean to say the LC doesn't "work like a library"? If, on the one hand, it suggests that the Library of Congress diverges from the oftentimes more altruistic goals of the nineteenth-century public library movement, on the other it directs us to "institution-building" in the information age as the logorrheic development of contrary tendencies. What the Library's many "mission statements" suggest, in fact, is a two-edged quality to emergent regimes of information; if one concerns the growth of technocratic expertise, the other is the growing ideological character of knowledge and knowing that exploits the *symbolic* properties of "efficiency" and "expertise."[13]

In examining the Library's spaces, artifacts and people in an anthropology of information science, I suggest the depth of that modernist scission between contradictory goals and constituencies is, far from ancillary to "information society," central to its currency in the late-twentieth century.

---

13  Though, of course, "mission statements" and all that they imply—labor-management "cooperation" and "vision"—are, strictly speaking, artefacts of 1980s corporate strategy (Hammer and Campy 1993).

CHAPTER 3

# From Knowledge Machines to Information Scapes: Tracing the Library's Places and Non-places

This Chapter examines the Library of Congress as a palimpsest of different *spatial orders* whose scale (and scope) is *skewed*, warped into an improbable topology that tells us a great deal about information society's intrinsic instabilities. As an AT&T commercial forecasted:

> Have you ever renewed your driver's license . . .at a cash machine? Fixed your car . . .with a television? Or had an assistant . . .who lived in your computer? You will . . .(quoted in Ness 1994)

The promise (or threat) of information society (at least, according to AT&T) is a complete reconfiguration between the relations of people to the State, the relation of people to knowledge and the relation of people to each other. But these sweeping changes wrought by the modern can only be brought about through the "creative destruction" of what went before, the development of information society as the progressive scission of the reader from the read, and, ultimately, the space of reading from the politics of knowledge. As an institution charged both with the production of knowledge and the legitimation of the nation, the Library of Congress evidences all these fault lines, even as it moves towards the utopian synesthesia forecast (but never quite realized) by the "digerati." This Chapter chronicles the succession of crises upon which that "virtual future" rests, beginning with the spaces of the Nation.

## MAPPING THE INFORMATION EXPLOSION: THE LIBRARY OF CONGRESS IN SPATIAL CRISIS

> Four troves of books, that fill three city blocks,
> All gathered in one cluster, are so rare
> We feel like Ozymandias when he mocks:
> "Look of these works, you mighty and despair."

We have room for no more buildings anywhere;
We can only expand by growing small.
Newspapers have been shrunk to one inch square;
Ten million cards into one breadbox crawl.
We will shrink, like Milton's angels, the Readers last of all. (Boswell 1994)

The Library of Congress occupies three, wildly different buildings to the east of the U.S. Capitol: the Jefferson, Adams and Madison Buildings, facing First Street, Third Street and Independence Avenue, respectively.[14] Each is a testament to a particular epoch in U.S. history and suggests, moreover, a different attitude towards "knowledge" and "information." The Jefferson Building is the oldest of the three and was built at a time (1897) when the city was heavily invested in cultivating indigenous, intellectual institutions; the building's Beaux-Arts exuberance suggests, perhaps, the imperial ambitions of a Congress with its eye towards economic and military conquest abroad (Oleson 1976; Jacob 1994). By contrast, the Adams Building (1938) is notable for its stolid functionality reinforced by its sleek, Art-Deco detail and was said to "interest, never to distract" by its planners (Architect of the Capitol: unpublished memo). It reflects not only an interest in projecting *thrift*, but also the *professionalization* of a rapidly expanding federal bureaucracy which was moving from the Jacksonian nepotism of the previous century to a more formalized system based—at least ostensibly—on principles of Taylorist management (Johnson and Libecap 1994).[15] The last in the triad, the Madison Building (1980), is perhaps also the most architecturally incoherent, combining neo-classicism with a monolithic modernism that some critics have compared to Albert Speer's colonnade at Nuremberg (Richard 1967; Huxtable 1986). Dedicated in the first year of Reagan's presidency, the Madison Building suggests a return to a centralized federalism characteristic of the 1980s that hinged on what some commentators have characterized as a close control of information access, under, for example, the Office of Management and Budget (OMB); certainly, the many covert operations undertaken by the federal government at this time depended on it (Schiller 1988). The three buildings sit alongside the Cannon Office Building to the Southwest, the Capitol to the West and the Supreme Court to the North, forming, if you will, a "fifth branch" of government (alongside media). Viewed from the Mall to the West, the Library's Jefferson Building actually "shadows" the Capitol, a tarnished copper umbra to Meigs's and Walter's white

14  In addition, the LC maintains other departments and storage facilities off of Capitol Hill, e.g. the National Library for the Blind and Physically Handicapped in upper-Northwest Washington or the high-density storage facility at Fort Meade, Maryland and a motion picture storage and preservation complex in Culpeper, Virginia.

15  Although the Pendleton Act (1883) created a civil service premised on merit instead of the "spoils system," only one-in-ten government jobs were at first covered by it. However, subsequent acts and attendant reforms have gradually incorporated more and more government jobs into the Civil Service. The reform of the Civil Service, if the Cook Class Action suit is any indication (see below), continues.

dome. In fact, when the Jefferson Building opened in 1897, its gold-leafed dome was said to *overshadow* the Capitol and part of the decision to remove the gold leaf from the Library dome in 1931 (leaving only its gilded "flame") was due to what many felt was an invidious semiotic competition between the two buildings (Hilker 1972:251-252). Beneath the ground, the connections between the LC and the different branches of government are even clearer; a warren of tunnels, conveyors and pneumatic tubes link buildings together into a "cybernetic" network of power and knowledge that is not nearly as evident above ground.[16] The next development contemplated by the Architect of the Capitol is a vast, underground amphitheater (the United States Capitol Visitor Center) linking the U.S. Capitol and the Jefferson Building which would be utilized for exhibits and tourism.

Like the library in Borges's fable or the Aedificum in Umberto Eco's *Name of the Rose*, the Library of Congress is a fantastic, sometimes wonderful and sometimes horrible space that never fails to impress visitors with its size and complexity. I would, in fact, suggest that much of the LC is *designed* to induce awe and dread in the sense of the Romantic aesthetic of the sublime. It's not surprising that a former LC staffer wrote three mystery novels set in a library closely resembling the Library of Congress; the buildings inspire a certain sense of mystery.[17] This feeling is only heightened by the Library's policy of *closed* stacks; sitting at your desk in the Adams or Jefferson Building, you sense the immensity of the collections in the stacks surrounding you. You can even *smell* them—the Jefferson Building's decks are designed to draw air up through the cellar for ventilation and, walking by the doors leading into the book-decks, you can actually feel the sepulchral wind from the Library's stacks redolent with book mold and old paper. All of this combines into an air of mystery and even helplessness. In fact, users are often baffled by a system of book circulation and stacks control that makes a monograph available one day but "Not On Shelf" (NOS) the next, to the extent that, in the 1990s, deck attendants produced a rather patronizing brochure rendering the otherwise hermetic processes of book retrieval more transparent ("Let's Follow the Request Slip!"). The Library is, in a word, sublime. Walking alone down a corridor at night before closing, my feet slapping the tunnels connecting the Adams with the Jefferson Building, I can well imagine some heinous crime taking place and sometimes rather dreaded meeting another person. A common story people shared with me, particularly before the "security clampdown" in 1993, was the experience of getting lost in the Library's labyrinth tunnels and deserted corridors or their fright at meeting someone alone in the bookstacks. One person recalled screaming aloud when she pushed the timed light button to an aisle in

---

16  Although the image should be one of Fordist, factory production than of "post-Fordist" flexible accumulation (Harvey 1989).

17  Charles Goodrum wrote three mystery novels about a "Werner-Bok" library in Washington, D.C. with—like the actual LC—a Gutenberg Bible and a slightly autocratic "Director." There's little doubt that he was referring, in part, to his own experiences at the LC (Goodrum 1977).

the stacks and surprised an employee taking a nap on the floor! All of this lends a certain credence to Goodrum's climatic scenes in the Library stacks:

> By the time she stepped out of the elevator onto Deck Seven she had generated a firm case of the jitters. The deck was dark in both directions except for a single line of fluorescent tubes running down the center of the aisle. (Goodrum 1977:115)

And like the library in Borges's "Library of Babel," the Library of Congress's holdings seem impossibly large, "with 108 million items on 532 miles of shelving," as Head Librarian Billington frequently stressed throughout the 1990s(Fineberg 1995d:1).[18] With its vast infinitude of materials, entropy seems never far behind. Deck attendants spend large amounts of time moving materials back and forth across shelf space, making room for new schedules, new accessions or building renovations.[19] Talking with deck attendants and staff detailed to "collections services," I was struck by the Herculean (or Sisyphean) task of managing impossibly large collections and the unlikelihood of ever attaining *control* (in the bibliographic sense) over their endlessly fecund materials.

> Well, you figure there are over a hundred million volumes and there's an amazing number of things that aren't shelved or are misplaced or somebody had been reading them and threw, they basically just throw them behind something and then if they move something they find a lot of it. They're constantly moving shelves, sections. I've seen this stuff! (interview, Constituent Services, Public Service and Collection Management II Directorate)

Sometimes library employees despaired over the imminent chaos they perceived just below the surface of the Library's apparent order. However: others (*not* the deck attendants charged with maintaining the order of the collections!) found the sprawl in some ways romantic.

For example, there's a tradition common to all libraries but particularly prevalent at the Library of Congress of "discovery narratives" where the librarian-as-hero stumbles upon rare and valuable treasures in some entirely serendipitous way. In 1992, *The Gazette* reported on reference librarian Joan Higbee's chance discovery of valuable manuscripts and broadsides in the Harry Houdini collection.

> While on top of a ladder, she looked down at some dirty papers lying loose on the warehouse shelf and found some valuable posters under them. Serendipity continued to be with her, for coming farther down the ladder she found a long-

---

18   In a tradition reaching back to Spofford, Head Librarians seem to stress—particularly before Congress—the unfathomable, transcendent dimensions of the Library, repeatedly citing the immensity of its holdings which are always, in the utopian sense, "beyond imagining."

19   Although that seems less of a problem now that the Architect of the Capitol has finished its ten-year renovation on the Jefferson and Adams Buildings.

missing catalog from the McManus-Young collection under some crumbled papers. (Ohnemus 1992:10)

While in some ways such a discovery might be considered one of the high points of a librarian's career, and, by all accounts, made Higbee into a "library celebrity," in another way it is an admission of defeat, an acknowledgement that utopian order will continue to recede ahead of cataloging and processing efforts. After all, we might well wonder what piles of "crumbled papers" were doing at the Library Landover warehouse in the first place and how these rare (and expensive) posters and catalogs ended up in what amounted to a pile of garbage! In the best of all possible worlds, there would be few discoveries like this, since knowledge *about* collections would be coincident with the collections themselves. Nevertheless: well-publicized discoveries like this interject real publicity into the quotidian workings of the LC and it's entirely likely that Head Librarian Billington began his long program of "arrearage processing" in the late 1980s with the hope that well-publicized discoveries like the Houdini materials would justify the LC's budget and increase the overall cachet of the institution. And, indeed, many of the people I talked with worried over the unprocessed collections in their divisions for just these reasons; any interesting or valuable item in a collection is in danger of being lost, damaged or stolen the longer it remains undiscovered. For example, one staff member described a collection of almost 100,000 paperbacks published over the last fifty years packed away in boxes. The longer they stay in boxes, she felt, the greater the chance they'd be moved or disposed of. "I don't think people know there's anything here. [In fact] We have a couple of staff members who want to get rid of the collection" (interview, Collections Services, Public Service and Collection Management I Directorate).

To be realistic, such travails are inevitable in a library the size of the Library of Congress. As the largest library in the world, it manages resources that not only vary quantitatively from other research libraries, but *qualitatively* represent more materials in different formats than other libraries. The LC's *collection policy* encompasses what Head Librarian Billington calls—with the exception of agricultural materials collected by the National Agricultural Library and medical materials at the National Library of Medicine—a "universal collection of human knowledge" (Billington 1995:7).[20] Many scholars, in fact, define the LC by its special collections *alone*—i.e. those photographs, maps, motion pictures, manuscripts and so on that deviate from the usual coin of the library circulation, the monograph.[21] Acquiring, processing, cataloging, shelving and retrieving these collections, in addition to the customized research, reference, special programs, exhibits, publications and tours sponsored by the Library, extend far beyond the usual purview of a national library.

---

20   The "Collections Policy Statements" for the Library are available at *http://www.loc.gov*.

21   Long experience and considerable corroborating evidence from other users suggests that the LC may be a rather poor place to find a *monograph*. As reference staff continuously intone, the LC is a "library of last resort" and, because, of the volume of acquisitions and processing, recent books are generally not yet available.

## THE LIBRARY OF CONGRESS AS A NATIONAL LIBRARY

> It should be noted, too, that a legal deposit is inseparable from the notion of a national library and that most national libraries throughout the world benefit from such a requirement. It has been said, with tongue in cheek, that the way to recognize a nation is by the fact that it has a national library and that a national library exists by virtue of legal deposit. (Ladurie 1995:xxxv)

But the LC, even though it manages copyright deposits for the Nation, clearly undertakes a broad range of activities and functions unassociated with these legal and bureaucratic functions.[22] It is not too much to suggest that the history of the Library of Congress is the history of incrementally broadened functions. While the expanding purview of the Library from the nineteenth to the twentieth centuries has had the effect of making the LC the largest library in the world, it seems unlikely that the primary goal of Head Librarians was the mere quantitative increase of the collection.

Instead, let me suggest that the growth of the Library and its accrual of different departments and divisions relates to the interpellation of a certain kind of *national knowledge subject,* by which I mean a certain attitude and relationship to texts that is projected into the "imagined community" of the nation. It is the intent of this chapter to elucidate those relationships through a short, synopsis of the Library's growth from the late-nineteenth century to the present.

I will suggest that the Library's exponential growth leads to a succession of spatial changes that are continuously couched in the language of crisis, an invidious discourse legitimating all sorts of draconian measures across government, from cuts in social welfare and education to warfare and jingoistic legislation. While some have concentrated on the threat prolonged crises poses to the legitimation of a *status quo,* it seems more the case in the twenty-first century that the *state of crisis* and, in particular, *the language of the state of crisis,* has become normative and is used as a tool of everyday governance (Habermas 1973; Held 1982).

## SPACE AND TIME AT THE LIBRARY

During the first 3-4 months of my field research, I considered the question of "space" versus "place" with the goal of elucidating "sites of resistance" amidst the LC's official spaces. Although I found myriad examples of what Michael de Certeau has called "spatial poaching" about the Library's reading rooms and corridors—people taking naps, itinerant strangers wandering about on their own errands, mystagogues engaged in research quite outside of academia and so on—I was struck by the relative unimportance of these diverse tactics. To

---

22  Besides, deposit is technically not required to guarantee copyright, although most publishers still deposit copies with LC (Lessig, Post and Volokh 1996).

what extent, after all, were they discomfiting the official orders or the Library? To what degree could these acts be considered bonafide resistance? After all, an *institution*—by definition—legitimates a locus of operations, practices and discourses. To leave that sphere of the permissible and the pronounceable is, in actuality, to leave the institution. This is especially the case at a bureaucratic machine like the Library of Congress, which is defined, however amorphously, by a series of operations broken down into defined inputs and outputs.[23] The mere fact that some people deign to sleep on the job instead of shelving books or cataloging serials in no way affects the hegemony of the cybernetic equation and to imply otherwise is to seriously underestimate the power of the institution.

But this is not to say that the tyranny of the institution is complete or *totalizing*. Rather, following Goffman, individuals both conform and "express distance, detachment, and defiance" (Williams 1976:90). With the widespread currency of Foucault's *Discipline and Punish*, this is frequently forgotten. For the Foucauldian critic, every specular surveillance, from airports to cupolated domes, assumes characteristics of the Benthamite Panopticon. Nevertheless, while much of the late-modern, citadel culture penchant for surveillance and reconnaissance overlaps in striking ways with Jeremy Bentham's prison spaces, it is still stretching Foucault's analysis to locate *Panopticons* in every aspect of the built environment (Davis 1992).[24] For one thing, Bentham's constructions are not only built environments, but also social organizations and discursive regimes. Assigning an absolute coherence to the strategies of space is, in the end, as egregious as its antiphrasis in the plucky tactics of place: both presuppose a general social anomie. As Henri LeFebvre reminds us, however, "space" is less a force "in itself" than part of a constellation of social productions.

> Spatial practice regulates life—it does not create it. Space has no power 'in itself' nor does space as such determine spatial contradictions. These are contradictions of society—contradictions between one thing and another within a society, as for example between the forces and relations of production—that simply emerge in space, at the level of space, and so engender the contradictions of space. (LeFebvre 1991: 358)

That is, a successful built environment will forge a correspondence between otherwise disparate spheres of social life, production and knowledge and organize practice accordingly. At that level, space can organize "people, things and ideas," but it cannot do so without contradiction, disjunction and crisis

---

23 *Defining* those varied operations has always been problematic for bureaucratic management and the Library, like other Federal agencies in the 1980s and 90s, has produced myriad "mission statements" codifying "products" for each department and division in its organization.

24 Can we consider a metal detector in a high school a Panopticon (Devine 1995)? Is a windowed cupola "the centerpiece of a panopticon built on a grand scale" (Leone 1995:256)? While useful, perhaps, as a way of analyzing structures of social inequality inherent in architectural formalism, "panopticon think" invests hegemony with too much coherency and homogeneity.

(Markus 1993:19). In a manner similar to Althusser's "ideological state apparatus," correspondences forged through spatial strategies cannot adhere across time.

What emerges at the Library is a series of contradictions in the "practical relationship" of spaces, things and people. But this is less of an effect of epiphenomenal resistance than the "normal" operations of the institution. It is into this spatial catastasis that we go next.

As the first "postcolonial designed capital," Washington, D.C. was supposed to reinforce the ideals of democracy and representative government through both its buildings (the neo-classical elements common to Federal architecture) and its urban planning (wide, diagonal boulevards facilitating the specular "communication" of rulers and ruled) (Vale 1992). That it does neither of these things is due to an admixture of accident and *realpolitik*.

> Though Jefferson and his supporters sought to use architecture to invoke Greco-Roman democracy, L'Enfant and the architects of the Capitol alluded more to the Roman Vatican than to the Roman forum. Thus, the experiment in democracy initially spawned no parallel experiment in planning or in architecture. (Vale 1992: 67)

Of course, the fledgling state only problematically embodied these Greek ideals of participatory democracy and, in many respects, D.C.'s design reflects this ambivalence to power, inviting the *res publica* to witness the spectacle of government rather than participate directly in it, setting a design trend for capital cities that has lasted into the present.[25]

The administrative and public buildings that circumference Washington, D.C.'s capacious Mall seem to recall older, Baroque ideals and seem designed to impress visitors with the power of the State rather than inviting participation; this is as true of the Capitol as the more recent construction of the Federal Triangle area. The federal city is—perhaps unsurprisingly—*federalist* in spirit. And yet, even the most authoritarian design needs to balance control with the legitimation of control: thus the monolithic Capitol also implies participatory egalitarianism in its dome. This moral drama of authoritarian control and participatory democracy is figuratively and spatially enacted in every federal building in Washington, D.C. and will frame my discussion of the Library of Congress complex.

---

25 This spatial split between rulers and ruled has been a continuous one in the District of Columbia. From the District's beginnings as a jumble of disconnected residential zones surrounding the Capitol and the Navy Yard in the early 1800s to the present dismissal of a much-maligned southeastern quartile, D.C. politicians have belligerently reduced the complexities of the *city* to the functions of its federal *functions*, ignoring the rich patina of history, community and identity that constitutes Washington's identity (Young 1966).

## LIBRARIES TODAY AND TOMORROW

One of the ways we—as resolute moderns—have understood the manifold contradictions of modernity is through variations on the "myth of the fall" raised to level of an often-repeated coda rehearsed in every country, in every milieu and accompanying every change. It is not surprising, therefore, that libraries should evidence a similar diluvial past, a benchmark between a mythopoetic time of Edenic plenty and a present beset with fractious chaos. Of course, if the past was a time of "grace" and if the present represents a "fall," the future will mark its Elidean return, as was the case with McLuhan's notions of a return to a more mechanical society (in the Durkheimian sense) through the adoption of "cool" media (Czitrom 1982).

In the case of libraries, at least two factors are said to have contributed to this modernist scission from a period of past plenitude: 1). the size of collections and 2). the (related) failure of a "classed" library classification to keep pace with the succession of "information explosions" rocking society from the inception of print capitalism.[26]

> The centuries-old direct link between shelves, books, staff and readers, as in Wolfenbuttel, was fractured. Sweeping consequences followed from the acceptance that books would have to be stored in stacks, that readers needed reading rooms, and staff their own spaces. (Markus 1993:177)

Early classifications assigned books stack locations according to general (classed) subject schemata (Petee 1946). Baconian classification, for instance, formed the basis for cataloging up until the nineteenth century; encyclopedae, libraries and museums were all variations on a "great chain of being" with roots in eighteenth-century classificatory rationalism (Lovejoy 1933). However, the various information explosions from the eighteenth century to the present made such fixed locations unwieldy and even obsolete once the various classificatory hierarchies began to disentangle under the weight of rapid growth in the volume of public scientific knowledge. What was needed to keep pace with this growth was a dehiscence of the classed catalog, where classification, subject indexing and location all went their separate ways.

> Free of the limitations imposed by the fact that books as physical things can occupy only one position in space at a time, classification provides a deeper subject analysis when applied to entries in catalogs than to books. The depth of the analysis is limited  only by the needs of the library, its classification, the competence of its staff—and, important today, its budget. (La Montagne 1961:8)

Insofar as it is a library, the Library of Congress is imbricated in the same "myth of the Fall" constituted by massive collections spiraling out of control. And yet, as a national

---

26  A classed system is a *proximal* one placing 1). like materials with like materials and 2). *classes* of materials in a rational order compared to each other (Petee 1946).

institution, the LC is bounded by another set of constraints. The following recounts the story of the Library as knowledge organization and as national institution.

## BECOMING THE LIBRARY OF CONGRESS

At its inception in 1802, the Library of Congress was little more than a handful of reference books and law texts housed in the (unfinished) Capitol for the occasional need of Congress. This was to change, however, with the purchase of Thomas Jefferson's encyclopedic collection of books in 1815 after the British burned down the Library in 1814 (along with part of the Capitol). Unfortunately, the Library suffered another fire in 1851 but was moved into vastly renovated quarters in the Capitol building in 1853 (Cole 1993). Designed to serve Congress, their families, visiting constituents and visiting luminaries, the Library represented—along with intellectual societies and social clubs—another of the select spaces developed for D.C.'s elite during the nineteenth century and had more in common—both in design and spirit—with a private club than with the public library movement that would transform American libraries by the end of the century. Its design—a "gallery and alcove" style providing a highly sociable and well-lit promenade—prompted one admirer to dub it "the most beautiful room in the world" (Cole 1993:81). Desks for Head Librarian Spofford, Congress and other users fell about the room in a pattern suggestive more of an acephalous equality than a compartmentalized bureaucracy; although Congress, staff and readers theoretically occupied separate spaces with Congress and staff to the south and other readers to the north part of the chamber, in practice all three groups spilled out onto any available surface. An "iron cage" compartmentalizing and operationalizing all into separate departments would have to wait until after the Civil War.

The early classification of books at the LC in many ways reflected its flattened hierarchy. Following the 1815 purchase of Jefferson's books, Librarians of Congress adopted a modified version of Jefferson's classification, a *method* grounded in Baconian thought that divided all of human knowledge into 44 "chapters" based on human faculties.[27] At the time, libraries utilized a bewildering number of different methods in their classification, cataloging and shelving. Many of them, however, were variations on the "classed" scheme (Pettee 1946).

> Book classification was also in a primitive condition. One sign of that condition was a general dependence on class entry as the principal method of subject classification and the lack of precision that this method entailed. Instead of entering books under terms that matched the particular topics that books treated, books were placed in large and undifferentiated classes that were broader than those particular topics. (Miska 1984:7)

---

27  Although, as Miska points out, the early Librarians of Congress who annotated Jefferson's method were less interested in forming "an intellectual map of universal knowledge" than with the *pragmata* of managing a large and expanding collection (Miska 1984:5-6).

All of this changed during Head Librarian Spofford's term with 1). the publishing explosion following the Civil War and 2). the passage of the 1870 Copyright Law mandating the deposit of copyrighted works at the Library of Congress. Both of these helped push the LC's holdings from 63,000 volumes in 1860 to 246,000 volumes in 1872 (Cole 1971; Library of Congress 1872:9).[28] Nearly overnight, the Library became the "greatest chaos in America" as collections began to spill out over inadequate shelving. Spofford began to press Congress for a separate building and an increased staff to manage the burgeoning deposit, a request they finally assented to in 1886 (Cole 1972:292).

Various designs for the new Library were debated both within and without the Library community and generally fell across a predictable spectrum of opinion. There were those, particularly among librarians, who felt that the new library should subordinate *form* to *function* and reflect recent advancements in the newly enfeoffed discipline of library science. As the Head Librarian for the Newberry Library opined, "These rooms will have no alcoves or galleries; for alcoves I regard as useless and galleries are an unpardonable nuisance" (Poole 1881:75). Others stressed the "national" character of a "national" library and regarded the Library of Congress as an important symbol of federal unity as well as a spectacle for Washington tourists. One of the Library's eventual architects, John Smithmeyer, was an enthusiastic advocate of a monumental building.

> There have been made objections to wide passages in a library [ . . .] but such objection is not tenable as to a National Library, which is essentially of a public character, and in which the mere observation of its arrangement and its management is in itself an object of interest and study like a museum, and there are enough separate provisions made for the pleasure and curiosity of the mere spectator, so as not to interfere with the ease and other claims of the reader and student. (Smithmeyer 1881:79)

In the end, while the Library incorporated some features of "modern" library science, the more decorative impulses won out over the raw pragmatism of book storage and retrieval, among them a vaulted reading room at the Library's center in the style of British Museum (Cole 1972; Library of Congress 1872:10). After discarding various neo-Gothic, neo-Classical and Baroque quotations, the committee in charge of the LC's design competition decided on an "Italian Renaissance" (really Beaux Arts) style of building submitted by architects John Smithmeyer and Paul Pelz, a marked departure from the heavy-handed classicism of much of the national architecture and a sore point for many critics who saw the Library building as "contradicting" the spirit of L'Enfant's plan (Hilker 1972:253).[29]

---

28  These "counts" of total holdings are—as always—slightly suspect. For example, by its own admission, the LC had no idea of the "number" of its manuscript holdings until the 1940s.

29  One might argue that "L'Enfant's plan" had already been well-departed from by the time

## THE COLUMBIAN EXPOSITION AS A MODEL FOR THE LIBRARY

Given the relative uniformity of the Capitol complex of buildings, it is worth asking why the Library of Congress diverged from the general speciation of "classical" themes common to the rest of the Mall. It can be attributed to the late-nineteenth and early twentieth century vogue for "Beaux Arts" design that crested in Washington with the "City Beautiful" movement and the 1901 McMillan Commission Report, a thirty year stretch of construction that gave D.C. the Library of Congress, the Central Library, the District Building and Daniel Burnham's Union Station in addition to a number of mansions and embassies. But the Library is more than a nod at a particularly ostentatious architectural style. Rather, it signals a shift in the way the U.S. government communicated with its citizens via the Federal City. Moving away from the combination of Athenian democracy and Roman republicanism that characterized the more Baroque Capitol, the Library's design reflected ideological imperatives based on the legitimation of empire and monopoly (liberal) capitalism in a time of unparalleled ethnic, racial and class strife.[30] It was a time—some have called it the "museum age"— when the State took an active interest in developing intellectual institutions as part of its central functioning, particularly in Washington, D.C., where an intelligentsia grew up around the Capital and in many ways served to legitimate centralized government (Flack 1968; Kohlstedt 1987:168).

The blueprint (and, perhaps, the apogee) of this synthesis was the Columbian Exposition of 1893. There, the ideational and the academic were interpolated into popular exhibits, signaling the triumph of a nineteenth century evolutionary dogma that derogated "primitive" peoples and ethnic and racial minorities to low rungs on a Social Darwinist ladder. It was, to cop a useful term from Emily Martin, a moment of "saturation" where the hateful calculus of "scientific" race and racism penetrated societal spheres far removed from the social or physical sciences, altering the way people conceptualized their world (Martin 1994). That saturation of Chicago's midway with the hegemony of class, race, ethnicity and empire was achieved at the level of *habitus* by structuring not only the representation of others, but the conditions of that repre-

---

the Library's building was under construction. Certainly, L'Enfant's simple, open design had long been superseded by Ellicott's more military boulevards and intimidating public architecture. The "City Beautiful" movement, at least, affected a largely symbolic return to the L'Enfant city (Weeks 1994; WPA 1939).

30   The federal government attempted to work this ideological fusion of progress and renaissance humanism into the design of many of its buildings from the late-nineteenth century to the 1930s. Some were less successful than others, as, for example, the 1856 the "Electricity, Fidelity, and Steam" reliefs on the Tariff Commission Building showing cherubim guiding lightning bolts and steam engines (Goode 1974). Likewise, it is no surprise that much of the imagery utilized in computer advertising today draws from the European Renaissance; certainly, the symbolic equation of *profit* with *human progress* is as widespread today as it was in the late-nineteenth century.

sentation, a metonymical chain of racist signification reinforced through the instantiation of the promenade itself.

> Brotherly love and understanding between nations was the single most labored aspect of exhibition diatribe, the sentiment usually being ridiculed by displays of military technology, imperial conquest, and abject racism at the sites themselves. (Greenhalgh 1988:17)

One of the most important ways this synthesis of sentiment and sentience was achieved was through *art*; the Columbian Exposition deployed a whole army of American artists, sculptors, architects, engineers and scientists to render the fair's evolutionary claims visible (hence *sensible*). As with the present, the nineteenth century's World's Fairs rarely distinguished between fine arts, the hard sciences and the demands of *commerce*, a capitalist synesthesia unwelcomed by those who saw menace in this age of liberal capitalism (Kuznick 1994). While some deplored this conflation of the fine arts and the theoretical sciences with monopoly capitalism, on another level their synthesis—through the syntax of nineteenth-century nationalism—was a necessary and sufficient condition for that superiority that "civilization" entailed. On some level, the civilizing mission dovetailed with the *consumption* of technological wonders, a fusion the Columbian Exposition achieved through grandiose Beaux Arts designs everywhere festooned with technological wonders and (potential) consumer products.[31] Whatever the excesses of the American translation of the Beaux Arts style, it was taken as a model for public architecture, beginning with the new Library of Congress building (Rice 1982:17).

> The main building of 1897—the building of Smithmeyer & Pelz, of General Casey and Bernard L. Green—was consciously designed to satisfy the aesthetic needs of the American people as represented by their government—and it did so. Its completion followed closely on the Columbia World's Fair of 1893, and it epitomized the exuberance which has led to that artistic coming of age. (unpublished memo, Architect of the Capital:2)

Although the overall management of the project was placed under the stewardship of Brigadier-General Thomas Lincoln Casey and his assistant Bernard L. Green, the "general decoration" was overseen by Elmer Garnsey and Albert Weinert; Garnsey had overseen the riotous colors and details at the Columbian Exposition.[32] Like the Exposition, an army of American painters, sculptors and masons were engaged to work on the new building. Having rejected more

---

31 The Beaux-Arts style was reviled almost at its inception in the United States as bombastic and reactionary. Despite some postmodern nostalgia over the last twenty years, most architects and architectural historians consider Beaux-Arts in the United States as just an interruption of Louis Sullivan's Chicago School (Aranson 1986).

32 I want to thank Peter Bartis for initially pointing out some of the design parallels between the Jefferson Building and the Columbian Exposition.

conservative classicism for a florid quotation of Renaissance architecture, the proposed Library was a large canvas for all manner of decorative cartouches, murals, mosaics, statuary and arabesques (Small 1901).

Those varied artists were charged with nothing less than representing the hegemony of the nation: its imperialist ambitions and its rampant Republicanism. In rendering the nation sensible to itself, the artists utilized a number of images and symbols couched in the language of evolution and Social Darwinism; these ranged from the thoroughly racist evolutionary heads for the keystone arches above the exterior windows to Martiny's Grand Staircase in the Main Entrance Hall, where four babies representing "America," "Asia," "Africa" and "Europe" face off in a neonatal pageant. It is worth quoting the full text from the *Handbook of the New Library of Congress*:

> The four continents are typified, very delightfully, by little boys, about three feet high, seated by the side of a large, marble globe, on which appears the portions of the earth's surface which they are intended to personify. *America* is an Indian, with a tall headdress of feathers, a bow and arrow, and a wampum necklace. With one hand he shadows his eyes while he gazes intently into the distance, awaiting, one may fancy, the coming of his conqueror, the white man. *Africa* is a little negro, with a war-club and his savage necklace of wild beasts' claws. *Asia* is a Mongolian, dressed in flowing silk robes, the texture of which, as the visitor will notice, is very perfectly indicated by arranging the folds of the marble so that they receive the proper play of light and shade. In the background is a sort of dragon-shaped jar of porcelain. *Europe* is clad in the conventional classic costume, and has a lyre and a book; and a Doric column is introduced beside him— the three objects symbolizing, specifically, Music, Literature, and Architecture, and, more broadly, the pre-eminence of the Caucasian race in the arts of civilization generally, just as the dragon-jar on the other side of the globe stands for the admirable ceramic art of China and Japan; and, also, as the wampum and bow of the Indian indicate his advance in culture over the stage of evolution typified by the rude war-club and the savage necklace of the negro. (Small 1901:25)

Also in the Main Entrance Hall are odes to the triumph of the publishing industry, John Alexander's East Corridor tympanums illustrating "the Evolution of the Book" as well as various paeans to the justice and superiority of the State, in particular Elihu Vedder's tympanums illustrating the moral evolution of government from despotism to rational administration (Small 1901:36). All seethe with characteristic class and race antagonisms; they are so many bald-faced assertions of interests of a central elite to those of a rank-and-file, the recognition of the *rulers* and the *ruled*. This reaches a certain height on the dome's collar in the Main Reading Room, where Edwin Blashfield has illustrated the "evolution of civilization" through twelve enigmatic figures representing the accretion of progress from distant, allochronic beginnings in the "East" to the growth of the European nation-state and the North American ascendancy.

The twelfth and last figure, bringing us once more around to the east, is that of *America*—represented by an engineer, in the garb of the machine-shop, sitting lost in thought over a problem in mechanics he has encountered. He leans his chin upon the palm of one hand, while the other holds the scientific book he has been consulting. In front of him is an electric dynamo—recalling the part which the United States has taken in the advancement of electrical science. (Small 1901:75)

In the Main Entrance Hall atop the balustrades of the Grand Staircase are two bronze figures of women holding an "electric torch." They epitomize the chief *leitmotif* of the Columbian Exposition: art and science yoked to consumerism and the State. More than a simple repository for books, the new Library represented the superior capability of the machine. Perhaps more than the figurative triumph of American "know-how" over European civilization, the Library—like the Columbian Exposition after which it had been patterned—was meant to memorialize the machine and its power to unite the Nation in the pursuit of profit. The mechanics of the Library—evocations of the dynamo's power—were, perhaps, better proof of American superiority than any allegorical representation of "good government" over "anarchy."

> Much admired by reporters, too, was the machinery— especially the "railroads" that carried books from the stacks to the reading room and from the Octagon to the Capitol via the underground tunnel. (Hilker 1972:244)

Electricity was in no way commonplace in the last decades of the nineteenth century. It is perhaps easy to forget that the first electric lights in the Capitol were installed in 1879 and the first in the White House in 1890; it would be decades into the twentieth century before electrification reached more rural corners of the United States (Truett 1968:500-501). David Nye has convincingly demonstrated the importance of *electricity* to the popularity of the Columbian Exposition and the same could be said of the Library; it was the first, major Federal building to be designed with electric power in mind and its space would have simply been impossible without it.

> Evenings, the light is furnished by incandescent lamps, with which the passages and the corridors are abundantly equipped, and here again the polished decks serve a most useful purpose in diffusing the brilliant illumination throughout the whole system of shelving. (Small 1901:84)

Could its complex murals, friezes and mosaics have been legible without the aid of the incandescent bulb (particularly in places like the North Corridor Entrance Hall which are tucked well away from natural, ambient light)? Even the Main Reading Room, with its heavily leaded glass, is heavily shadowed during even the brightest afternoon.[33]

---

33  Much of this is due to the gradual *filling in* of the Jefferson Building's courtyards and the extension of the top decks above the original line of the roof.

## TECHNOLOGY AND THE DEMOS

I think we have to see the entire Jefferson Building as in some ways a monument to the power of applied technology to palliate the many problems of a "democratic" government extended across the space of a continent. For one thing, like its prototype in the British Museum, the domed enclosure of the Main Reading Room placed the reader-citizen at the center of the "bibliopolis" (Thomas 1983). At the center of the Library's knowledge-universe, readers could—literally and figuratively—call upon the resources of the *nation*. In many buildings, *depth* connotes *power*; the deeper the penetration of people into a building's interior, the more power they have relative the institution. "This looks like a good analogue for some of the towns and factories within their walls, gates and towers, shallow workers' housing, increasing depth representing increasing power and control. The spaces of maximum productive value lie deep within" (Markus 1993:261). As Head Librarian Billington has suggested, "In many ways, the Main Reading Room is the symbol of this nation's commitment to learning as the basis for democracy" (Billington 1990:9). Since, however, the Library of Congress—like other national libraries—has closed stacks, readers are unable to procure these "democratic tools" for themselves. Rather, to extend the metaphor further, Library readers must depend upon the largesse of the State: truly democratic participation would not, after all, involve the intercession of an institution. What Thomas Markus writes of the British Museum's library is also true of the Library of Congress, in many ways its intellectual issue:

> The dome with its central oculus was modeled on the Parthenon and had a diameter of only two feet less. It has cosmic meanings as elemental as those of the original. The physiognomy of the cylinder is constituted by the books, a mere sample of the knowledge hidden in stacks and accessible through the catalogue and staff intervention. The centre, under the eye of the dome, represents power both in the total surveillance it exercises and in being enclosed by the ring of catalogues into which all knowledge is compressed. (Markus 1993:179)

The "trick" of the British Museum's domed reading room is the way it can *connote* freedom while at the same time (necessarily) *impelling* obedience; this, of course, is the brilliance of "panoptical" thinking. What energizes this democratic/authoritarian apparatus at the Library of Congress is electricity; this was the medium through which one could build a national-technical hegemony, a "body electric . . .connecting all souls" (Nye 1991:2). Even in 1897, the size of the Library's holdings, after all, precluded instant access to holdings; it was already the largest library in the United States (Billington 1996). In the Joint Committee hearings that preceded the adoption of the Smithmeyer and Pelz plan, Members of Congress had worried about the inconvenience of a separate Library building and had even suggested raising the Capitol dome as a way of extending the Library's bookstacks, a scheme that E.J. Applewhite has kindly termed "amateurish" (Applewhite 1981:257).

> But it was technology that would (virtually) connect the Capitol back to Congress's library. It is calculated that, by means of the pneumatic tubes and book-carrying apparatus, it will require no more than six or seven minutes to bring a book from the stacks, from the time it is called for. Valuable, however, as the use of machinery is in connecting widely distant portions of the Library, it is even more important as a factor in bringing together the Library itself and the Capitol, where hardly an hour passes, during a session of Congress, but some member desires to draw books for immediate use in debate or committee work. The distance between the two buildings is about a quarter of a mile (twelve hundred and seventy-five feet). This is covered by a tunnel having at one end a terminus in the basement almost immediately beneath the Distributing Desk, and at the other end in a room in the Capitol about midway between the Senate and the House of Representatives. (Small 1901:79)

The conveyors began as independently operated belts connecting the Main Reading Room with the North and South Stacks through the basement level, bringing the books down the stacks and up to the Reading Room by means of a series of plates, and a third belt running east from the Library to the Capitol conveying two large trays (Small 1901:79).

The pneumatic tubes connect the Main Reading Room to the surrounding decks by means of terminals on each deck, routed from the Reading Room at a "Central Sorting Station" in the Control Room of either the Jefferson or the Adams Building rather like a telephone switchboard with tubes for each deck, although at the Library's inception the tubes were connected to a giant (and noisy) terminal at the Main Reading Room's circulation desk.[34]

> Along the front of the deck, also, is a row of twenty- four pneumatic tubes for the transmission of messages, either in cylindrical pouches, as in the case of the written applications which those desiring to draw books are required to make out, or verbally, by means of a mouth-piece with which each tube is equipped. Nine tubes go to the South stack, or one for every floor. Four go to the East stack, or one to every other floor. An attendant for any portion of the stack system can thus be reached at a moment's notice. (Small 1901:78)

Many readers complained at the clanking of the book conveyor and the bursts of compressed air that powered the pneumatic tubes, what one irate reader termed their "consumptive coughing" (Nelson and Farley 1991:24). What, perhaps, those early critics failed to appreciate was that they were not only at the center of a library, in the classic, Alexandrian sense, but the center of a machine powered by the dynamo and deeply enmeshed in the production of an ideology of national, technocratic progress. One might even argue that the

---

34   The Madison Building houses only special collections, hence users requesting those materials cannot have them delivered by means of the conveyors.

purpose of the Main Reading Room, with its mechanical clanging and marble floors echoing every footstep, was designed as a sort of tribute to the growing hegemony of the industrial spirit and to the spirit of engineering applied to the metaphysics of knowledge. After all, weren't the original architects of the project—Smithmeyer and Pelz—gradually distanced from the project in favor of Brigadier General Thomas Casey, an engineer? It certainly fit an age when wealthy industrialists became cultural brokers of United States life, influencing education, communications and the language of representation in a way unsurpassed until the present.

## CRISES OF SPACE/CRISES OF KNOWLEDGE

"The increase of the Library of Congress will forever be on a grand scale, and, like the annual growth of our country, will be greater and greater in every succeeding year." (Justin Smith Morrill, quoted in Library of Congress 1947:261)

A built environment is not just a static *tableau* of surface, structure and corresponding *semiosis*, a connection of objects and their "emitted signs." Rather, a building—a built environment—suggests changing patterns of use, different practices of space and shifting (and possibly contradictory) environments.

The answer returns to the idea of an unfolding serial event, a building as a narrative. From the moment it is conceived, through its design, production, use, continuous reconstruction in response to changing use, until its final demolition, the building is a developing story, traces of which are always present. (Markus 1993:5)

The Library, like any building, develops a gap between the ideologies associated with different functions, with, in this case, the *national* prerogatives and the *technological* prerogatives of progress. Unlike L'Enfant's Baroque city, which rested on a vision of power achieved through diagonal avenues and monumental building (as opposed to a reciprocity of power), the 1897 Building, true to its renaissance stylings, embodied a built environment where readers were placed at the epicenter of knowledge in the Main Reading Room rather than a more subservient (and shallow) position along the Library's periphery (Leone 1987). It is a powerful image—and a powerful practice—to sit in the Main Reading Room equidistant from all of the tools of knowing, potentially in the midst of limitless knowledge and able, through the imposition of technology, to access any part of it at any time. However: the Jefferson Building (or the Main Building), like any built environment, does not remain a static repository of structure and meaning over its lifetime, like a beacon endlessly broadcasting the messages about space and practice, but shifts over time as new conditions, renovations and practices change the relationship of people and technologies to their built environment.[35] In 1962, Head Librarian Quincy Mumford looked back at the design of the Jefferson Building with nostalgic longing.

> This has necessitated some major changes in the Main Building, whose "pavilions" and "curtains" speak of more spacious days. They have been encroached upon, adapted, and readapted until their beauty has largely been lost and the dark subdivisions seem, in summer, more like steam cabinets than rooms. (Library of Congress 1962:xii)

I will suggest that the "loss" Mumford mourns is not merely cosmetic—e.g. the erection of office cubicles in arcaded exhibitionary space—but also ideological. The "beauty" of the Main Building rests not only in its gilding and colonnades, but also in the ideas it manifests about the relationship of library users (citizens) to library materials (the Nation).

Gradually, however, this fusion of reader, machine and library dissolved into modernist scission for a number of reasons. The ones frequently cited in annual reports and committee hearings to Congress include: 1). a "spatial crisis" precipitated by the geometric, then logarithmic, growth of publishing in the United States; 2). the variety of "container types" collected by the Library; and 3). the successive "revolution" of informational technologies, each requiring different architectural arrangements to accommodate their physical design. Whether or not these are actually causative agents is not particularly relevant to this analysis. The primary records of the Library's growth—annual reports, contracted studies and committee hearings—are hardly innocent windows on conditions prevalent at the LC. Rather, their presentation of "the facts" is always a tendentious affair usually pointedly trained towards self-preservation. What's more important, I believe, is tracing the development of a "language of crisis" around a perceived "information explosion." What follows is a summary of different threats to the Library's order during this century.

The post-war publishing boom during the late-nineteenth century quickly filled the new Library of Congress building. By 1905, only 8 years after the building's completion, Head Librarian Putnam struggled to shelve a growing corpus of bound newspapers, eventually finding temporary storage in the basement (Library of Congress 1905:103). Not only did the sheer number of newspapers strain the Library's resources—testament to the growth of journalism—but their size prohibited efficient shelving in the main stacks. While thought extremely flexible at the time, the Library's shelving could readily accommodate typically-sized books—folios, octavos or duodecimos—but not other, non-standard sizes.

---

35 Curiously, much of anthropology relegates the built environment to just this sort of anhistorical ubiquity, assuming—even as they focus on historical processes—that the architectural features of, for example, a colonial encampment always "mean" the same subservience of native Other to European domination even though the relations of the State may have changed (Rabinow 1989).

In the next place, it should now be said that in none of the original estimates of the book capacity of the building does account appear to be taken of the fact that there would be a continuing necessity to devote great shelf areas to the storage of material other than books, pamphlets, and bound newspapers counted as constituting the "collections." (Library of Congress 1918:113)

Head Librarian Putnam estimated the bulk of the bound newspaper at twelve times that of a typical book (Library of Congress 1906:75).

As stated in the last annual report, the larger part of the present collection is now temporarily shelved in the cellar of the Library building. The place is wholly unsuitable, but the only one now available. It is too hot, damp at times, dusty, most inconvenient and slow of access, and dangerous from possible leaks in the steam and water pipes of the mechanical apparatus which abound and which the space was more especially intended to accommodate. The service to readers is correspondingly slow, and the volumes not only unclean, but are unavoidably subjected to rough handling, which is accelerating the gradual ruin of the collection. (Library of Congress 1906:75)

While the Head Librarian's complaint centers on the threat to the preservation of the Library's collection—a universal concern in all libraries at all times—there's another part to his remonstrations that have more to do with the confusion of library "apparatus," the combination of the LC's physical machine with the "reading machine" upstairs and the lengthening of delivery times.

That classificatory apparatus was also strained by the growth of the collections. Even though the LC has long abandoned more medieval "fixed location" systems of book classification (although bookstores, for example, still utilize them), the LC Classification still required that books classified together be shelved together, a mixture, really, of relative and fixed stack locations (Miska 1984).

First, economic library administration requires that all the material on a given subject shall be shelved together, so that the investigator may find assembled in one place all the library's resources in that subject, and the attendant may not need to go to many widely separated places to find the books wanted by a single reader. (Library of Congress 1918:112)

Like the breakdown of the Library's physical apparatus, the classificatory apparatus frayed both at the number of books and the variety of container types, each which separated schedules from the classification that, by all rights, should be classed together.

Putnam's answer to the overflow was to press for new bookstacks in one of the Library's four courtyards, created by the four stacks radiating off the Main reading Room and providing some natural light to the stacks and reading rooms. The southeastern court was filled in with a bookstack in winter of 1909, a stack that improved on the design of the original 1897 stacks through a technological expedient (Library of Congress 1910).

One of these is the large stack occupying the entire southeast court of the building for the special accommodation of bound volumes of newspapers and for other books of all kinds. It is to receive its mechanical automatic book carrier of necessary special design and construction, running in a vertical shaft at the side of one of the elevators throughout the nine stories of the stack. This will ensure the greatest practical speed of service between the stack, main reading room and other parts of the building. Its construction is under way at a total cost of $4,800. The other stack is that for the Division of Music, in the north curtain, basement. It was begun near the close of the previous fiscal year, and was completed and equipped during the past year at a total cost of $10,871.27. Like all the other stacks in the building, its design and construction is especially and economically adapted for its purpose and fireproof throughout. (Library of Congress 1911:86)

The over-size newspaper folios required a specially constructed book conveyor while the Music Division—a corpus of recordings and sheet music deposited at the Library for copyright since the enactment of the 1870 legislation—required different techniques for storage and access that made the library's more conventional bookstacks impractical.

Nevertheless, Library collections continued to outpace available space and Head Librarian Putnam clamored for new stacks only a decade after building the southeast bookstack.

On many hundreds of shelves are two rows of books, one hidden behind the other. The classification has been broken in many places; related material has been separated and groups of books relegated to distant parts of the building wherever a bit of room still remained available. The resulting conditions are deplorable. There is constant delay in producing for use books needed immediately. The assistants at the reference desk have constantly to bear in mind these irregularities, so that call slips shall be sent to those decks where the desired books ought to be shelved, but to other decks and even to other stacks. (Library of Congress 1918:114)

Again, the complaints devolve not so much upon the number of new accessions to the Library's collections, but to the way new materials strain the Library's classificatory and management systems: the way readers, staff and Library apparatus (i.e. pneumatic book-tubes) work together.

In 1926, the Library began constructing another stack of book decks in the northeast courtyard, finally completing them in March of 1927. This time, the Library couldn't install a system of book conveyors connecting back to the Main Reading Room.

The system of conveyors (book railway) common to the two other large stacks could not, for physical reasons (precluding terminals in the reading room) be carried into the northeast courtyard; so that, except for the lifts, the service of the new material from the new stack must be by messenger. (Library of Congress 1926:6)

Other compromises to the Library's circulation were to follow, however, even with the extension of the height of the east and southeast stacks an additional three stories.

> The congestion in the bookstacks reported in previous years is now becoming a very serious problem incident to the accession each year of about 170,000 volumes (equivalent to the capacity of one whole deck room). Only recently we have been compelled again to pack in boxes and store in the cellar many additional thousands of volumes (chiefly folios) in an endeavor to relieve the situation. (Library of Congress 1935)[36]

By 1935, Head Librarian Putnam had convinced Congress that an annex to the Main Building was necessary, and construction began across 2nd Street on the site of a bank of residential housing.

The design of the new building was—in contradistinction to the Beaux Arts exuberance of the Main Building—a restrained affair, essentially a shell of offices, reading rooms and carrels surrounding a dense layering of bookstacks. Instead of placing readers in a vaulted center, the Adams Building, as it came to be called, consigns them to the outside; the *center* (following Markus, the place of most power) is occupied by *control rooms*, that is, conveyors, book trucks and the staff that loads one onto the other. Having the control rooms there, it must be said, is certainly more efficient.[37]

> Here are no great halls such as Washington has come to expect. The beauty which must arise from their work must come solely from the fitness of form to function; from the movement of lines expressive of the well- considered plan and unity of a building which was viewed in prospect as a mere storehouse: from the effectiveness, not the lavishness of ornamentation. (Architect of the Capitol: unpublished memo)

Already a cliché in the 1930s, "the fitness of form to function" meant sublimating the iconographical (and ideological) functions of the Main Building to the *storage* of books. Indeed, the Adams Building holds twice the number of books as the Jefferson Building (almost 10 million to the Jefferson's 5 million). Following that, the Annex (now the Adams Building) elides much of the imperialism marking (or marring) the Jefferson Building, the sole exception being Lee Lawrie's restrained, arte moderne bronze door reliefs of the world's inventors of alphabets: Ogma for the Irish, Itzama for the Mayans, Thoth for the Egyptians and so on. Instead of dogmatic tracts on racial superiority, the murals in the fifth floor North Reading Room depict scenes from the Canterbury Tales and those in the South Reading Room the life and thought of Thomas Jefferson.

---

36  It should go without saying that to *box* up Library materials is the antithesis of the Librarian's mission, an admonition of defeat.

37  Of course, the control rooms in the Jefferson Building are also in the *center* of the building, but occupy the lower levels of the building, beneath the grandeur of the Main Reading Room.

Despite the extension of a pedestrian tunnel and book conveyor to the new building, the completion of the Annex in 1938 still necessitated the division of the Library's collections.

> As between the Annex and the Main Building the general subdivision of the collections will be as follows: To the Annex, the groups embracing Bibliography, Agriculture, technology, Medicine, and Science (including the Smithsonian deposit); bound files of newspapers (some 98,000 volumes); Official Documents of foreign countries with certain   exceptions; and certain bound serials, e.g. trade journals. (ibid.)

Interestingly, the division of the collection sets up several dichotomies between areas of knowledge that were, in the Main Building, at least symbolically contiguous. The most distinct division is, of course, between the *sciences* and the *humanities*, prefiguring C.P. Snow's often-cited (and often exaggerated) treatise on the division of the "two cultures" (Snow 1959). But the division of the collections also suggests other patterns: 1). the separation of different container types (bound newspapers and serials versus more conventional monographs); and 2). the banishment of "exotica" from the Main Building (foreign documents). By 1969, the Annex contained the Orientalia Division and the Slavic and Central European Division (Truett 1968:175-176) and by 1993 it housed the African and Middle Eastern Division, the Asian Division, the Chinese Section, Hebraic, Japanese, Korean, Near East and Southern Asian sections while the "Western" collections resided in the Jefferson Building, a division, by the way, propounded by the Jefferson's location west of the Adams Building. It's important to note that the elaboration of "orientalized" divisions for these collections coincided with their growth and the formalization of collections policies for their acquisition.[38]

Whatever the symbolic significance of these subject divisions, the division of collections into two broad moieties—humanities in the old building and science and technology in the new—introduced a *gap* into the machine of library retrieval. Despite the book conveyor linking the two buildings—by all accounts more efficient than its predecessors in the Main Building—it took longer to access books shelved in the opposite decks and, by the 1960s and 1970s, this time-gap had been exacerbated. "Regrettably, the time between request and delivery has been growing longer and now approaches one hour per volume" (Goodrum 1974:118).[39]

The end of World War II saw the Library actively enriching its collections with increasing amounts of European and Asian materials, a goal immeasur-

---

38 This spatial "orientalization" has been ameliorated somewhat by the completion of renovations to the Jefferson Building in 1997 that have allowed some of these errant divisions to "return."

39 At present, the Library posts a ninety-minute delay between the two buildings and—from personal experience and anecdotal evidence—appears to often take much longer than that.

ably helped by the conversion of profits from agricultural sales abroad into local currency for the purchase of published materials authorized by the Agricultural Trade Development and Assistance Act of 1954 (Library of Congress 1963:xv).

By the 1970s, the Library had field offices in India, Kenya, Egypt, Indonesia and so on, each acquiring and in some cases cataloging foreign monographs and serials. One Brazilian librarian expressed some shock at the LC's seeming cupidity.

> The obsession with amassing every single document ever published anywhere on the planet sparked my amazement when I attended the 1992 International Federation of Librarians Association's congress in New Delhi and discovered that India's Library of Congress employs 115 staff members exclusively to collect material produced in the country's eighteen official tongues. (de Sant'Anna 1996)

The end of World War II brought 1). a publishing boom; 2). an unprecedented number of international acquisitions from countries recovering from the World War; and 3). a growth of staff commensurate with the increased levels of acquisitions and processing, from 960 in 1939 to 1,975 in 1958 (Library of Congress 1959:52). The post-War "information explosion"—here not just a *proliferation* of information sources, but also an increase in the *demand* for sources—led to a dramatic growth in the Library's Legislative Reference Service (founded in 1915 and later re-named the "Congressional Research Service" in 1971). Heretofore a source of more mundane reference work for Congress and Congressional staff, the office burgeoned from a small room with a few reference books to a full research bureau, producing briefs on current issues, issuing law reports and, for all intents and purposes, taking on the responsibilities of a think tank (Goodrum 1974:43; interview, Congressional Research Service, Management).

By the 1950s, Library officials were complaining that this surfeit of new materials, new staff and new responsibilities introduced in the post-war information explosion had precipitated another bibliomantic crisis.

> It arose out of normal growth, but especially out of the great influx of materials that had been pent up during World War II, and the Library's need to adjust its organization, program, and collections to the changing requirements of the Government and the world of scholarship with respect to such developing areas of crisis and interest as Southeast Asia, Eastern Europe, and the Near and Middle East in such subjects as science and technology. (Library of Congress 1962: xi)

Although the Legislative Reference Service had developed into an almost completely autonomous organization with its own library and (later) proprietary information systems, the rank-and-file scholar, LC Management intimated, was not so fortunate.[40]

> It is apparent to all—to libraries and perhaps more acutely to their users—that if arrangements for guiding the inquirer to the sources of information were inadequate before the war, they are intolerably inadequate now. It is true that many excellent time- tried techniques exist for bringing to an inquirer's attention the sources of the information which he requires—in bibliographies, checklists, indexes, abstracts, catalogs, union catalogs, bibliographical centers, etc. [ . . .] But when all is said and done, presently available guides to the sources of information are overlapping in their coverage and far from sufficient in total coverage. (Library of Congress 1948:12)

Some of the Library's problems, management suggested, stemmed from the surfeit of non-book materials in the Library and new techniques of information storage and retrieval, including the development of microfilm and microfiche readers, which the Library increasingly invested in after World War II, and photocopy machines (*photostat* and, later, *xerox*), which the library was using by the late 1930s. All of these new machines, and the new collections they helped engender, strained a system trained towards the storage and retrieval of mainly monographs and serials, on the one hand, and the accommodation of readers and tourists, on the other.[41]

> The relocation of certain non-book collections in a third building is particularly favored because of the inflexible type of equipment for housing such collections in the present building. A modern building  could be made more adaptable to varying needs and  conditions than the two present structures, and such  adjustments would relieve stress in the activities which  remain in the present buildings, where necessity has  produced some fairly critical distortions in the locations  of collections and staff. (Library of Congress 1959: 52)

Head Librarian Quincy Mumford articulated what—by the mid-1960s—he saw as in some ways an insoluble tension between the Library's decorative filigrees and its responsibilities towards the efficient delivery of information.

> And were Mr. Young alive today, attempting to fit  computers among the cupids and catalogers along the  curtains, he might be tempted to say amen. The Li-

---

40   One of the reasons the Congressional Research Service developed into a more-or-less autonomous think tank vis-à-vis the rest of the Library was precisely because of this perceived deficiency in Library information systems. As one researcher suggested, "We're only here by accident; it was decided that the Library needed researchers to compete with the Executive Branch. For years we had nothing to do with the Library."

41   It was during this time—the late 1950s to the early 1960s—that the "reader" is supplanted by the "user" in Library literature and committee hearings. This has much to do not only with changing container types but with a world of knowledge and education increasingly concerned with the instrumental "usage" of information rather than with the more accretive "reading" of knowledge.

brary's primary responsibility has been the function of the building rather than its design. (Library of Congress 1967:16)

By the 1950s, the Librarian had begun to lobby for a third building and had, in the short term, leased a number of properties all over metropolitan D.C., eventually occupying twelve buildings all over the city and one in Ohio. With the division of materials and departments all over the city, Library management began complaining of an excessive fragmentation and displacement of Library services and collections, as the Library's Card Division and Bindery were moved out of the main buildings altogether (Library of Congress 1961:50).

The building it proposed would be substantially different than its first two, reflecting both the need for *flexible* spaces accommodating different container types and changing information technologies as well as the need for an increasing *specialization*.

> An equally important factor is the specialization of the age. Many of the great libraries built at the turn of the century saw no need for office or work space; at best, they provided an office for the librarian. Work areas, simply enclosures to separate the operational activities of a large institution from its service, had to be carved out of halls, exhibition areas, even reader space. The Library of Congress is no exception. In a research library the demands for special subject areas, for special collections, for special staff to satisfy the reference requirements of library users, have in turn made impossible demands upon buildings whose granite walls and marble floors were not designed to grow with growing needs. (Library of Congress 1965:xxxvi)

With these perhaps contradictory aims—a high degree of specialization of function and a flexibility to accommodate rapidly changing technologies and container types—Library officials along with the Architect of the Capitol and the Joint Committee on the Library began to plan for a third building.

## THE MADISON BUILDING: NATIONALISM IN THE AGE OF TECHNOCRACY

In 1965, Public Law 89-260 provided for the construction of a third Library of Congress building additionally memorializing the fourth President of the United States, James Madison, on Square 732, a plot directly south of the Main Building. Years before, George Stewart, then the Architect of the Capitol, had submitted plans for a smaller Library building *east* of the Annex, but a series of events and compromises (including vociferous protest from Capitol Hill residents in the path of the proposed site) led Congress to combine both projects into one building.

In 1960, a "James Madison Memorial Commission" was formed to plan for a memorial similar in design to John Russell Pope's 1943 Jefferson Memorial, i.e. a neo-classical temple strongly reminiscent of the Athenian Parthenon. Beneath the proposed Memorial was to be a three-level complex dedicated to the archiving of presidential papers falling under the jurisdiction of the Library of Congress's Manuscripts Division, which had collected them since 1903, when it acquired Andrew Jackson's (Library of Congress 1993b:18). The Library itself, on the other hand, was to be granted a plot one block east of the Annex, on residential property that would have to be condemned before the construction took place. Neighborhood opposition to the incursion, in addition to an interest in thrift, led the Subcommittee on Public Buildings and Grounds to recommend combining a Memorial and third Library building on the 732 site, just south of the Jefferson Buildings and across the street from the Cannon Building. In doing this, they apparently overrode the objections of the then-Architect of the Capitol, J. George Stewart, a former Member of Congress who had been granted the political appointment of Architect during the Eisenhower Administration even though he lacked architectural credentials. The combined-use building would house a "James Madison memorial" in one wing and the overflow of Library holdings in the rest (U.S. Congress 1965).

Unlike the Annex, which was explicitly designed as an extension to the Main Library's decks, the James Madison Memorial Building espoused an entirely different philosophy. Confronted by a growth of new types of containers—e.g. magnetic tapes and new audio formats—and the rapid fragmentation of the Library's organization into highly specialized departments, the new building was designed as a superstructure essentially without permanent features—movable partitions instead of marbled curtains and motorized, high-density bookstacks instead of steel-and-marble decks. Its designers gave up any defining architectural features for a maximum flexibility in function, so much so that some critics suspected the building would revert back to the Congress for office space.

> Because the building is intended to be flexible with regards to book space and office space, some Members questioned if the addition would be used as another House office building. Consequently a provision barring the building from ever being converted into a fourth HOB [House Office Building] was added to the bill. (Langworthy 1970)

Even with the utilitarian focus of the subcommittee on public buildings and grounds, however, the new building maintained a sometimes ironic dialogue with the old Jefferson Building. For example, the vaulted, heavily embellished Main Reading Room in the Jefferson Building was reduced to an "Interior Court" surrounded on all sides with the smoked windows of offices and processing laboratories rather in the style of a corporate office lobby. In addition, "pursuant to the federal policy encouraging the inclusion of works of art in government buildings," the new Library still had to feature a certain amount of decorative flourishes, the least of which was the marble statue of James Madison in the Memorial Hall off the foyer.[42] Art and sculpture were, however, limited to five assemblages: a marble statue of James Madison by Walker Hancock, a bronze ornamental screen entitled "A Cascade of Books" by Frank Eliscu, a fountain for the Interior Court by Robert Cronbach, a series of incised, gilded quotations from James Madison and an enlargement of a medallion of Madison with his birth and death dates beneath his low-relief portrait.[43]

While the original Library combined nationalist iconography and a "democratic ethos" of knowledge and power with different library materials, the Madison Building in many ways represents and structures the scission of that (apparent) nineteenth century unity. To begin with, the sometimes suffocating patina of sculpture and tympanum celebrating the apotheosis of the United States above both "civilized" European nations and "primitive" indigenes is, if not altogether missing, at least distanced from the quotidian tasks of Library staff and users. The James Madison Memorial Hall, for example, is consigned to a small addition off of the main lobby and, while sometimes used for exhibit space, seems very much separate from the rest of the Madison building. The reading rooms and departments in the Madison Building—Copyright, Law, Geography and Maps, Manuscripts, the Congressional Research Service, Motion Picture, Broadcast and Recorded Sound, Prints and Photographs and the Performing Arts Reading Room—are free of reference to James Madison and, for the most part, the United States altogether.[44]

A comparison of the central rooms in both buildings dramatizes these differences. In the Jefferson Building's Main Reading Room, users work (literally) under the shadows of the a patriline of "founding fathers" and (canonical) forebears—Columbus, Robert Fulton, Isaac Newton, Joseph Henry—in the form of "portrait statues" along the balustrades of the Rotunda and, as mentioned above, Blashfield's utopian typology of nations and civilization painted on the crown of the dome above. In the Madison Building, although the lobby seems to gesture towards the doors to the Interior Court, the large, double doors at the southern end of the lobby lead, literally, nowhere. Instead of a grand, rotunda of books, marble and decorative frieze "symbolic of democracy," the Interior Court was almost empty; it seemed designed neither for research nor exhibits nor, even, repose.[45] As in the Adams Building, the central spaces of the Madison Building are taken up, by and large, with offices and stacks housing

---

42   From an unpublished memo, "Fact Sheet: A Cascade of Books, James Memorial Building, Library of Congress." No date. Archives of the Architect of the Capitol.

43   From an unpublished memo from Dewitt, Poor & Shelton, Architects, to Mario E. Campbell, Assistant Architect of the Capitol, 1/24/73. Archives of the Architect of the Capitol, Washington, D.C.

44   There are, however, some exhibits in the connecting hallways of the Madison Building, e.g. the LC's permanent exhibit, "By Securing To Authors: Copyright, Commerce, and Creativity in America," by the Copyright Office or the globe on the mezzanine floor next to the Law Library.

45   Indeed, when I began coming to the Library in 1991, the Court was quite empty; the fountain had been removed.

the collections, many of them specially insulated. While the Jefferson Building seems given over to vaulted spaces, the Madison Building is strikingly insular and myopic, with relatively few windows and a history of "sick building syndrome" that has affected the lives of many of the people I talked with.[46] Following Markus's logic that equates *depth* with *power*, the consigning of Library users to rooms along the periphery of the building and the staff to a dense, honeycombed labyrinth of interior offices suggests a different attitude towards power, knowledge and nationalism, one premised on an more rigid division of staff from users, or, as I shall argue below, of producers from consumers (Markus 1993). Nothing brought this difference home more than the masses of tourists who have crowded into the Main Hall of the Jefferson Building since it reopened in May of 1997; the Library estimates it has at least twice as many visitors than it did when only the Madison Building was readily accessible by tourists, suggesting that, everything else being equal, the Jefferson Building is easier to equate with "the nation" than the Madison (Fineberg 1997:1).

Whatever the shortcomings of the Madison Building as a national space, it *did* solve the Library's immediate need for more room, at least in the short term. In the late-1980s and 1990s, the Library, as a result of both its routine accessions and its "arrearage reduction" begun by Head Librarian James Billington shortly after he took office in 1987, again began to press Congress for more Library space in a way strikingly similar to decades-earlier testimony from Head Librarians Putnam and Mumford.

> Crowding in the Library's general collections stacks has reached a crisis stage, and the Collections Management Division (CMD) is now implementing short- term emergency measures to deal with the problem. "Traditional maintenance procedures are no longer effective or cost-efficient. We are just about completely out of space, and books are now being placed on floors throughout the stacks," said Joe Puccio, public services officer, CMD. "In addition, new books keep coming in at a rate of over a quarter of a million volumes per year." In the Jefferson Building, CMD has started double- shelving materials in certain areas of the stacks. Parts of the PZ collection on Decks 35 and 36 have been double-shelved on wide shelving originally intended for the storage of folio volumes. This will free space for overflow areas on those decks to accommodate materials that cannot be shelved in other areas of the building. ("Stacks Crowded: Library Needs More Storage" 1995: 1,4)

Although the symptoms of over-crowding are presented in the same way, i.e. the gradual occlusion of the LC's classification through double-shelving, putting books on the floor and moving collections out of their logical, metonymical sequence and the concomitant difficulties this may pose to the researcher, the Library's solution to its latest spate of over-crowding is patently not the

---

46 Although, government evidence about the deleterious effects of the Madison Building are inconclusive (National Institute for Occupational Safety and Health 1991).

same as in decades past. Available plots in the federal complex surrounding the Capitol have been, with the exception of small plots south of the Capitol, filled (Architect of the Capitol). The Library will not get a *fourth* building in the Capitol complex, although it will expand underground with the "Capitol Visitors Center" stretching between the Capitol Building and the Jefferson Building (Fineberg 1995c:10). Hence, solutions to spatial shortages have revolved around the development of high-density, secondary storage facilities in warehouses on "downsized" military facilities (as in Fort Meade).

> Linked with the Library arrearage reduction project is the development of a secondary storage site to house properly processed materials and to provide for growth of the collections through the first part of the 21st century. The Library, the Architect of the Capitol (AOC), and the Department of the Army agreed to a plan transferring up to 100 acres of land at Fort Meade, Md., to the AOC for legislative storage branch requirements. ("Officials See Library Gains in the Past Year":10)

This high-density warehouse stores books in large lots differentiated by only by arbitrary, accession codes and accessible, not through Library of Congress schedules, but through an "automated storage and retrieval system"("Librarian Requests 8.6% Budget Increase":9).[47]

Book warehousing in remote storage facilities is, however, the opposite of what the Library of Congress purports to do with its collections; even with the "automated storage and retrieval system," gaining access to materials in remote storage takes longer than materials housed in nearby stacks, sometimes as long as two weeks (although the system is said to deliver books within one day). Many Library staffers I talked with were staunch critics of the "Eaton/ Kenway" remote storage system, and thought it a clear abrogation of the Library's historic mission as a "universal" collection of human knowledge. The ideological function of a Library that places its citizen-readers at the center of a vast apparatus of knowledge, power and empire cannot be sustained with the widespread usage of warehouses for key Library collections. After all, as John Cole has suggested, we can see the library movement in the late nineteenth century as an explicit rejection of a passive, "storehouse" model of libraries and an adoption of a more active paternalism that reconceptualized the library's role as one of educating the citizen to make informed decisions in a democratic society (Cole 1979). If the LC fails in its educational (and ideological) function as the structuring of a certain relationship to knowledge, than much of its organization—the parts of the Library initiated by Herbert Putnam during the first decades of the twentieth century—is placed in jeopardy as well. The

---

47   The LC is not alone in the implementation of high-density book storage systems. The coincidence of budgetary shortfalls in universities and "deindustrialization" in many areas of the United States has made warehouse space particularly attractive to academic libraries hoping to clear materials from their overcrowded stacks (Kennedy and Stockton 1990).

otherwise quixotic 1996 report from Booz-Allen & Hamilton, Inc. that called for the Library to become an "information service" rather than an "information provider" (mentioned above) can be partially explained by the change from a model of the Library premised on nationalism to one structured by the more utilitarian concerns of the Library's technocratic apparatus—flexibility and specialization—structuring the functional austerity of the Madison Building. (Then) Speaker Newt Gingrich's defense of the LC is instructive here, if only because he firmly re-affirms legitimation as the primary function of the Library:

> I want to take this evening as a moment to state emphatically my disagreement with the effort of the management analysts who looked at the Library. They assumed that in a time of limited budgets as we have entered the information age that this Congress should diminish and shrink and divide the greatest knowledge asset this country has. I believe just the opposite . . . I believe that we should encourage the Library to boldly reach out, to seek, to expand, and grow as a repository of knowledge, and to seek, to spread even more widely. (Newt Gingrich, quoted in Billington 1996:53)

But how do you figure the Library of Congress as a unified, *national* asset when—according to its own testimony and periodic reports—its spiraling acquisitions threaten to *separate* and *fragment* collections, staff and users into a mélange of separate, specialized departments and container types strewn across dozens of high-density warehouses?

## THE NON-PLACE OF LIBRARY AND NATION

Over the course of my field research, I was witness to an instructive shift in the way the Library of Congress represents itself to outsiders. When I first came to the Library as an intern in 1992, I watched—as an introduction to the institution—*A Tour of the Library of Congress*—a 22 minute film run on a tape loop in the Library's visitor's center in the Madison Building (Library of Congress 1986). Besides the expected summary of Library departments and functions infused with a strong dose of self-aggrandizement, the video ended on a mysterious image: a slow pan towards a disconnected bundle of fiber-optic cable protruding from a reader's desk. What the director—Jim Cummins—wanted to imply was that the Library was ready for the future, whatever it might bring. On another level, however, the cable suggested profound misgiving over the coming "information society." What would the Library's function be in the coming "age of the computer"? Would "readers" be *reading*? Would the Library still be engaged in its work of classification, cataloging and reference? Budget cuts under such agencies as the Office of Management and Budget had proved especially maleficent to institutions that were not directly involved in Reagan's unprecedented military build-up and Gramm-Rudman-Hollings had just reduced the Library's budget by some twenty percent.

In 1997, in honor of the re-opening of the Jefferson Building's Main Entrance Hall, the Library produced a new film that, while no more coherent,
strives to answer some of the questions raised in the first. After an obligatory
introduction to the Library's different functions—to serve Congress and other
federal agencies, to serve scholars' needs—and its different departments—the
Congressional Research Service, the Copyright Office, the Preservation Directorate, etc.—Head Librarian Billington comes on to talk about the Library's
new, flagship program—the National Digital Library. In the past, he explains,
"Users had to travel to D.C. Now, with the National Digital Library [ . . .]
Much of the same resources are available online." While there's some question about the level of access to the online collections, Billington goes on to
rhapsodize on the National Digital Library in a way strikingly similar to the
way previous librarians had perorated on the physical Library. "These [online]
documents illustrate our nation's [ . . .] creativity [ . . .] These are all the primary records of the American people [ . . .] They tell us who we are."

The two films suggest, at least on the level of rhetoric, a "return" to the ideological function of the Library of Congress as a not only a place where information is sorted and gathered into "knowledge," but where a certain *knowledge*
of nation and nationalism, empire and imperialism, is cultivated, packaged
and inculcated (Billington 1996:38). As I was finishing a second draft of this
section in June of 1997, I attended the first, public tour of the Digital Library
Visitor's Center in the Interior Court of the Madison Building.[48] The fountain
that had once graced the middle of the Court was long gone, replaced by a
maze of purple, particle-board cubicle dividers called "veal-fattening pens" in
Douglas Coupland's *Generation X* (Coupland 1991). In each of the cubicles
sat computer hardware somehow evocative of the work of the National Digital
Library (NDL): desktops, scanners, multimedia CD-jukebox servers. In the
back of the Court, to the far south, was a small stage with two television moni-
tors and a larger, projected screen all facing a few rows of chairs. Taking a seat
with three other people, I looked above to the smoked windows enclosing the
Court; behind each glowed a dull, fluorescent light illuminating office cubicles
not unlike those around us.

I made small talk with a man whom I realized must be the National Digital
Library Visitor's Center docent; he was worried about the sparse attendance
and I reassured him that more people will come once the word gets out. The
young woman next to me asked, rather peevishly I thought, how long the tour
would take and I realized that, besides me, the "audience" had been drawn
from the ranks of the Library's summer interns; not all of them, it appeared,
had come willingly.

The docent moved to the stage and welcomed us to the Center. His talk—

---

48   I had, of course, been there before. The Center had been "open," after all, since October of
1994, but, as one of the Library Police exclaimed, "Yeah, it's open. I just don't know *who* it's open
for."

one half-hour—introduced the Library's home pages (the "Front door to the Library of Congress"), the digitized collections (the Houdini Collection, "California Gold: Northern California Music from the Thirties"), the Library's search engines (including the "Experimental Search System" (ESS)) and the Library's online databases (LOCIS). After demonstrating each, he took questions (we asked none) and then invited us to move to the computers around the room and try the National Digital Library collections for ourselves. None of us stayed to try the collections.

And so our "tour" ended. I wasn't surprised that no one stayed to ask questions or browse the multimedia collections. Why should we have? We all had offices very like these simulacra around us with the same desk-top computers and the same access to the Internet. Each of us could browse as many of the Library's collections as we wanted or, for that matter, anyone else's collections, should we find the Library's inadequate or tiresome. In fact, I was unclear why we had to sit in this room at all. It wasn't for aesthetics: the Interior Court looked like the abandoned quarters of a telemarketing firm that had rented furniture from a bargain, corporate furniture store. But it really didn't matter: after all, wasn't the Library's home page (http://www.loc.gov) the National Digital Library's front door and not the National Digital Library Visitor's Center? Wasn't the National Digital Library, by definition, accessible from anywhere and, by extension, located nowhere?

The Visitor's Center was an attempt to clothe a distributed system (the National Digital Library) in the *place* of the nation, to center the Library *user* in the midst of a national system of telematic information in the same way the Main Reading Room interpellates the Library *reader* amongst universal collections of books. If the Visitor's Center seemed strikingly inept, it's because the sorts of nationalism implied in the Jefferson Building across the street doesn't necessarily translate into the telematic future of which the Visitor's Center is merely a synecdochic trace.

It is no mistake that the "Visitor's Center" had, by 1999, become the "National Digital Library Learning Center," an auditorium used to present the "American Memory" collections to k-12 teachers. Similar its forbear, however, the "Learning Center" remains unused much of the time, an ambiguous space tenuously linking ideologies of virtual knowledge to ideologies of spatial knowledge.

Like the Jefferson Building's overwrought shrines to nineteenth-century imperialist expansion and Social Darwinism, the National Digital Library's "American memory" collections "reflect" the American. Through composite lenses of photograph, document, music and motion picture, the collections attempt to "tell us who we are." "American Memory" is comprised of "unique Americana that will be of greatest value to students, researchers, and educators" and includes civil war photographs, suffrage pamphlets, Works Progress Administration life stories, broadsides and pamphlets from the Daniel Murray Pamphlet Collection; in short, a wide range of materials speaking to many different experiences and histories in the United States from the entirety of its history ("National Digital Library Visitor's Center Frequently Asked Questions"). This, I believe, has much to do with the ingenuity of the staff in choosing selections from different collections that present a slightly more complex picture of the United States than, perhaps, the linear, epochal march of "American civilization" presented across the street in the Jefferson Building.

And yet, the collections documenting aggression abroad or the global scapes of American capital (e.g. United Fruit) are entirely missing, as are images or collections of more "transnational" immigrants to the United States, whose varied experiences cannot be contained within the protocols of "Americana."[49] We are told, often enough, that the Library's collections are mostly in languages *other than* English; those twisted histories, however, are not part of the National Digital Library. While the "hagiology of the citizen" may now include blacks and women, it is still a hagiology, albeit one rendered in WAV and JPEG files rather than in sculpture and painting. The images that challenge the tired shibboleths of bourgeois identity, nucleated families, compulsory heterosexuality and melting-pot assimilation are missing from the NDL (although the Library has started to cooperate with other digital libraries in its "Global Digital Library" project).

What the Visitor's Center attempts is nothing less than the salvage of the Library's unraveling strategic mission to both legitimate the nation while classifying an increasingly rationalized and specialized universal collection. In a sense, it redeems the Madison Building—that temple to technocracy—and, while doing that, redeems the mission of the bureaucratic apparatus structured by the Library to "media-te" what it means to be a citizen and what it means to have a past in the United States. In short, the Visitor's Center is an attempt to fix the contradictions on *anthropological place* in the digitized utopia of *non-place*.

Nevertheless, it is in the umbra of "non-place" that the Library can reconcile the centrifuging speciation of "information society" with the parochialisms of the nation. As the Library discovered in the 1980s, its role as a *national place* becomes more important in a world of instantaneous information.

> We thus approach the central paradox: the less important the spatial barriers, the greater the sensitivity of capital to the variations of space within place, the greater the incentive for places to be differentiated in ways attractive to capital. (Harvey 1989:295-96)

Contrary to computopian essays forecasting the imminent demise of the nation in the global scapes of an online world, the *place* of the nation has become

---

49   The one exception that I found was the "California Gold: Northern California Folk Music from the Thirties," a mixed collections of photographs, sound and written documents from ethnographic work in northern California. With recordings in a polyglot of languages and musical styles from a dozen different traditions, it seems the one National Digital Library collection that elides the strict sensibilities of "Americana."

more, rather than less, exclusive (and excluding). The wages of nationalism, and the cost of abrogating its legitimation, are high. Like all federal institutions, the Library of Congress undergoes yearly appropriations hearings in front of Congress. Every year, its future is thrown in doubt and, every year, it is forced to undertake an endless process of self-publicity and federal lobbying in order to secure its appropriations for the next fiscal year. In these times of selective economy, Congress's favor has been hard-won and the LC seized on the technologies of the nation as a way of both palliating a fickle Congress while attracting corporate donations through the Madison Council, the Librarian's philanthropic "advisory committee." So far, these strategies seemed to have worked, thanks in part to the utopian constructions of the nation and the citizen in the "non-place" of the National Digital Library, where the past, present and future can be inscribed as a message of the "American" and the fictional melting pot of assimilated traditions, classes and races.

# CHAPTER 4

# Ghosts in the Information Machine

One recurrent refrain throughout the twentieth century has been the forecasted replacement of the printed, (Gutenberg) book by smaller, cheaper and more easily reproducible mediums. However, to paraphrase, the death of the book has been greatly exaggerated, despite the apotheosis of the World Wide Web. Why is that? For one thing, publishing involves a good deal more than just the production of *print*; there are printers, bookstores, warehouses, distributions: a whole vespiary of systems and organizations involved in the formation of our textual world. To move into a "digital age," these institutions, organizations and relations must also be replaced, superseded or revolutionized and that, as copyright lawyers have reiterated, remains extremely problematic (Cf. Lehman 1995). In addition, it would be a grave mistake to contrast a "gutenberg age" to a "digital age" as if they were absolutes, one stage succeeding the other in linear succession. The truth is more complex; our "information age" evidences a (sometimes uneasy) coexistence of printed and electronic information and tracing their interdependence call tell us much about information society.

"Information society" is often portrayed, in both popular and academic writings, as very nearly synonymous with *information technologies*, particularly by computopian critics and scholars granting technology causal determinacy. In turn, those "information technologies" most often cited as most formative of our "information age" are the computer and its associated accoutrements: networks, processors, memory capacity and so on. But libraries—and, to some extent, all bureaucratic institutions—have always struggled to process, control and communicate their materials. To that end, they have developed myriad techniques and technologies generative of *order* and *control*. But what do librarians strive to order? What do they struggle to control?

Today, the LOC uses an "integrated library system" that knits together diverse materials (e.g., print and digital) and diverse departments (acquisitions, cataloging, copyright). Although not seamless (e.g., the "keyword" search in the Library's OPAC is not the flexible, "open text" search engine Google users may be accustomed to), it is nevertheless an apparent improvement over the heterogeneous systems used in the 1990's to track a book from CIP (cataloging-in-publication) to the user's desk. And yet, these older systems have not really disappeared either; their traces still haunt the Library's ILS today, and the key to understanding information as a social and cultural artifact lies in uncovering those more primordial forms. In the age of the more-or-less seamless protocols (and least from the perspective of an end-user) that govern the decoupage of networks we know as the Internet, we are urged to accept our online world as an endlessly synchronic (if protean) *present,* and forget the miscellaneous files, softwares and systems that make up complex, online ecologies.

In this chapter, I excavate "information's past" at the Library of Congress from its imposition of the card catalog at the turn-of-the-century to more recent experiments with the World Wide Web in the 1990s. Rather than signify some unilineal patriline of technocratic progress, I argue that these different information machines express different institutional imperatives structured, in part, by fiscal imperatives.

Each, in turn, affects a distinct "politics of information." More than just another way of thinking about something called "information," the "information artifacts" I trace below are *productive* of certain kinds of knowledge, certain kinds of work and certain kinds of social relations. Furthermore, the superimposition of one over the other is less a matter of "evolution" than tendentious ideology. As Head Librarians and managers struggle to secure the LC against the variegated chaos that threatens to engulf it, they utilize different, even contrary systems and rather than tell a "just-so" story of the progressive control of spiraling, truculent collections, I want to suggest that the Library's different, artefactual machines reflect and shape those different administrative and organizational imperatives.

The following attempts to trace the uneven imposition of "information society" at the Library of Congress through a situated analysis of the Library's artifacts—card catalogs, online catalogs and World Wide Web collections. I want to suggest that the McLuhan-esque notion that social change inexorably follows new technology and that the digital world is the natural successor of Gutenberg patrimonies is a gross simplification (McLuhan 1962). By this I do not mean to return to the pastorale of the book, but to question the narrative productions that reduce the play of "print" and "digital" to a false (and hypostatized) antinomy of past and future.

The "subjects" of this chapter include the artifacts themselves (card catalogs, MARC and the World Wide Web) as well as the people charged with the production and maintenance of the LC's information systems and information technologies. Providing a "meta-commentary" on the whole are more or less authoritative accounts from the U.S. Congress and Head Librarians drawn from Annual Reports, transcripts of hearings and memoranda. This is not to imply that "information society" cannot or should not be studied from "the bottom up," as many anthropologists have done in their study of institutions and work, just that, although many of the decisions in an information age are mandated by top-level administrators and managers, this does not mean that they are *coherent* or *homogeneous* (Kellner 1990).

In April of 1996, the Government Accounting Office issued a report calling for the Library of Congress to phase out its hundred year-old mandate to acquire, catalog and organize knowledge and instead become a "passive clearing-house of information" (Weeks 1996). As a "clearinghouse," the Library would liaison between users and information providers, pointing them in the right direction, but not organize knowledge in any appreciable, value-added way. The Librarian of Congress—James Billington—was quick to dismiss the recommendations and marshal Congressional support for a "'more ambitious concept of sustaining a universal library and getting more people to use it in more ways'" (Fineberg 1996a:10). But perhaps this was the unintended consequence of Billington's reorganizations of the Library into a paragon of the information age where "librarians" are replaced by "knowledge navigators" and books become so many streams of data in the space of flows. And it certainly was an ironic echo of the many efforts Billington has made over the years to move cataloging outside the Library of Congress onto private vendors. In other words, the difference between these two visions of the future—the GAO's and Billington's—are complementary.

The *book*—together with its multifarious signified, *text*—has always presented an ontological problem. Foucault traced the genealogy of the West in the ordering of the body and the disciplining of the flesh, but he could just as easily have generated his apologue on Enlightenment technologies from a discourse on the formation of the *book*, or that other body whose ebb and flow, order and disorder, shadows the work of nations. The present bibliomantic dreams of hypertext that informed both the GAO's report on the Library and Head Librarian Billington's defense of the same seem another (pre)face to the problem of the book, i.e. another wrinkle in the problem (and problematization) of the West. In short, all of our meditations on books, reading, information and knowledge amount to nothing less than a metaphysics of the West, the theorization of authenticity, origins and theodicy that underlies social and political policy as much as literary discussion.

At the close of the twentieth century, we are awash in the mobile, labile and ultimately fungible image of information bought and sold, collected and collated, produced and productive, networked and connective. Our ultimate dream is "a child sitting at home able to access an entire universe of knowledge that is applicable to whatever the child wants to do" (Library of Congress 1993a [online]). But what does that mean? Both the notion of a "passive clearinghouse" of information and the dream of a universal, "level playing field" of digitized information betray an almost sinister polysemy. Can information exist in a pure state to be packaged and processed into "value-added" services, formats and programs? Doesn't "information" already imply conscious screening, sorting, organizing and framing? Isn't it already a social product riven with power, with struggle, with *disciplinarity*?

Popular media certainly haven't helped clear the intransigence, instead generating endless programming on the information society, the coming (or co-eval) "information age" and the wonders (or horrors) of utopian (or dystopian) "information technologies." By degrees, "information" has made its way into our discussions of biology (Goonatilake 1991; Rabinow 1996), health and illness (Martin 1994) and, inevitably, into cultural anthropology itself; it is now indisputably part of our (second) nature (Nelson 1996; Downey *et al* 1995; Franklin 1995). Information has become the philosopher's stone of modernity, retroverting culture and history into a commodified glossolalia. It has reached what Emily Martin calls "saturation," a kind of overdetermined multidirectionality (Martin 1994).

But "it"—"information," the "Information Age," the "information economy" and "information society"—however objectified and disciplined, lacks tangible, independent form. Rather, it can only exist in the midst of the social relations, material struggle and cultural production that condition its fitful existence. The magic of "information" lies in the regimes of power and production legitimated by expert knowledge and the "de-skilling" and "proletarianization" that cower just behind its slick virtuality (Aronowitz and DiFazio 1994; Braverman 1975; Kroker and Weinstein 1994). "Information" is the name for what Lakoff and Johnson term "ontological metaphors," key means through which gross abstractions are clothed in (metaphorical) corporeality (Lakoff and Johnson 1980:26). Only through metaphorical and metonymical maneuverings are we able to see, to grasp and to act on something as inchoate as "the Internet" and give its scattering of computers, networks, administrators, backbones, hackers and everyday users solidity, coherence and homogeneity. It is "as much an artifact of discourse and imagination as a thing of glass, metal and plastic" (Pound 1995:527).

## UNRAVELING INFORMATION SOCIETY'S ARTIFACTS: GENE-ALOGIES AND HISTORIES OF INFORMATION OBJECTS

"Information" occupies a half-life between object and abstraction, sometimes described as a measurable substance while at other times slipping between a bundle of metaphors—always suspended between competing fictions alternately illuminating processes, objects and social relations (Latour and Woolgar 1979). This is a source of apprehension for practitioners of the comparatively young discipline of information science; there may be 134 different usages of "information" in information science (Schrader 1986). It seems unlikely that the nascent field will ever attain the status of a *science* per se, if we understand science to involve—particularly during its normal, paradigmatic stage—consensual objectifications of the world (Kuhn 1970).

Point, click, ship, track, confirm rates, prepare export documents, check sales in Europe, manage accounts receivable, reorder inventory, pre-program customer orders, etc. . .etc. . .etc. . .If it seems like more information than you've ever asked from your shipping department, well that's exactly the point. Introducing UPS online. Powerful software to help you manage not only your shipments, but your business as well. From tracking shipping activity by department to tracking product sales by market. From monitoring inventory to managing costs and cash flow. The truth is, to keep pace in business you're going to need more and better information instantly at your fingertips. (Wired 4.10:79)

What's striking about this otherwise quotidian advertising copy is the tremendous variety of activities, actions and substances grouped under the sign, *information*. The "information" available through the aforementioned UPS online service includes *things* (inventory, sales, accounts, documents), *actions* (re-ordering, exporting, tracking) as well as *communications* (confirming, managing). "Information" shuttles back and forth between object and idea, practice and effect.

But rather than simply implode under its connotative gravity, "information" becomes increasingly turgid, encompassing more and more under its apparently seductive simplicity. But more important, we are interrelating data in more ways, giving them context, and thus forming them into information; and we are assembling chunks of information into larger and larger models and architectures of knowledge. (Toffler 1990:85)

Alvin Toffler's arithmetic progression, whereby a quantity of data is gathered into quanta of information, which in turn can be assembled into a vast edifice of knowledge, will probably not satisfy the epistemologists and analytic philosophers of the world. Nevertheless, Toffler's logic fits certain technocratic/rationalist expectations and preserves the quality of "information" as an open sign applicable to any situation and any politics. Perhaps even more important, this empty formulation allows for the resurrection of tarnished metanarratives of scientific progress, now firmly locked in the "emancipating" embrace of advanced capitalism.

The "information age" can be construed as the end-point of a linear development beginning with the age of print, fueled by the engine of universality and the dream of the encyclopedia and, as Chartier (1994:62) reminds us, as old as the West itself:

The dream of a library (in a variety of configurations) that would bring together all accumulated knowledge and all the books ever written can be found throughout the history of Western civilization.

Indeed, it is relatively easy to construct vast evolutionary hierarchies, finding precursors of "hypertext" in the early encyclopedae, indices and bibliographies of Renaissance and Enlightenment Europe (Anderson 1992; Wolf 1995). Just as Europe signified the height of civilization to Victorian anthropologists, so the World Wide Web represents the crowning achievement—and the Elidean return—of democratic individualism.

The Library of Congress characterizes its own dalliance with different technologies in just such a manner.

> The LC started down a one-lane road toward the information highway 30 years ago. The Library began to develop the MAchine Readable Catalog (MARC) system in 1966, installed the first reading room computer for public use in 1975, and operated the first microprocessors, in the Congressional Research Service, in 1985. (Fineberg 1995a:3)

In the ringingly familiar language of ineluctable progress, the "march" of information society begins with the first steps towards "automation" and ends in the telematic present.

Clearly, though, card catalogs are not proto-World Wide Web search engines. This is evident at the Library of Congress which, in its day-to-day activity, uses artifacts from both ends of the putatively evolutionary spectrum; card catalogs and dictionary catalogs jostle alongside CD-ROMs and computer networks. Each technology implies different social relations and practices in the context of the historical development of the State, labor, and the Nation. Similarities between the past and the present are, in the end, less telling than the differences. Each *form* information takes embodies and "bodies" distinctly different ideas of power, knowledge and practice. And while looking at "information" in this manner may make it difficult to render paeans to the gods of the information age, it may reveal contradictions and inconsistencies that explode equally vapid narratives of information salvation and information damnation.

## INFORMATION AND ARTEFACT

Latour's and Woolgar's *Laboratory Life* shows the social construction of scientific fact, the way contested narratives gradually become a single, authoritative account of "reality" (Latour and Woolgar 1979). The end product of this long process is either the *fact* or the *artefact*, a piece of "real" nature or its opposite, a creature of scientific fancy drawing sustenance from "noise" in the data, faulty instrumentation or human error. True scientific discovery emerges from just such an apposition of fact and artefact. Is this subatomic particle or this endocrine reaction "real" or a product of instruments, bias or noise? The establishment of "truth" depends upon operations that wrest facticity from the netherworld of the scientific *imaginaire*.

As I've suggested above, "information" never resolves into the clear light of fact. As the pre-eminent, periphrastic trace for the late-twentieth century, "information" bounds pixie-like from economic value to political empowerment to "T3" connections to the communicative interactions of macrophages and

T cells in the body's immune system (Martin 1994). Simply, information is always an artefact of its construction; it never exists independent of the institutional discourses that enfold it.

By virtue of its hyperbolic signifieds, we would expect information systems or information technologies to evidence high degrees of variation in design, operation and intent. Clearly, this is the case; information technologies suggest a wide variety of "worldviews," many of them mutually exclusive. For example, as Bryan Pfaffenberger (1988), David Noble (1986) and others have pointed out, the rise of mainframe computing in the late 1960s and early 1970s co-incided with a move towards corporate centralization. As part of that reorganization, mainframes were purchased and implemented in order to clinch control over key productive forces in business and government (Pfaffenberger 1988:42). In the 1980s, designers of the personal computer explicitly set out to challenge the centralized domination of the mainframe with the "empowering" democratization of hardware and software. As Pfaffenberger points out, however, the difference between an old UNIX-based mainframe and a Novell-network of personal computers with firewalls and "spying software" is moot; the "democratic" PC may lead to even more invidious instances of managerial control! However, these contradictions often go unnoticed and consumers can blithely accept the often-repeated, little-demonstrated claim that personal computers (and their contemporary counterparts, iPhones) are the key to participatory democracy, hanging their own middle-class dreams of the bourgeois public sphere on a technological fix that promises a return to a small town of American life and politics. "Like other master symbols, computerization has come to stand in for a very broad range of often contradictory developments" (Hakken and Andrews 1993:87).

Not only do these "artefacts" of the information age betray certain constructions of information, knowledge and power, but people position themselves vis-à-vis these artefacts in contradictory ways. Each artefact—by definition—is pierced by imagination and desire—a certain attitude towards the Other of knowledge.

## LIBRARY SCIENCE/DOUBLE SCIENCE

From its inception in the Enlightenment "Science of Man," anthropology has been caught up in the logocentric rejection/desire for power of the "savage" and the "oriental." The "Other" word for anthropology is mimetology, a fascination with representation and with the sublation of difference in mimetic *orders*, the evolutionary chains, the craniometric distributions, the catalog of phenotypes. Only in the most simplistic sense are these "mirrors of man," to use Kluck-hohn's formulation. Rather, they imply both a movement towards the "Other" and the subtending of low mimetics into other orders altogether, i.e. both "Being" and "Becoming," "mimesis" and "kinesis." If "mimesis" means to "become and behave like someone else," it also suggests another movement towards an (alter)native. For instance, Coombe's study of trademarks suggest the way these artifacts of consumership "mimic" the other, as well as appropriate the imputed power of the Other to mimic, i.e. to mimic the mimicry (Coombe 1996). But "trademarks" do more than just set up a mirror—however distorted—of alterity.

> Laws of intellectual property generally—copyright, trademark, and publicity rights, in particular— constitute a political economy of mimesis in capitalist societies, constructing authors, regulating the activities of reproduction, licensing copying, and prohibiting imitation—all in the service of maintaining the exchange value of texts. (Coombe 1996:206)

That is, the imposition of "trademarks" like "Winnebago" campers and "Redman" chewing tobacco is, of course, a sort of *imitation*, a thoroughly racist, colonial rendering of Native Americans grounded in the orientalizing machine of savagery and desire. Only in its lowest form is "mimesis" the *imitation* of the real. Rather, a mimetic order entails a *movement* towards an alternative and, in the end, dominant order of being.

Libraries articulate systems of organization redolent with the language of deconstruction. Cataloging, after all, is a science of tracings, name authority, classification schedules and imprints; all these display all of the shibboleths of deconstruction—presence, authenticity, origins and denotative reference. There is a sense, perhaps, that library science is "always already" double science:

> This structure itself is worked in turn: the rule according to which every concept necessarily receives two similar marks—a repetition without identity— one mark inside and the other outside the deconstructed system, should give rise to a double reading and a double writing. And, as will appear in due course: a *double science*. (Derrida 1981:4)

While librarians inevitably sketch their discipline as the unilinear evolution of *information systems* from the simple dictionary to the dictionary catalog and beyond, there is a sense that the movement from one sort to the next is less dependent on some progressive *unfolding* than on an explosive moment of deconstructive reversal when the *catalog* overwhelms the collections it is to supplement. That is to say, the replacement of one form of arrangement over another has less to do with the logical adumbration of method than with the terms of Derrida's deconstructive moment: trace, arche-writing, preface, difference.

Like trademarks and copyrights, cataloging is a *form* of imitation where one can speak of cataloging records as either more or less correct based on their imputed closeness to an "originary" text. Cataloging constructs a record of a text that both *copies* it—renders a likeness in main entry and subject tracings—and links with it—through LC Classification, Dewey Decimal or LC Card Number (Taussig 1993). Cataloging constructs a "document surrogate" (Mandel 1991:65), a *doppelganger*, a *fetch* of the original whose purpose—benign or malign—is to impose a grid, to imply an attitude and an audience. And yet, cataloging is also an alternative discourse whose structure bears no necessary resemblance to a "text." That is, cataloging "copy" is only in the simplest sense a *reproduction* of text.

## BIBLIOGRAPHIC ORDERS

A book, a serial, a database, a videotape or motion picture, a photograph, a map, a recording: none of these exist by themselves. They are all *container types*, abstract designations of some thing given the force of reality through more or less consensual agreements among nations, copyrighters, users and catalogers. From these categorizations a *text* emerges, but only after the book or recording or whatever has been categorized, shelved or marketed. Library cataloging is the most complex and in many ways the *primum mobile* of these textual umbrae, involving a grid of interconnecting orders—a national order, a social order, a spatial order, a chronological order, a geographic order, a topical order and a disciplinary order.

It is difficult—and even futile—to trace a time when there was only the book. Likewise, there is little sense in seeking a time before the "order of books," if only because "books" are ontogenetically bound to their diverse orders.

The Library of Congress did not always have a system of cataloging as we know it now. Of course, it *ordered* its books, initially by size—folios, octavos, duodecimos—and later by book catalogs, though these were sadly outdated by the end of the nineteenth century (Nelson and Farley 1991). In 1900, however, the library installed a *card catalog* in its Main Reading Room. It could be argued that the *card catalog* was simply the spatialized form of the book catalog, but there are, I submit, important differences. Unlike the attenuated entries in book catalogs used at the LC, cataloging cards "included careful authentication of authorship, both subject and added entries, and close classification, all of which required expert professional attention" (Rosenberg 1993:44-45). The installation and later dissemination of cataloging cards marks the brachiation of an *order* of books. The card catalog was not merely a record of the Library's holdings. Rather, it expressed a series of different orders—ways of thinking about subjects, authors, geographies—that were only indirectly related to the materials they traced. Although the Library's catalog, for example, can *index* the Library's collection, it expresses a fundamentally different order than the LC's Classification scheme (Mann 1993).[50] In fact, the LC's Classification

---

50  That is, the LC Classification locates an item in a single *place* grouped according to schedules while the *catalog*, through its access point, orders books according to author, title, subject and so on.

scheme itself expresses a fundamentally different philosophy than did earlier, more Baconian (and classed), orders. Rather than lump books by strictly pre-coordinated subject headings, the LC's system is designed to be flexibly pragmatic, growing with the collections.

> Rather it is an enumerative classification with a number of separate schedules devised entirely on subject grouping of the collection of books in the Library of Congress. (Wynar 1972:245)

Roger Chartier has suggested that the genesis of these supplemental orders lies with the 15th century book-length inventories of books and authors called "libraries." One of these—Doni's *La Seconda Libraria*—listed books that had not yet been written (Chartier 1994:73). But the cataloging card, whatever the true "origins" of the order of books, gradually takes on a life of its own, particularly in 1901 when the LC developed a "Cataloging Distribution Service" (CDS) whose mission was to distribute *cataloging* to subscribing libraries in the form of 3x5 cataloging cards (Edlund 1976). At its height, almost 600 employees worked in the Cataloging Distribution Service (Edlund 1976:417). In fact, one might consider this distribution of standardized cataloging at per title rates the beginning of one version of "information society" at the Library of Congress.[51]

Just off the LC's Main Reading Room, split off into the close confines of Decks 16 and 33, sits the Reading Room's behemoth catalog, the Main Card Catalog (MCat). Part of it used to occupy center stage in the vaulted Main Reading Room and dominate the readers' desks around it, but it was moved away shortly after the Library switched over to online cataloging and installed terminals off the Main Reading Room in 1977 (Nelson and Farley 1991:51). Now, when you enter the dimly lit decks to look at the catalog, the atmosphere is palpably different from the Main Reading Room next door. Looking out of place and not quite fitting the cases they're packed into, the card catalog is not used very often, especially when compared to the online records which are accessible from computers all over the library (and beyond). It was discontinued between 1978 (for subject cards) and 1980 (for author and title cards).

The cards themselves, whether typed, printed or touchingly hand-written, are heavily worn now; some are missing. They fall into three categories. The first and second sort are filed alphabetically by "main entry," usually a title or an author's name printed across the top of the card. The third sort—marked from the first and second by a red bar—is filed alphabetically by Library of Congress Subject Heading (LCSH), an alphabetical structure of terms, concepts and places assigned to most of the Library's collections in all formats. These three types of cards constitute the *access points* to the catalog, the "portals" through which you enter and "travel" from one card entity to another. Some items have

---

51  This version, spotlighting the transformation of different areas of life into commodities of *information*, will be explored in greater depth in Chapter 6.

been given fewer than three access points, as in the case of many serial titles, while others have been given more than three, as in cases of "added entry": additional personal names, corporate names, titles or series information. Although there is theoretically no limit to the number of added entries given any one cataloged item and hence no theoretical limit to the number of different places a card might be filed in the catalog, *space* has worked to minimize the number of tracings.

Like most libraries built before the twentieth century, the Jefferson Building of the Library of Congress was never designed to house card catalog cabinets. Space was a problem from the outset: the Main Catalog displaced readers and its 21,000 drawers eventually took over rooms outside the Main Reading Room (Goodrum 1974). However, the Library switched its Cataloging Distribution Service (CDS) to MAchine Readable Card (MARC) records during the 1960s and early 1970s and was already offering online terminal access to its Congressional Research Service. After a pilot program in the 1970s, the LC "froze" its card catalog and put dumb terminals in its place. It would have discarded the Main Catalog altogether were it not for a concerted drive on the part of scholars and librarians to preserve it as an alternative to digitized (and especially PREMARC) records (Goldberg 1986). By 1980, the LC had worked up a revision of the *Anglo-American Cataloging Rules* (AACR) and was preparing to switch over to the *Anglo-American Cataloging Rules Revised Edition* (AACR2) in 1980. Staff members predicted that, under the new rules, almost half of the cards would require revision, far too much work for the Library to undertake with its existing resources (Fasana 1980:9). Automation was, according to this version of events, the only possible recourse.

## MARC

A MARC record automates the card catalog, i.e. codes cataloging similar to that in printed records so that it can be downloaded onto PCs or even printed out on 3x5 cards. MARC records are strings of codes and characters without discernable structure (at least to someone not trained in MARC). However, with the help of coded designations, divided into *tags, indicators* and *subfields*, computers processing MARC records divide the record's intelligible parts following the logic, if not the actual form, of the cataloging card (Furrie 1994). The MARC record, then, consists of strings of characters or numbers along with the designated codes that structure the records for users.

The following example of MARC cataloging is taken from the LC's MUMS (Multiple-Use MARC System) application, a program initially developed for use by the Library's own catalogers and since supplanted by the Integrated Library System (ILS), which still preserves the structure of the original MARC record (however augmented under MARC21 cataloging rules). At the time computer terminals were introduced into the Main Reading Room, readers used a different application—SCORPIO—that was thought more "user-friendly." It was not until 1987 that both MUMS and SCORPIO were available in the space of the same search (Library of Congress 1988a:15). Since other cataloging software—both at the LC and without—truncated the record in some way, dropping fields that may be of little interest to most library users, MUMS had the advantage of showing a MARC record in a relatively unmodified form.

The record below shows a series of numbered lines—010, 020, 030, etc.—after which follows an "&" symbol and at least three additional numbers. The first three numbers after the "&" act as a *tag* for the *field* that follows. Field "245," for example, designates the "title information" field, while the "650" tag towards the end of the entry designates a "topical subject heading" (as opposed to, say, "600," a personal name subject heading). The "245" tag is followed by "00" and then "#abc." "A," "b," and "c" in this example refer to the presence of the three *subfields*, each marked off from the other by a *delimiter* (#). The first subfield is the title itself, *Thinking Robots, an aware internet, and cyberpunk librarians*. The second provides title information, and the third subfield denotes additional title information, in this case the book's editors, who are also listed under the "700" tag below as personal name added entries.

— 020 &955#a#pc03 to la00 07-31-92; lj09 07-31-92; lj07 08-10-92; lj05 08-11-92; aa12 08-12-92; CIP ver. pv07 04-12-93%

— 030 &05000#ab#Z678.9#.T46 1992%

— 040 &24500#abc#Thinking robots, an aware internet, and cyberpunk librarians :#the 1992 LITA president's program : presentations by Hans Moravec, Bruce Sterling, and David Brin /#R. Bruce Miller and Milton T. Wolf, editors.%

— 050 &260-#abc#Chicago :#Library and Information Technology Association.#1992.%

— 060 &300#ac#iv, 200 p. ;#23 cm.%

— 090 &440-0#a#"A collection of background essays prepared for the 1992 LITA president's program, 'Tools for knowing, environments for growing: visions of the potential of information technology for human development'"—Cover.%

— 100 &504#a#Includes bibliographical references.%

— 110 &020#a#08389766255 (acid-free paper)%

— 096 &70010#a#Mu, Queen.%

— 099 &08200#a2#001.9#20%

— 100 &040#acd#DLC#DLC#DLC%

— 120 &005#a#19930817084246.8%

— 140 &985#a#APIF/MIG%

Like catalog cards, MARC records are designed to be retrieved through a series of *access points*, including *main entry* (100 field), *subject entry* (600 field) and *added entry* (700 field). All of these may or may not be present in any given

MARC record. The example below, for example, has no *main entry*, but it does have two *topical subject headings* (650 field), "Libraries—Automation—Congresses" and "Information Technology—Congresses," five *personal name added entries* (700 field), "Moravec, Hans P.," "Sterling, Bruce," "Brin, David," "Miller, R. Bruce" and "Wolf, Milton T." and one *corporate name added entry*, "Library and Information Technology Association." Different records may be assigned different numbers of *access points* depending on the 1). the container type, 2). the sorts of cataloging (Collection Level Cataloging, Minimum Level Cataloging) and 3). the needs of individual subscribers and vendors (900 fields). For example, an item cataloged under MLC (Minimum Level Cataloging), may only be assigned a single access point, i.e., *main entry* only (100 field).

## THE DEVELOPMENT OF MARC

The MARC program is considered by many as the launching of the LC's "information age" and the direct precursor to its "library without walls." While I take issue with this characterization, I don't want to diminish the excitement and optimism that surrounded the different MARC programs in the 1960s and 1970s. Funded with money from the Council on Library Resources (CLR), MARC represented—to many in the Library and Information world—the best of centralized, government research. If something like MARC was to become a reality, informants recounted, the LC would have to do it. There was, at least in the hindsights of participants I spoke with, a sense of being part of a program vitally important to the continued survival of libraries in the United States. And, although "downsizing" was possible with the instigation of MARC, the program began without the pall of bitterness and suspicion that accompanied the development of "American Memory" and the digital library (see Chapter 6 below).[52] While general naiveté could be behind the generally enthusiastic reception of MARC (and not everyone was enthusiastic), I think that other factors were at least as important. For one thing, MARC began as a way of *distributing* cataloging information. Only later did MARC threaten to replace the card catalog. Secondly, MARC is a *cataloger's* technology, produced by an in-house staff who communicated, to some degree, with the catalogers they were trying to help (but not replace). The "American Memory" project, on the other hand, developed amidst an atmosphere of administrative hostility to such labor-intensive practices as descriptive and subject cataloging and was, in the minds of some managers, supposed to obviate the need for some of the meticulous work of cataloging.

In the 1950s and 1960s, many Federal agencies in Washington, D.C. were "automating," introducing automated payroll systems, inventory

---

52  I should qualify that MARC, as a world-wide system of distributing cataloging information, *was* met with by a good deal of suspicion by many outside of the LC.

control and record keeping with an eye towards emulating scientific models of management and organization practiced in the private sector and grounded in advanced Taylorist thinking (Asbell 1965; Rosenberg 1992).[53] The GAO (Government Accounting Office) and various branches of the DOD (Department of Defense) were already heavily invested in "automation" before the Library began to consider it in the early 1960s. All of these agencies, however, had at least two goals in common: 1). the foreshortening of heretofore manual tasks with the help of some mechanized process and 2). the downsizing of what was already considered a "bloated" Washington, D.C. bureaucracy. At the LC, the cost of keeping millions of cataloging cards in the master stock was thought prohibitive, as was the cost of the labor required for the indexing and filling of card orders. As then-Librarian of Congress Quincy Mumford told a House Subcommittee in 1967:

> In the card distribution service specifically, it is anticipated that we will be able to reduce the number of employees substantially, once we have introduced mechanized procedures. (U.S. Congress 1967:395)

During the 1940s and 1950s, the LC discussed different plans for automation—beginning with the "memex" and microform reproduction—and, in 1963, published the "King Report," a feasibility survey recommending the implementation of an automation program. The "automated system" proposed by the King Report was comprehensive in scope, encompassing *acquisition, cataloging* and *circulation* (King 1963). At the time, the Library maintained separate card catalogs for each of these functions. For example, the *shelflisting* catalog would track books sent out for rebinding, but the Main Catalog would not. The Copyright Catalog recorded all materials copyrighted by the Library, but didn't trace other acquisitions or existing imprints. As a result of the favorable report, the Library received funding to hire three employees in information systems to develop the pilot project for automated catalog. "MARC 1" ran from 1966 to 1968 and initially involved 40 participating libraries (Avram 1968, 1975). Subscribing libraries would receive magnetic tapes coded with MARC records and batch-load them onto their own systems, accessing the records with either commercial or in-house software. Largely successful, the pilot program resulted in important modifications to software and to an expanded set of MARC fields. By the end of the pilot program in 1968, the LC launched a full-scale MARC Distribution Service, eventually producing magnetic tapes for all LC cataloging and authority records. Importantly, this move towards "automation" did not mean that the LC was online.

---

53 The lexical shifts from "automation" to "computerization" and "digitization" are, I believe, vitally important to our understanding of the information age. They signal more than just the triumph of *computers*, but a shift in the discourses, expectations and practices surrounding them. "Digitization" is one more step in the distanciation of knowledge from its producers, connoting, as it does, an autochthonous accretion of information while "automation" implies the social processes at the root of expert systems.

We are using the U.S. Mail in effect as a medium for the transmission of this information. There would be no reason, if the economic conditions are such, that this same information could not be sent automatically by wire to the same libraries. (U.S. Congress 1969:11)

Three general themes emerge from the programmatic reviews of MARC I, MARC II and the various committee hearings deciding MARC's funding: 1). the centralization of Library personnel and services; 2). increased access to the collections for Library users and 3). expanded cataloging records.

Like many agencies in the U.S. government, the Library of Congress carefully couched requests for Congressional appropriations in "automation" and "mechanization" programs in the language of *crisis*, emphasizing the encroachment of entropic disorder in its collections.

We have reached the place where our traditional methods of doing things, the mere proliferation of catalogs— for example, reference was made yesterday to the enormity of the catalog of the Copyright Office— will not suffice, and we must undertake to make use of what the modern age has produced in way of machines, and to seek automation of bibliographic data. (U.S. Congress 1964:267)

With automation, the Library managers hoped to stem what they suggested was a bureaucratic chaos out of control. Not only was there the enormity of the Card Division's 5.5 million-card stock, but there were separate card catalogs kept for acquisitions, shelflisting and copyright besides the smaller catalogs kept for special collections. Even the Library's organizational charts during that time—usually unreliable artefacts of management—suggest the tortuous peregrinations of cataloging record from the receipt of an item to its shelving in the Library's collections.[54] That dendrification was even evident in the *spatial order* of the Library itself which, due to overcrowding, had located different departments and parts of departments in twelve locations in and around the D.C. metropolitan area and one in Ohio. This was ameliorated somewhat with the completion of a third Library of Congress building in 1980 (Library of Congress 1970:71).

Consistent with managerial tendencies towards centralization, Library officials conceptualized automation as a "brain" connecting its errant departments: "We also find that in general they have a central machine generally referred to as the brain, and then they have peripheral equipment which feeds data into this machine" (U.S. Congress 1964:268). For the cataloging record, automation meant a central database of common information manipulated by each department involved in acquisitions, cataloging, shelflisting or circulation, effectively cutting across the Library's increasingly byzantine organiza-

---

54 The 1964 "Library of Congress Organization Chart," for example, different divisions are listed *alphabetically* under the Library's six departments rather than *functionally*, unintentionally providing an object lesson in the cognitive dissonance produced by competing information orders (Library of Congress 1965).

tion. Librarians strained to conceptualize what MARC would mean.

> The study pictured a system where one of these tiny, binary "documents" would be created when a book was ordered, expanded as it was cataloged, annotated as the book was charged in and out or sent for rebinding, and in general manipulated so as to reflect everything that happens to a book through its lifetime in a library. (Goodrum 1974:229)

While this might conjoin the Library's "separate principalities" and even effect the streamlining of its burgeoning labor force, the real "winners" of automation were said to be the users who, by the mid-1960s, were only getting sixty-percent returns on their requests for the LC's materials (Library of Congress 1964:108-109). That is, four out of ten requests for books and other materials were returned "Not On Shelf" (NOS).[55] With the help of a computer terminal, the user could locate any item in the LC's holdings and, theoretically, determine whether or not that item was on the shelf (although this goal was never, in fact, achieved). "Ideally an automated system should place the full resources of the Library at the immediate disposal of the user" (U.S. Congress 1964:266).

The linchpin of all of this was the MARC record itself. Its design—revolutionary for the time—combined *fixed* and *variable* fields for a record that was both predictable in structure *and* flexible enough to accommodate different cataloging needs and continuously evolving container types (Avram 1968). It was the possibility of the latter that excited Library management.

> One of the big arguments for the conversion of the bibliographic apparatus to computer form is that we could do indexing in greater depth. Whereas we now assign one, two, or three subjects to a book, we could assign a dozen subjects if it seemed desirable. We could include the table of contents of journals, titles of articles, et cetera, that we are not now able to do manually because there is too much manpower involved and because it means the proliferation of our catalogs. (U.S. Congress 1966:430)

Using variable fields, catalogers could expand infinitely on the record, multiplying the number of added entries in any MARC record (6XX and 7XX fields) or including any additional notes in the 5XX field. The MARC record itself seemed to in no way structurally limit the depth of cataloging entry.

Or did it? What's interesting about these predictions (or projections) is how quickly they were discarded once MARC had been institutionalized. This is not to say, however, that MARC was a failure. From the point of view of the technotopian dreams of the time, though, MARC cataloging failed to realize the possibility of instant access and centralization.

---

55  This is actually even worse than it sounds. Since many researchers at the LC request *series* of reports, catalogs, phone books and serials, I suspect that the "NOS" rate for monographs was (and is) much higher.

For the different departments and divisions involved in the control of library materials to become in any way *centralized*, they had to share, in essence, the same electronic record, updating it at each stage in the life of the book, from the publisher's desk to the reader's desk, as it were. But that's not what happened. As Library officials testified in 1970, "Compatible databases are being created throughout the Library with a view to building toward the Central Bibliographic System" (U.S. Congress 1970). These included MARC, CBS and LOCATE, among others; in the 1990's, additional applications included ACQUIRE, a tracking system used in acquisitions, COPICS and COINS, a copyright system (Library of Congress 1968:17; Library of Congress 1995). Although the Library had some limited success linking departments to its accounting system, all of these, from the late 1960s to the adoption of the LC's Integrated Library System in 1999, were highly localized, proprietary systems and utilized either purchased or in-house software that resisted easy integration. Accordingly, some at the Library questioned the utility of this centralized automation.

> We can't have anybody programming this and hanging things on it independently. It has to be done in a centralized manner. On the other hand, so-called stand-alone systems that are not tied to the mainframe, distributed systems, in copyright and National Library Service for the Blind, and CRS, which will appear in the budget, and we feel that is appropriate—the hardware and the software for that—because that is where the costs are, that is where the benefit is, in other words. (U.S. Congress 1987:488).

This defense of "decentralized" systems seemed consistent with a growing distaste for hierarchical networks in the 1970s and 1980s. Ultimately, of course, this sort of logic seems a tautology; divisions utilizing separate systems for separate bureaucratic functions are unlikely to have developed operations that require substantive "sharing," as is the case with the Library Copyright Office. As one of the early, MARC developers explained,

> It isn't easy. It's harder at times. It's more than a Library. Everybody in the place is dealing with information; we all have different functions. It's not the same function. Copyrighting deals with information; they could care less whether the names are the same. You know, they have no authority control and that means nothing to them—all they want to do is get at that one item and find out if they had copies. (Interview, Collections Services, Acquisitions and Support Services Directorate, Management)

But this was not always the case. MARC records, for instance, were developed in the Library's Processing Services Division (now the Acquisitions and Bibliographic Access Directorate) and, ultimately, stayed there, even though the MARC record became, over the intervening decades, increasingly important to other divisions of the Library like the Congressional Research Service (CRS).

In the beginning when we started this, you know, [we] developed the network development office in 1975. Nobody in the Library was talking about that, only processing [services]. So it was pretty natural to keep it there. Now it should really be at
the Library, that is, somewhere where it covers the whole Library. (Interview, Collections Services, Acquisitions and Support Services Directorate, Management)

In addition, this fragmented development of different automated systems
meant that—at least according to this logic of centralization—MARC's usefulness to library users and to Congress was also diminished. It was impossible
to deduce the status of the Library's holding from the cataloging record; the
cataloging record was not, in other words, a *circulation* record.[56] Also, the electronic catalog remained inexplicably incomplete, due to 1). a failure to assign
electronic records to some special collections and 2). the hurried and largely
regretted attempt to "retrospectively convert" the Library's older holdings to
MARC records.[57] Because of a series of unfortunate mishaps involving contract labor, administrative mistakes (i.e. the K.G. Saur microfiche) and a lackadaisical attitude (prompted by economics) towards editing, the "PREMARC"
database of the Library's holdings was considered suspect by some and completely useless by others (Mann 1991).[58] These complications had the effect of
stymieing the "union catalog" ambitions of MARC, a privilege derogated—by
default, perhaps—to OCLC, a commercial cataloging vendor (Buckland and
Basinski 1978).

But the MARC record itself remains a lasting, cataloging breakthrough.
While some might argue that MARC undermines some of the metonymic
serendipity of the old Main Catalog, it erects another system in its place with
some advantages over the old. Composed of different fields that can be subjected to qualified searches or specific, "compressed" commands, MARC records
have their own structure, rooted in the 3x5 cataloging card but extending it
in different directions. Lacking integration with other systems or "full text"
fields like tables of content or indices, MARC records nevertheless emerge as
cataloging records with rigorous standards that have been adopted worldwide
as well as a certain flexibility for accommodating different container types and
different customized usages, from collection-level records of photographs or
sheet music to computer databases. It is a system of agreed-upon protocols
(e.g., authority records that fix standard spellings for names and subjects) that
make bibliographic searching highly predictable for researchers and librarians
who know how to utilize these records. But like the card catalog that preceded

---

56 Once, that is, the item is out of processing. As the monograph, serial, photograph, database,
etc., is being processed, codes and descriptors are assigned to the record that track that process
(e.g., APIF).

57 This even seems the case for the National Digital Library.

58 In the days before the adoption of the LC's ILS, doing any amount of research at the Library
brought you up against PREMARC's many miskeying errors. For example, I found four *different*
spellings for Leibniz.

it, the MARC system forms a largely separate structure only indirectly (and sometimes obliquely) referring to *full text* (through LC Classification, Dewey Decimal, accession numbers, etc.). That is, "full text" is not part of the record. But not everyone sees this as a shortcoming.

> That's my idea of the digitized library, the catalog will reflect and tell you how to use and do all the rest of it, of what you would use. [ . . .] Let's say it was put together like the catalog would say, "If you're interested in this material it's out at Stanford. This is what you do." Or it could say "We have this file. There's this and this is what you do to get it." And, to me, the catalog would change. It would have other things in it. (Interview, Collections Services, Acquisitions and Support Services Directorate, Management)

Since copyright remains a serious, if not ultimately crippling, impediment to "full text retrieval" in cataloging, catalogers have been augmenting the cataloging record in other ways. For example, in the mid-1990's, Blackwell North America (BNA), began including tables of contents in the 505 field (Contents note) for books with substantive chapter headings and for edited volumes. More recent "enrichments" include URL links to digitized content. Depending on your opinions about natural language versus controlled vocabulary, this enriched record may or may not be an improvement over the MARC cataloging that has developed over the last 25 years. An abstract or a table of contents adds *words* with no particular relationship to the rest of the cataloging record, that is, names are not "tagged" as personal name added entries, titles as "series different title," etc. In fact, the semantic value of added summary notes or content notes can only be known *after* retrieving the record. By definition (i.e. as "uncontrolled" natural language), they cannot be predicted in advance.[59] What that does to "access" and "retrieval" depends much upon the needs and experience of the user. In either case, however, the architecture of the MARC record is changed.

---

59  See Mann (1993) for an interesting discussion of "precoordinated" versus "postcoordinated" searching.

CHAPTER 5

# "Getting the Champagne Out of the Bottle and Into the Six-Pack": Laying the Foundations for the Virtual Library at the LC[60]

With the establishment of a World Wide Web home page (http://www.loc.gov) in June of 1994 and a legislative information site called THOMAS (http://thomas.loc.gov) in January of 1995, the Library placed itself on what it considers the forefront of the "National Digital Library." Whatever the ultimate fate of the "library without walls," it seems to have captured the collective imagination of Congressional appropriations committee members. Amidst budget cuts for 1996 that quite literally ripped apart federal bureaucracies, the Library's budget actually *increased* and was, in fact, the only legislative branch agency to have received one (Ohnemus 1995). In the years since then, the National Digital Library has proven a magnet for private philanthropy.

At the end of fiscal year 1987, Dr. Daniel Boorstin stepped down as Head Librarian. At his last appropriations hearing before Congress, Boorstin and his staff came under some criticism for what the Subcommittee saw as the centrifugal multiplication of closed systems at the Library.

> Also, we are concerned about the growth of so many individual programs in the Library. We want you to have a high level of programs. At the same time, we want you to have one that integrates all of the operations of the Library to the extent that it is possible. (U.S. Congress 1987:487)

On the tails of severe budgetary cutbacks from the Gramm-Rudman-Hollings Balanced Budget and Emergency Deficit Control Act (1986), the subcommittee was also interested in the pecuniary savings associated with *automation*, particularly in terms of downsizing and deskilling.

It fell to Boorstin's successor, Head Librarian James Billington, to revive these ideas. Like Mumford before him, Billington connected automation

---

60 Head Librarian James Billington used this strange metaphor at a meeting I attended in April of 1995.

with both work-force reduction and increased efficiency. After assembling a "Management Planning" (MAP) Committee, Billington's office issued a report calling for both "flexible" workers and decentralized information processing.[61] This included attempts to link heretofore disparate systems, for example copyright and cataloging (Library of Congress 1988b:490). And like Mumford, Billington saw the electronic *record* as endemic to the attainment of these other goals.

> We will apply the experience gained over the past century to support the Library's information systems, and to create an expanded, enhanced, and enriched catalog that will serve a new generation of users. We will reconceptualize the bibliographic record, moving beyond the model of the manual card catalog, and fully embrace the electronic age. We will substitute digital image of title pages, in some cases, for elaborate bibliographic descriptions. We will increase subject access by including tables of contents, back-of-the-book indexes, abstracts, and links to evaluative essays such as book reviews. (Library of Congress 1992:12)

We should not miss the implicit threat to descriptive and subject cataloging in the above citation, i.e. the replacement of "elaborate" cataloging with "natural" language gleaned from tables of contents and indices. Billington's tenure as Librarian of Congress (1987-present) has been marked by numerous challenges to the "Cataloging Directorate" (now the "Bibliographic Access" division of the "Acquisitions and Bibliographic Access Directorate") a division that—whatever its name—has, since Quincy Mumford's time, been singled out by Library management and Congress as in need of winnowing, despite its prominence as the leading source of cataloging for the United States. Billington has been the first to actually "downsize" the cataloging division, first through its re-organization (e.g. "Whole Book Cataloging") and then through the implementation of various kinds of *truncated* cataloging, e.g. Minimum Level Cataloging, Copy Cataloging, Core Level Cataloging, etc., that, in effect, lower the LC's cataloging standards and, in the classic, Braverman sense, "de-skill" the cataloging process (Braverman 1975). Although I can't speculate on the effects of these changes on the integrity of the catalog, it has certainly been de-moralizing to the great majority of subject and descriptive catalogers, who work under a sigil of uncertainty and doubt (Library of Congress 1997; Library of Congress Cataloging Forum 1993). Ironically, of course, much of the "natural language" that is supposed to supplant "pre-coordinated" cataloging ultimately derives from Library of Congress Subject Headings anyway, e.g. subject indices in the *Social Sciences Index* or Outline of Cultural Materials in the *Human Relations Area Files*.

In the first years of Billington's stewardship of the Library, the key to this

---

61 These buzzwords—"flexibility," "decentralization"—were the 1980s equivalent to post-World War II "centralization" and "automation." Both were purported to result in increased efficiency and savings.

"abridgement" of cataloging and heterogeneity was thought to lie with the "optical disk," the generic name for CD-ROM technologies. Of course, throughout the twentieth century, libraries had experimented with techniques for miniaturizing their burgeoning collections. In the 1940s, the LC had begun microfilming its collections and, particularly after World War II, collections housed in European libraries. By the 1960s and 70s, microfilm or microfiche was thought to have made the "physical library" obsolete, as all of the LC's collections could easily fit into a couple of filing cabinets (Mann 1993:104-105). In the late 1970s, however, the LC began experimenting with optical disk technology, combining the miniaturization of microfilming and microfiche with the assumed permanence of digital technology. Users sitting at high-speed terminals could access and print whole articles or books that had been scanned into the reader; like the microfilming that preceded it, "optical disk" promised instant access to limitless collections. The Library began a pilot program to study the potential of optical disks in 1982 and installed its first optical disk reader in 1984 ("Three Speakers Tout LC's Optical Disk Program": 9). But although the Congressional Research Service used optical disk technologies to store and retrieve selected journal articles, the optical disk program was never adopted as a regular service for the remainder of the Library, due to its expense, the copyright problems associated with digitization and serious doubts as to the permanence of both optical disks and the machines on which they're read (Lawton 1991; Saffady 1988).

But the LC found another use for its digital imaging, in the form of digitized collections of primary (and public domain) historical documents disseminated to selected libraries and schools. Emphasizing Library collections centered on well-known epochs in American history, the pilot program was known as "American Memory" and featured primary textual documents, visual and sound materials that could be viewed together and interactively (Library of Congress 1991a:14). Although the program was touted at its inception as an educational and an outreach tool, Head Librarian Billington and his staff gradually began to conceive of "American Memory" as a way for the Library to increase its public visibility and serve the "needs of the Nation" by placing "potential high-use, high-value collections that are logical units to facilitate access to their contents and make these materials more widely available across the nation" ("Summary of MAP Committee Recommendations":493). It was the optical disk and American memory that prompted Billington to testify that "Technology—the electronic storage, selection, and transmission of information—will make it possible for the Library of Congress to become a Library without walls" (U.S. Congress 1990:1990).

However, the idea of an "electronic library" steadily took on a different connotation, first as the provision of "interactive links" to Members of Congress and gradually, as the Library began to experiment with Internet applications, to the public-at-large (Library of Congress 1992a:27). In 1992, the Library began experimenting with making some of the collections it had digitized for "American Memory" available through File Transfer Protocol (FTP) and through one of the then-emergent commercial Internet providers, America Online. "File Transfer Protocol" is just that, a command structure that allowed the transfer of selected files from open systems. The "AOL" site, on the other hand, was an experiment in multimedia.

> It started in 1992. The Librarian is a Russian scholar [and] there seemed to be a possibility of getting some interesting documents from the Soviet archives. I had a conversation with him where I said it was time that the Library launched electronic exhibits and he said, "Let's work with AOL and see if we can't launch an electronic exhibit." (Interview, Cultural Affairs, Management)

AOL and the LC arranged an "electronic exhibit" paralleling but not reproducing its "live" exhibit, "Revelations from the Russian Archives." Using texts culled from the exhibit, the AOL site allowed visitors to "tour" different documents.

The AOL site was an ambitious experiment in interactive exhibits, combining documents with online discussion groups and feedback from reference staff at the LC. However, by 1995 the LC had ceased monitoring the site or uploading new material.

> I have posted several questions, but for the life of me I have not managed to discover IF anybody answers, and if so, WHERE or HOW I can find their responses. Is there a big "person in the sky" I just can't see without my special glasses? Is there a hidden answer post in an unnamed-menu? Somebody let me in on this! (AOL post, 6/10/95)

What had happened, of course, was that nobody at the LC had been detailed to the reference work of answering user questions.

> I spent a lot of time on AOL [but] it was almost impossible to get Public Affairs to update their documents. AOL is interested in us becoming more active; I'm for becoming more active or getting out of it altogether. (Interview, Cultural Affairs, Management)

Employees at the LC were already working on their own Gopher server, LC MARVEL. Volunteering their time, a group investigated different sorts of "Campus Wide Information Systems" (CWIS) and in July of 1993 had come up with recommendations for a Gopher server, a simple, client-server software displaying content in a hierarchical fashion, from "top-level" directories down to files that need not be housed on the root server (Marine *et al* 1993; Miller 1993b). As at the AOL site, LC management never detailed staff to the Gopher client, which remained in the flexible hands of various employees who acted as "owners" of various files on the server, updating them whenever they had time. As a campus-wide system, the Gopher was meant to serve both employees and users with texts supplemental to the LC's printed collections and employee information. And since Gopher clients employ simple, ascii script, LC employees tended to upload documents they'd already published in print form, including press releases, finding aids, texts of journals (LC Information Bulletin) and memoranda from the Librarian's office.[62] An exception to this was the "Global Electronic Library," a classed-subject directory of Internet resources organizing materials in hierarchies from general to specific. Not only did the "Global Electronic Library" organize materials *outside* of the LC, but it did so according to a system of *classed* subjects that had little in common with the *dictionary* arrangement used at LC.[63] The system of "classed" cataloging, however at that point perfunctory, nevertheless suggested different ways of organizing information than conventional cataloging at the LC.

Since linking with the "selector strings" representing different documents on different gopher servers effectively takes users outside of the LC's server, designers of the structure of LC MARVEL were concerned over the preservation of institutional identity.

> We want to be clear. We want to be clear what we're providing and what other people are providing. This was [his] feeling; whatever was ours he wanted to be clear. He wanted to be clear what was here and what was outside. (Interview, Cultural Affairs)

---

### Library of Congress (LC MARVEL)

<menu>  About LC MARVEL
<menu>  Events, Facilities, Publications, and Services
<menu>  Research and Reference (Public Services)
<menu>  Libraries and Publishers (Technical Services)
<menu>  Copyright
<menu>  Library of Congress Online Systems
<menu>  Employee Information
<menu>  U.S. Congress
<menu>  Government Information
<menu>  Global Electronic Library (by Subject)
<menu>  Internet Resources
<menu>  What's New on LC MARVEL
<menu>  Search LC MARVEL Menus

---

LC MARVEL's top-level directory
(Gopher://marvel.loc.gov)

---

62  "ASCII" text is the unembellished, "plain" text standard used in programming. It lacks, among other things, diacritics.

63  That is to say, "classed" subjects present materials according to a logical order isomorphic to the organization of that discipline, while "dictionary" catalogs present it alphabetically. Of course, the LC's dictionary catalog still preserves some of the characteristics of a "classed" catalog, though this logical structure is somewhat occluded by the computerized catalog.

There were at least two reasons for this caution: 1). an overarching concern that the "unbridled" growth of the Internet would inundate LC sites and materials and 2). the recognition that LC MARVEL—ostensibly an "information" server—was also a public relations booster, presenting the "identity" of the Library as an institution to a public not necessarily familiar with its mandates, workings and organization. The eventual structure of LC MARVEL (above) shows a careful hierarchy of knowledge, arranged by importance from public services to LOCIS (the SCORPIO/MUMS catalog *outside* the gopher client) to employee information (featuring, among other things, proprietary memoranda not accessible to the general public), "Government Information," the "Global Electronic Library" and "Internet Resources." It is no mistake that the last three directories take users beyond the purview of the LC's server and that none of the foregrounded directories contain selector strings for any of the latter sites. This stratified approach—in a way antithetical to the "resource sharing" ethos of Internet-users up to that time—was to become an important element in the LC's design of its "National Digital Library" (below).

At the same time that volunteers were compiling documents for LC MARVEL, a multimedia artist and programmer named Frans van Hoesel had discovered some of the online files from the Library's "Rome Reborn" exhibit and had decided to put them together into a multimedia exhibit accessible through the recently released NCSA Mosaic browser.[64]

> It turned out that the Library of Congress made those pictures available through anonymous ftp. In fact, they had a huge collection of small text files and about 200 image files, which all together formed the online version of the exhibit, 'Rome Reborn'. This exhibit was already available via gopher or ftp, but users needed a long time to retrieve the images and the separate text files. To me it was very obvious that those text files and images were just waiting to be merged together into one big exhibit. Such an exhibit could be created using the simple multimedia language used to create documents. (van Hoesel)

Van Hoesel arranged several Library of Congress exhibits—"Rome Reborn: the Vatican Library and Renaissance Culture," "Revelations from the Russian Archives," "Scrolls from the Dead Sea" and "1492: An Ongoing Voyage"—before the Library put up its own Web server in 1994. For their part, people in the LC's Information and Technology Services (ITS) Directorate assisted van Hoesel with knitting together the dissimilar files types into a working whole, and in particular a style van Hoesel termed a "Real World Look and Feel" approach to online exhibits simulating a "walking" tour of a museum. "I wanted to give the visitors a feeling of being there, just like in the old style text adventures" (van Hoesel). The exhibits were ordered, not by "classed" hierarchies from general to specific, but by a thematic metonymy more typical of early- to mid-

---

64  Released in 1992, NCSA Mosaic was the first widely available, hypermedia browser for document sharing on the World Wide Web.

twentieth-century museum exhibits.

Although the Library had, to some degree, supported van Hoesel's experiments, they began to distance themselves from him in 1993-1994 as they developed their own World Wide Web server.

> They tend to make their own exhibits now, not in EXPO style. I asked them if they would like it if their work was modified for EXPO, but their answer was very formal that they could prevent me from doing it. For me that was the same as they wouldn't like it, so I did not. (online "interview" with van Hoesel)

With this seemingly abrupt departure from the 1992 altruism of "anonymous ftp," the LC began to craft a "presence" on the World Wide Web, starting with its display of "African-American Culture and History."

In June of 1994, the Library launched its "lcweb" server. The first documents placed on the site were exhibits, followed by "American Memory" collections until then only available on optical disk ("The Guts of the Digital Library":263). Its organization bore a striking resemblance to the LC MARVEL site, with a top-down hierarchy of links to directories and files foregrounding exhibit materials first. At first, nothing not already published, exhibited or collated somewhere else was placed on the server, but the Librarian's office began to develop plans for the World Wide Web.

In October of 1994, Head Librarian Billington presided over the opening of the Digital Library Visitors Center, an austere space filled with a labyrinth of removable office stalls resembling nothing so much as the leased quarters of a slightly shady telecommunications company and featuring different desk-top computers running different LC applications. It was to be the Library's model of its future: the National Digital Library. Often characterized by both critics and supporters as a "visionary," Billington struggled to conceptualize the Library's new role in the age of "information superhighway."[65]

> Dr. Billington presented an egalitarian view of providing the Library's collections electronically to those who cannot come to Washington, D.C., for on- site research. "Our goal is to preserve, organize, and digitize the intellectual cargo." (Fineberg 1995d: 10)

Months later at the employee introduction to the Visitor's Center in April of 1995, Billington grappled with similar metaphors.

> 'We are not in the highway construction business or the trucking business,' he said, 'We are in the content business. Our main mission is to digitize our core Americana collections and make them available.' Dr. Billington proposed offering, free to the Internet, LC's digital information in complete archival packages—what he calls 'plain vanilla'—allowing librarians

---

65 There is an apocryphal story that I have no way of verifying that one of Head Librarian Billington's first suggestions upon taking the office in 1987 was to construct a "moving sidewalk" around the Main reading Room so tourists could examine the room's elaborate statuary. True or not, it is an index of the rank-and-file's exasperation with him.

and educators to refine LC's digital resources for their own purposes. (Fineberg 1995a:9)

All of Billington's metaphors, of course, seem drawn from a world of private commerce, an image he strengthened by calling for the LC "to be a benevolent wholesaler for the local institutions which will retail knowledge and information to teachers, students, and the public" (Library of Congress 1996:118). It may be true that he couched the Library's role in the development of multimedia products and Web sites in the language of "supplier" to palliate corporate sponsors like Xerox who might have been planning multimedia products of their own.

His slightly cryptic blend of cliché and mixed metaphor, however, generated confusion in staff members. After all, the Library's web site was anything but "wholesale plain vanilla intellectual cargo." In fact, all of the collections on the site had been carefully selected, arranged and explicated as either "museum exhibits" or educational tools. Having derived at least some of the architecture of their Web site from van Hoesel's earlier efforts, LCWEB was obviously meant to *attract* people by digitizing and arranging collections in an enticing way. The main source of confusion at the meeting I heard about centered around Billington's notion that the LC should "digitize our core Americana collections," a process that seemed redolent of editing. One of the employees asked if important Latin American, South American or Canadian collections would also be digitized, particularly those that had some bearing on the history of the United States, only to be angrily reproached that "Americana" meant the "United States." The criteria, he suggested further, was that "one, it must be institutionally important and, two, it must be deeply interesting."

> That conceptual confusion persisted into the pilot program itself. But this came up [ . . .] it was early on when they opened the first meeting. They were talking about 'plain vanilla' this and 'plain vanilla that' and I kept saying 'Look, whatever we put out just deciding what we put out is an extremely important editorial decision because just because we decide something we are creating much more access to it [ . . .]  What we take it to mean—what I take it to mean— the working definition that our group kind of sorted out was you convert the collections, you provide essential finding aid data for that. But there are so-called partners in the private sector if they want to take you know a section of Abraham Lincoln's papers and add in songs from the time and add in lesson plans and market it for K through 6 that's great.   (Interview, Collections Services, Cataloging)

Presenting true, 'plain vanilla' would mean something more along the lines of the 1992 ftp server that presented a top-level directory of files that could be downloaded. The Library of Congress Web site, on the other hand, gradually became more and more oriented towards the identity of the institution and the packaging of collections as "exhibits." A substantial reorganization of the Library's home page in summer of 1995, for example, relegated sites outside the Library to the bottom of the page while keeping "exhibits" at the top of the hierarchy. A 1996 reorganization even introduced "The Learning Page," a series of finding aids organized around the needs of educators and students and, apparently, offering just the sort of "value-added" services decried by the Librarian two years earlier. If anything, the "National Digital Library" grew more and more concerned with the presentation of a strong, institutional identity. And like LC MARVEL, "Digital Library" collections were hermetically contained hierarchies of image and texts that never led to related sites on other servers.

> Although the Library has adhered to the standards for "browser" software, it was considered to be essential that remote patrons could instantly identify a Library of Congress site through its unique and attractive graphics as high quality information. Toward this end, and NDL task force completed the plans for developing an interface design to present the "look and feel" of the Library of Congress. (Library of Congress 1996:26)

The Library's search for an appropriate "look and feel" coincides with the explosion of corporate advertising—from canned foods and coffees to universities and insurance agencies—on the World Wide Web. Since the Library—like most government bureaucracies in the 1980s and 90s—sought to emulate private business, much of this concern could stem from the imitation of strong corporate Web sites like "Microsoft" and "Disney."[66]

## THE QUESTION OF FILE LOCATION

Part of the reason for presenting the collections in such a parochial fashion lay not only in the relationships between the collections and the Library, but also in the relationships *among* different parts of a collection. Again, unlike atomized, "plain vanilla" files, different historical collections were meant to be viewed in some kind of metonymic order: the "Evolution of the Conservation Movement, 1850-1920," for example, is an *evolution*, a chronotype of events one after the other. And yet, keeping files together proved a difficult task in the early days of the National Digital Library.

While writing this chapter, I needed to check on an online source that I'd consulted, "The Expo Story" by Frans van Hoesel. The site's "Universal Resource Locator" (URL)—a unique name specifying a hierarchical pathway from top-level files and indexes to individual documents—was "rugmd4.chem.rug. nl:80/hoesel/expo/part1.html." Linking to that URL, however, did not give me "The Expo Story" but a message from the rugmd4.chem.rug.nl server, "404 Not Found," meaning that van Hoesel's file was no longer at that URL.

---

66  For a series of publications calling for government to reorganize under "total quality management" and other flexible styles produced under the auspices of the "National Performance Review," click onto the LC's THOMAS site (http://www.thomas.gov). This was brought home to me on a 3/17/97 National Public Radio broadcast when a Government Accounting Office auditor lambasted the Internal Revenue Service for using "1950s processes" with "1970s technologies."

The World Wide Web has a temporary, shifting character and only with a great deal of imagination can it be considered "archival." Files are routinely changed, moved or removed altogether. While it may be easy enough to update personal home pages, an institution digitizing eleven million "items" (by 2006) on its website may experience special difficulties.

> So we've got stuff out there all over the place. Well don't you do the same thing as Benjamin Franklin to [sic] instead of putting the pamphlets over here well we put the TIF over here and the BIF over there and the JPEG over here and ACE over there and we've got names for it. Well don't you think we should try to control this?[67] (Interview, Information Technology Services, Management)

That is, it's not just that the LC had different files on different directories, but that it had different *file types* on different *servers*. The notion that online collections somehow transcend the problems of *container type* is not exactly accurate. "Location"—here a relative term designating a *path* to a specific file rather than a physical space—becomes in some ways as problematic as the classification of physical collections and presents, perhaps, a limit to the unfettered multiplication of files on applications such as World Wide Web. At the very least, the structure of the World Wide Web seems in many ways incompatible with the sorts of *access* and *reference* practiced in libraries. For one thing, Internetworked files are resolutely *synchronic*—that is, the hierarchies of servers, indices and individual files exist in that moment when you instruct your browser software to contact a server using a Universal Resource Locator (URL) but not necessarily afterwards, when the files may have been moved or removed.

The Library's solution to these twinned problems—file type and the uncertainty of file location—has been to develop tagged, descriptive documents for each of its online collections structuring access to materials that might be resident on different directories and different servers. This has been immeasurably aided by the sorts of collections the Library has heretofore digitized; instead of placing whole monographs or serials online (arguably the popular idea of a 'digital library') the LC has instead placed *multimedia collections* on its server drawn from its enormous holdings of photographs, prints, motion pictures and recordings.[68] Unlike monographs, many of the digitized items have not received a full, cataloging record. For example, "Washington As It Was: Photographs by Theodor Horydczak, 1923-1959" is a collection containing some 14,000 photographs, none of which have been cataloged at the same level as most monographs. Rather, they "inherit" cataloging attributes from a *finding aid*, a "class of documents that, in general, consisted of an optional title page, the description of a unit of archival material, and optional back matter" ("Development of the Encoded Archival Description Document Type Definition").

---

67 "TIF," "JPEG" and so on refer to file formats using different methods of compression to condense image or audio files.
68 This is, of course, the Library's answer to the copyrighting dilemmas posed by digitizing documents.

The genius of the LC's plan was to adopt finding aids to digitized collections as a way of ordering diverse files and structuring predictable access to a range of materials. The standard for these "marked-up" finding aids is known as the "Encoded Archival Description Document Type Definition." Using Extensible Markup Language (XML) (replacing earlier experiments in SGML) to tag and structure finding aids, the "EAD DTD" allows for a document with predictable parts structured in relation to each other: a segment describing the finding aid itself and a segment describing the material itself, i.e. the content of the finding aid ("Development of the Encoded Archival Description Document Type Definition").

With a standard way of structuring and "marking up" finding aids, the LC could both place files on different directories and servers as well as change their location as their computer systems changed, relying less on "absolute path names" than on "relative path names." Whichever server hosts, say, the "Portraits by Carl van Vechten, 1932-1964" is, in the end, immaterial, since the collections are linked to the World Wide Web *through* the finding aid, which, while hardly an archivist's dream of permanence, nevertheless provides a more-or-less predictable location for different multimedia collections.

> One of the key factors in selecting a collection is: Does a finding aid exist and if so in which form? You know, they'll be able to process it if the issue of converting it into SGML format and also linking the Internet to the finding aid. (interview, Collections Services, Cataloging)

The usefulness of finding aids for online collections seems to have solved the Library's immediate, organizational problems and has led some staffers to predict the end of other organizations of knowledge altogether.

> They keep talking about MARC: about MARC online, updating MARC. I think it might be outdated. That's going to solve the standardization problem. We may not need to worry about cataloging as much. It may be all we need to do is put up our finding aids and not worry about cataloging as much. (Interview, Cultural Affairs)

But dismissing conventional cataloging seems to collapse two distinct, though interrelated, issues: 1). the organization of collections vis-à-vis themselves and collections outside the LC and 2). access to collections. It is the second of these considerations that has proved in some ways problematic for the Library's "electronic library."

## SEARCHING FOR THE LIBRARY: PRATFALLS OF ACCESS IN THE INFORMATION AGE

For some time now, the contention among some in LC management (inevitably those closest to Head Librarian Billington) has been that searches undertaken on Internet search engines are overtaking library catalog searches.

> Today, a large and growing number of students and scholars routinely bypass library catalogs in favor of other discovery tools, and the catalog represents a shrinking proportion of the universe of scholarly information. (Calhoun 2006: 5)

Those of us who work in settings with large numbers of undergraduates know that Google searches have waxed in importance over the last 10 years. And yet, is it true that these students "sitting there" in their "cozy computer-equipped dorm room," ignore "your library entirely, and going online to, say, a commercial search service such as Google" (Marcum 2004)? Perhaps it is, but it's not clear that these are the only people the LC should strive to serve.

In any case, Calhoun's contention that the catalog qua "product" has outlived its "product cycle" (Calhoun 2006:10), has enraged many in the library and information sciences in general and at the Library of Congress in particular, many of whom resist the idea that libraries should capitulate to Google. But this is only a recent salvo in two decades of special reports designed, it seems, to under-cut LC cataloging:

> And so the Library's management in recent years has consistently disparaged the work of its own professional catalogers, has invited a string of outside speakers to tell them how irrelevant and outmoded their work is "in the digital age," has changed Library priorities to avoid hiring new professional catalogers as old ones retire, has restricted catalogers' ability to extend the subject headings system, and has generally sought to promote the belief that authority control, standardization of headings, and the shelving of actual books in subject categories—that all such practices are now no longer necessary because keyword searching in Google Book Search is, or soon will be, an acceptable substitute. (Mann 2006)

The argument, however, is rarely so absolute. Usually, polemics against traditional cataloging argue for 1) *supplementing* the catalog with full text and other links or 2) *integrating* the catalog with other searches available on the Internet, e.g., linking an Amazon record to the book record. Of course, while it is clear that commercial vendors would welcome the opportunity for free advertising, it is less clear that the commercial world would give equal weight to libraries.

In any case, suggesting that the catalog should emulate Internet search engines and commercial information vendors confuses two different *orders* of information—two different ways of structuring, institutionalizing, practicing, and, ultimately, *defining* information. In way of illustration, let's consider two different searches for "Chinese immigration in California"—one on what (for lack of something better) passes for a union catalog in the digital universe—WorldCat On Google Book Search (books.google.com), the other search on regular Google (www.google.com). Dropping the "in" from the search string, my Google Book search (November of 2007) generates 1870 hits; courtesy of a combination of content, page ranking and relevance scores (among other things), there are several good possibilities in the first page, among them *The Anti-Chinese Movement in California* by Elmer Sandmeyer and public domain, historical documents from the 19th century. But where is the Library of Congress? As a place, it's not so obvious—because I searched from my office in Baltimore, Maryland, the LC appears as one of the libraries where I might find the book (only 40 miles away!), but, as a function of distance, would appear much further down the list if you lived, say, in Texas. But, in another sense, the LC is everywhere: in the ISBN (the International Standard Book Number), in the name authority (*Elmer* rather than *Elmore* or *E*), in the descriptive cataloging (number of pages), in subject headings for the library record (e.g., Chinese-Americans—California—History) and even for the Google subject terms (e.g., Social Science/ Anthropology/ Cultural), which, however obliquely, are based on Library of Congress Subject Headings anyway.

Now, let's do the same search on regular Google. Here, there are 297,000 hits that include archival sites, scholarly articles (the *Brown Quarterly*), and para-scholarly digests (Wikipedia). Here, the Library of Congress figures prominently: the second result is the LC's "Learning Page," a collection of resources for k-12 educators based on selections from "American memory"; the fifth hit is "The Chinese in California, 1850-1925," a rich, photographic archive of the Chinese American experience.

Both "libraries"—i.e., the Library in its capacity as Cataloging Distribution and the LC as its "Digital Library"—are resoundedly successful. It would be difficult, after all, to imagine searching for a book (whether in a physical library or on Amazon) without the textual orders produced at the Library. Likewise, the results for Chinese immigration foreground the LC's content in a way that would make any .com envious. Indeed, not only has the LC digitized a large volume of content, but that content reliably comes up in Pagerank-driven searches; in other words, the National Digital Library is both expansive in scope *and* popular.

And yet, the two searches suggest very different institutional priorities. The first is very much the Library of Congress in its capacity of a public good—the kinds of standardization, cataloging rules, authority records that have shaped the landscape of "information society" from the 19th century up until the present. The second, while no less public (these are free and usually public domain materials, after all), pits the LC against a number of other for-profit and non-profit entities, among them "Thinkquest" (www.thinkquest.org), an educational service hosted by Oracle, "Mexconnect" (www.mexconnect.com), an online newsletter on Mexico and Mexican tourism, and "Wikipedia" (www.wikipedia.org), the sprawling online encyclopedia whose accuracy has been endlessly debated in academic forums like the *Chronicle of Higher Education*. While the LC has taken a leadership role in organizing digital information, here, in the space of Google search, it is merely one site in the marketplace of Web content, however successful. If we follow up on LC Management's recent characterizations of LC users as college undergraduates too enmeshed in their digital lives to leave their dorm rooms, than we can suggest that the LC will only succeed here in the marketplace of infobytes insofar as it enables undergraduates to grind out another five-page paper for a survey history class.

But the point here is not to mourn the abrogation of the LC's traditional role, but to suggest that the "Cataloging Library" and the "Digital Library" are fundamentally different visions of not only the institution, but fundamentally different operationalizations of "information" altogether. The chicanery here is to see one ineluctably succeeding the other, as if the MARC record, having served its purpose, should gracefully concede to the world of full-text retrieval and natural language, keyword searching. And yet this is precisely the argument that Library management makes.

In the 1990's, the manifold and perhaps irreconcilable differences between the structure and practice of libraries versus that of Internet applications like the World Wide Web have led the LC back to its developed cataloging systems, in spite of the many salvos it aimed at the "cataloging directorate" in the 1980s and 90s.

> But to know it exists it has to be represented in the traditional on-line catalog [ . . .] But I'm saying outside tools like the card catalog, other indexes, OCLC, because then people will know. At least they'll know that there's an entry, like, for THOMAS. You know [a person at an ALA Meeting said] "Please catalog THOMAS so I can put a card in my . . .", you know, she's a public librarian and, say, well at least put a card in the catalog so at least people will know about it and then they'll know they'll have to go out onto the Internet. But you know you still have to have—the idea is to have sort of a unified tool also, to bring these materials together because otherwise you could segregate. (Interview, Collections Services, Cataloging)

It's interesting to note that some people at the LC perceived a possible conflict between placing collections online and *democratizing access* to collections. Like the chaotic fecundation of autonomous, automated systems at the Library in the 1960s and 1970s, the online collection threatened to bifurcate the LC into *two libraries*, the "National Digital Library" and the non-digital collections housed in the space of the LC itself. Likewise, the dreams of *internetworked* systems of information bringing together research libraries, public libraries and national libraries across the nation and, ultimately, the world, seemed particularly hollow

While the justification for the digital library often rests on the promise of inter-connected systems of information that transcend single institutions and governments, the LC instead balanced the hyperlinked quality of the Web against the preservation (and even self-aggrandizement) of the LC vis-à-vis other institutions. At the beginning of the American Memory initiative, exhibits were resolutely parochial (e.g., "The African-American Mosaic"), confining themselves to materials housed at the LC itself. More recent efforts have begun (rather grudgingly) to direct site visitors to related materials off-site (e.g., "A Century of Creativity: The MacDowell Colony, 1907-2007"). But what has remained is a tension between networked resources and institutional identity in way strikingly similar to the tension between proprietary and public information in the era of digital information.

```
020 &955#a#vb22 to sj00 12-05-96; sj09 12-09-96; jhll 1-15-97%
030 &05000#auu#PN1968.U5#<1996 01525>#<MRC>%
040 &08210#a2#793.8#12%
050 &24500#ahbc#American variety stage#{computer file} :#vaudeville and
popular entertainment, 1870-1920 /#American Memory, Library of Con-
gress.%
060 &24630#a#Vaudeville and popular entertainment, 1870-1920%
070 &256#a#Computer data.%
080 &260#abc#{Washington, D.C. :#Library of Congress},#1996-%
090 &538#a#System requirements: World Wide Web (WWW) browser soft-
ware.%
100 &538#a#Mode of access: Internet.%
110 &500#a#Title from title screen dated Oct. 31, 1996.%
120 &500#a#"Groups of theater posters and sound recordings will be added to
this anthology in the future."%
130 &520-#a#Multimedia collection containing digitized versions of selected
Library of Congress holdings. Represents diverse forms of popular entertain-
ment, especially vaudeville, that thrived from 1870-1920. Includes 334 English
and Yiddish language playscripts, 146 playbills and programs, sixty-one motion
pictures, and 143 photographs and twenty-nine memorabilia items document-
ing the life and career of Harry Houdini.%
140 &5051-#a#Houdini — Theater playbills and programs —Sound record-
ings (coming soon) — Motion pictures — English playscripts — Yiddish
playscripts%
150 &650-0#azxyx#Vaudeville#United States#History#20th
century#Databases.%
160 &650-0#azxyx#Vaudeville#United States#History#19th
century#Databases.%
165 &650-0#azxx##Vaudeville#United States#Film catalogs#Databases.%
170 &650-0#ayx#American drama#20th century#Databases.%
180 &650-0#ayx#American drama#19th century#Databases.%
185 &650-0#azx#Yiddish drama#20th century#Databases.%
186 &650-0#azx#Yiddish drama#19th century#Databases.%
190 &650-0#azx#Theater programs#United States#Databases.%
195 &650-0#azx#Playbills#United States#Databases.%
200 &60010#adx#Houdini, Harry,#1874-1926#Databases.%
230 &8567#u2#http://lcweb2.loc.gov/ammem/vshtml/vshome.
html#http%
240 &952#a#Cataloged using WebExplorer browser software.%
250 &040#acd#DLC#DLC#DLC%
260 &043#a#n-us---%
```

In the 1990's, the development of mutually exclusive information systems within Library of Congress collections, on the one hand, and the "invisibility" of online collections to people using other online catalogs presented the LC with nagging dilemmas. How could it both accede to a position of leadership in the world of virtual libraries while still retaining proprietary control over its collections? Part of the solution has involved linking the MARC record into the online record.[69] Catalogers began to give online collections a full cataloging record with subject terms that refer both to non-databased materials as well as to other online materials. The above MARC record from the 1990s displays several noteworthy features: 1). It is a *collection level* record rather than a record of every motion picture, photograph, recording and playbill in the Vaudeville collection; 2). It refers back to the World Wide Web through the 538 field (technical details note), the 710 field (added corporate author) and the 856 field (added index term); 3). its subject added entries (650 fields) use the free-floating subdivision "Databases" both to describe "container type" *and* to refer users browsing subjects through a conventional, online catalog to other, contiguous subjects like "Yiddish drama—19th century" or "Theater programs—United States." Cataloging these materials has been an evolving process for the Library. For example, when they started MARC cataloging for "National Digital Library" collections, they produced records *without* URLs for the finding aids, perhaps a necessary evil of producing a permanent cataloging record for an ephemeral location, but nevertheless baffling users attempting to access World Wide Web collections from the catalog.

Second, the Library adopted the Z39.50 interface, a protocol—i.e., a set of agreed-upon syntactical commands—mediating the exchange of information between dissimilar systems using different command structures, providing a more-or-less seamless "client/server" interface. Using the Z39.50 protocol, a user examining files on the LC Web site could do a search of materials *not* on the World Wide Web at all using a simple, universal syntax for her inquiry. And yet, movement in the opposite direction has been difficult to achieve. A typical Google search does *not*, for example, yield a cataloging record (although it does yield article citations that utilize name authorities and Library of Congress-derived subject cataloging and free-floating subdivisions).

## THE AMBIGUITY OF INFORMATION AND ACCESS

The Library's experiences with "automation" and "digitization" from the 1960s to the present suggests not the gradual evolution of the printed word to the virtual word, but a succession of different and mutually contradictory constructions of "information." Thomas Mann, stalwart defender of the full cataloging record, describes this fundamental antinomy as one of *precoordination* versus *postcoordination.*

---

69  Although, to be fair, OCLC was the first vendor to produce cataloging records for Internet-worked files.

With a computer you take two or more separate subject sets (e.g., "Women" and "Mass media") and cross them against each other to determine if any record includes both headings; this is known as postcoordination. A precoordinated heading, by contrast, is one that in effect has already done such a combination for you; it expresses in one predetermined phrase the overlap of two or more subjects, so that you do not have to combine them yourself through postcoordinating computer manipulations. (Mann 1993:117)

In fact, this logic extends beyond topical subject headings to name authority, title and scope notes. In the MARC record, these have been carefully "precoordinated" and are accessible in a predictable, structured way. By contrast, the World Wide Web search indices and search engines are forever chasing files *after the fact*. Names, titles, and "natural language" keywords *already exist* in the document; search programs *chase* the elusive keywords, without "knowing" in advance—through authority work, descriptive and subject cataloging—whether or not they exist.

While the bulk of Web searchers seem mostly satisfied with these different postcoordinated searches, staff at the LC have not been altogether comfortable with the "rough and ready" fuzzy logic of Internet searching. Much of this has to do with the sometimes oblique, oftentimes direct threat the "digital library" has posed to the *physical* Library, exemplified in the Booz-Allen and Hamilton report on the LC for the Government Accounting Office recommending the cessation of the LC's traditional functions (see above), and more recently by the Calhoun Report commissioned by Library management (Calhoun 2006). But I submit that these differences also signal fundamental tensions in the way we think about "information," tensions that *saturate* information society at all levels.

More than just bad rhetoric, Head Librarian Billington's propensities towards paratactic metaphor may help us unearth those confusions. Billington told LC staff that "We are not in the highway construction business or the trucking business [ . . .] We are in the content business" (Fineberg 1995b:9). With his predilection for mixed metaphor, it is, perhaps, difficult to fathom his intended meanings, but I believe he was drawing a distinction between Internet service providers, multimedia publishers (e.g. Time/Warner) and government agencies providing what some might consider a "public good" (the LC). Hence, he describes the National Digital Library as the digitization of "plain vanilla" collections, that is, collections provided without the sorts of "value-added" superstructure evidenced by for-profit sites maintained by 'Net entrepreneurs. But as the preceding discussions of the LC Web sites and online collections show, the "National Digital Library" is anything but the "plain vanilla" presentation of historical material. Rather, the entire American Memory project from its inception in 1990 to its continued development today shows 1). a careful selection and organization of materials designed to both highlight the institution of the Library of Congress and appeal to the Library's "clients," especially Congress; 2). the maintenance of a collection's "integrity" and the organization of different "file types" residing in different directories and on different servers through the adoption of the Finding Aid Document Type Definition (DTD) and 3). the gradual distancing of access away from postcoordinated, "keyword" searching and towards precoordinated main entry and subject entry cataloging.

These amendments to the Library's Web site suggest the impossibility of separating "content" from "container" and "container" from "access." The notion that information exists as a *thing*, a rationalized and commodified object set apart from the systems that enfold (envelope) it and the practices that invigilate and fenestrate it, is one of the key assumptions of the "information age." Much ideological work, in fact, is accomplished by the elusive condensation and displacement of differing conceptions of information, resulting in, for example, the conflation of the *existence* of information with its communication and apprehension. For example, in January of 1995 the LC put up a legislative information site called THOMAS (http://www.thomas.gov) combining summaries of bills with the *Congressional Record* and documents explaining the lawmaking process. At a "ribbon-cutting" ceremony for the new site, Rep. Newt Gingrich opined that "Electronic technology gives government an unprecedented opportunity to empower the People with knowledge and information. The Electronic Village of 1995 may become, in the new Millennium, the Wired Electorate." Notice the rhetorical slippage here where the presentation of *information* gives way ineluctably to the "empowerment" of the "Electorate." This optimistic interpretation of information society is only possible by the subrogation of information as an institutional practice of knowledge organization, classification and communication by information as an *object*, a concatenation of text without the "dross" of people and bureaucracies.

A very similar process follows the development of the "National Digital Library" in the 1990s. Billington's tenure as Head Librarian of Congress begins in the midst of nearly crippling budget-cuts mandated by the Gramm-Rudman-Hollings Act of 1986. He, or his office, soon realized that the only way to secure increased budgets was to couch all requests for appropriation in the language of corporate downsizing (or 'rightsizing'). In the 1990s, he frequently described the Library's activities in automation, arrearage reduction and the "library without walls" as a way of "doing more with less," by which he meant—or so I believe—providing more *information services* with fewer employees making less money with fewer chances of promotion. This is in marked contrast to earlier Librarians who showed a more Taylorist approach to bureaucratic management. Archibald MacLeish, for example, acceded to post of Head Librarian under quite similar Congressional charges of mismanagement and bureaucratic waste. But, consonant with the times, his reorganization of the Library involved hiring *additional* people, rather than "downsizing" and "outsourcing" (MacLeish 1945). A convert to the models of scientific management espoused by Taylor, Ford and Veblen, MacLeish thought the palliative to the Library's ills was the engineer-manager. His reorganization created, in essence, a "middle management" for the Library (Banta 1993; Jordan 1994). By contrast, Billington's reorganizations of the Library have started from the opposite assumption, again in synchrony with the times a la Peter Drucker and his more syncopated approach to corporate hierarchy (Drucker 1993). In other words, when Billington says "do more with less," he's not so much registering a petulant complaint as prescribing a new social order: fewer employees will be able to do more!

This has had a profound effect on the constitution of the information arte-fact at the LC, separating the information "product" (cataloging record or Web page) from the context of its production and the systems that structure access to it. The "fantasia" of the electronic library is of a world of texts without con-texts, "plain vanilla" collections requiring neither processing nor maintenance nor administration (Foucault 1977). In fact, the intimation is that additional employees, processing or editing will act as a *barrier* to access, a "middle-man" impeding the utopia of instantaneous, full-text retrieval. The real dream of a "virtual library" is a library *without* a library: books, films, recordings and pho-tographs presented in their logocentric fullness without the "noise" of catalog-ing, classification and organization.

CHAPTER 6

# Corporeal Work at the Virtual Library: Research and Scholarship for a New Age

In this chapter, I struggle with the "society" element of "information society," i.e. the revolution in social organization and social relations purported to accompany technological and spatial shifts. Consonant with other utopian/dystopian projections common to theories of "information society," ideas of work and research in the information age fall into two, broad camps. The first sees information, information society and information technologies as a tremendous force for good, catalyzing a return to "town-hall" democracy and an eventually empowering "trickle-down" of information and technologies to historically disadvantaged peoples (Friedland 1996). With more information at our disposal, the reasoning goes, we will be able to "re-skill" constantly, resulting in a richer, more satisfying life distant from the drone-like manufacturing lines of the Fordist enterprise (Hiam 1992; Toffler 1990). The other camp, critical of the overwhelmingly capitalist quality of the "information explosion," sees a more dire future in the coming "information age." As more and more heretofore public institutions in government and education are denuded of funding, "information" will concentrate in the hands of multinationals. "Public information, like public schools, health care and libraries will become either less available or will be converted into circulable commodities, resulting in an increasingly disenfranchised plebeian class effectively "de-skilled" out of their jobs (Noble 1986; Schiller 1991).

My own beliefs are closer to the latter than the former. Clearly, present cutbacks in public and university library acquisitions and cataloging contravene the plucky optimism of many of the computopian theorists. That said, however, information society's critics—however correct—tell us little about that process of reification, commodification and hierarchy that transforms heretofore free "public goods" in schools, museums and libraries into commodities to be bought and sold. It is not, in any case, an even process. Whatever their politics or position, most people at the Library of Congress are staunch supporters of free (e.g. reader services) or subsidized (e.g. the Cataloging Distribution Service) library services. However: some believe that the best way to preserve the Library's public mission is to partner with corporations, while others see any capitulation to the mediatized, telematic information economy as the beginning of the end.

The interesting question here, though, is not so much *who* would "sell out" the incipient public sphere functions of the LC to Microsoft or Google as *how* different people at the LC use "information" and "information society" to articulate different, contrary visions of the themselves and the Library. How does "information society" come to express the problematic relationship of researchers to an institution they feel no longer concerns itself with the work of scholarship? How do the politics of the "information age" become a coin in an increasing acrimony of labor and management played out along racial lines? To me, this "information society" is a sack in which people place contrasting visions of the present and the future. In this chapter, I follow its perambulations in the 1990s, asking not so much whether or not the technologies that surround us are inherently *good* or *evil*, but, rather, how those fantastic machines become part of the *social* field of the LC.[70]

The impact of new containers, new systems and new organizations upon research, learning and knowing is an area of keen interest to library and information professionals. Indeed, since the moral mission of the information professional is to facilitate knowledge, these questions could be said to be at the heart of the library profession, from its inception in the subscription libraries of the eighteenth and nineteenth centuries to the full-fledged paternalism of the public library movement (Bial and Bial 1991; Rosenberg 1993:8).[71] Part of this moral mission involves collecting knowledge about the people librarians serve and evaluating the "fit" between library materials and library patrons. From the late nineteenth century to the present, librarians and library staff have produced a menagerie of "user studies" probing both the demographics of library users as well as the efficacy of library systems in satisfying library patrons.

For much of the twentieth century, those studies have involved some kind of a quantitative measure, whether that involved a simple accounting of user requests, books circulated or patrons present, or more complex survey instruments designed to measure the "information needs" of target populations in the library. Premised on what some have called a cybernetic model of library use—the algorithmic circulation of library materials and library users through an architecture of library systems, catalogs and reference materials—many of the studies confined themselves to the success of a reference interview or to the

---

70   I might point out that, while the LC has yet to become a subsidiary of Disney or Microsoft, there is a sharp (and critical) sense of the LC being overtaken by commercial interests.

71   One thinks, for example, of Ranganathan's five laws, four of which spell out a relationship between librarians, libraries and library users: 1). Books are for use; 2). Every reader his [sic] book; 3). Every book its reader; 4). Save the time of the reader; 5). The library is a growing organism (Ranganathan 1992)..

number of "hits" gleaned from a catalog or database.

> The model of information-seeking behavior that underlay most work at the time may be described as the information retrieval model [. . .] In this model, a user recognized an information need and came to the retrieval system with a request based on that need. (Ellis 1993:472)

Even studies that attempt to contextualize "information needs and uses" in instances from everyday life still privilege the system, consigning human interactions to so many stumbling blocks in the completion of a cybernetic circuit, as in, for example, much of the literature on information "gatekeeping" which identifies nodal points in organizational hierarchies that impede the free flow of information. Although such analysis may be grounded in the experiences of actual organizations and even actual events, human interaction still seems like an adjunct to pre-existing circuits of information storage and retrieval, a circuit-breaker to pristine info-scapes (Cf. Dosa *et al* 1988). If anything, the prominence of World Wide Web search engines has concentrated attention on the architectures of searching at the expense of the "practice" of information, the user reduced to her Boolean query (Cf. Meats *et al* 2007).

Beginning in the late-1960s, this "objectivist approach" with its oftentimes jejune assumptions of what and how people know had come under critique from proponents of qualitative user studies situating "information needs and uses" in wider contexts than the quantitative reductions of library retrieval (Case 2002). These studies sought to contextualize the "subjective" experiences of "information seeking behavior" in a holistic understanding of social practices that extended well beyond the bounds of a library or a database (Dervin and Nilan 1986). There are a variety of reasons for this self-described "paradigm shift." During the late 1960s and early 1970s, *information science* emerged as a more rigorous and professional approach to the traditional problems of library science. With roots in sociology, philosophy and linguistics and its own, individuated nomenclature, the discipline of information science—particularly in Scandinavian countries—ventured far from more conventional library science into areas of cognitive science, philosophical pragmatics and artificial intelligence (Olaisen, Munch-Petersen and Wilson 1995). Secondly, this broadening of scope beyond strict "storage and retrieval" questions germane to library science mirrors changes in the library profession itself, as more graduates find themselves employed in areas far removed from academic, public or special libraries and adopt the more inclusive monikers of "information manager" or "knowledge navigator" (Caulfield 1997; White 1996). Finally, the shift to qualitative and, indeed, occasionally ethnographic methodologies, can be socially and historically situated in the shifting demographics of urban areas, where the most well-developed public-library systems are and which are characterized by growing populations of people whose needs may vary from the bourgeois, middle-class model that usually informed more "objectivist" studies.

> In the 1970s, public libraries sought to determine and to eradicate the barriers preventing culturally diverse groups from gaining fuller access to information. One approach was the development of services designed to meet local information needs. Some researchers argued that traditional reference services did not meet the information needs of nonusers, and that new delivery systems were required. (Metoyer-Duran 1993:125)

Although the LC executes a variety of user studies in its different departments, it is almost exclusively invested in the earlier, quantitative approach. There are a variety of reasons for this, of course, including the rather obvious insight that the LC is not a *public* library and does not really need to be responsive to the changing demographics of urban America in the same way public libraries have. Rather, it assumes (though perhaps it should not) a baseline of scholars and politicians with needs that may shift according to puissant, current events, but whose overall "information seeking behavior" remains essentially the same. Library surveys ask participants to evaluate the overall experience of "collections and services" during their visit as a check to quality control and an outlet for user criticisms rather than an actual catalyst for change. Other instruments ask participants to check off research specialties and narrate their current projects. The Reader Registration System, the first Library-wide database integrating users and circulation, also asks users basic survey questions ranging from subject specialties to reading rooms consulted (Fineberg 1996b). Overall, the instruments seem crude compared to other survey instruments available; their purpose, however, seems more to provide Congress with evidence that the Library's reading rooms are being consulted than as a means of focusing efforts in the Library's user services. This is consistent with the tendency of LC management to adduce various, numeric measures in Annual Reports as proof of the LC's continuing relevance (e.g., numbers of "hits," readers, items processed, acquisitions, arrearage reductions, etc.). None focus on the (implicitly social) relationships between users and "information-seeking behavior" that lie at the heart of Dervin's and Nilan's user studies.

When I began my fieldwork in 1994, I had these user studies very much in mind for a number of reasons. To begin with, there were actually anthropologists undertaking "user studies," albeit on a level rather removed from my holistic/descriptive training. Secondly, Library staff seemed to accept me as a social scientist engaged in some form of "user study." Perhaps because of the relative paucity of qualitative studies at the Library, several told me they hoped I would "get to the bottom of things," meaning, presumably, patterns of library use. Even though I always explained that, although I was speaking with users about their research, my study was wide-ranging, many Library staffers still assumed that my work would help them to design better "front-end" applications for Library databases, while users generally considered me an advocate for greater access to library materials.[72] It was, of course, a source of discomfort that I was neither of these things.

For the most part, I confined my study to users and staff associated with the Library. However, for the first three months of my fieldwork, I tried to cultivate a community of online researchers as a way of doing an ethnography of the still-nascent "digital library." Posting inquiries to several different newsgroups—e.g., soc.libraries.talk, sci.research, sci.anthropology, sci.misc and comp.internet—I asked researchers to comment on their experiences with online indices, databases and search engines. The following exchange is fairly representative of the thirty-six researchers who chose to respond to my inquiries.

Q: Think of your most annoying search session… What made it particularly difficult? A: Trying too broad a search using veronica can be annoying. A lot of places I'm trying to get info from are busy or down. Searching databases in the Telnet window sucks because my software saves the entire Telnet session as one chunk, whereas I can save individual records in gopher. Accidentally ftping the wrong item used to suck, because the old version of my software didn't have a break command! Having the network down is annoying because then I'm stuck at home, fidgeting.

While I was (and am) tremendously grateful for the responses I got, it soon became clear to me that these exchanges were proving to be of limited usefulness for my evolving (though still imperfectly articulated) research program. Much of the fault lay with my questions; respondents probably thought I was working for a software engineering firm! Much of the problem also had to do with the conceptual murkiness of "information" itself, an idea whose Byzantine complexity I traced in Chapter 4 and 5 above. This hyperbolic valency surely extended to such chimeras as "information-seeking behavior," which seems, in retrospect, an ill-defined and somewhat misleading *apercu* onto highly contextualized instances of actual, social life. In asking respondents to comment on the databases and Internet applications they used, I was (unwittingly) playing into a casuistry of technological determinism where faster and more reliable Internet access meant more information. Even proponents of such studies recognize the dangers of confining "information seeking" to a narrow operationalized modality.

Most of these studies attempt to relate specific variables to particular information-seeking tasks or behaviors. While they further our understanding of elements of the information-seeking process, they leave us without an overall sense of what constitutes information seeking or a feeling that we know and understand an individual's

---

72 This (mis)construal of the anthropologist in the field is, by now, part of the apocrypha of the ethnographic experience. However, such experiences, while uncomfortable, seem to me very telling instances indicative of hierarchies of power and knowledge within an institution. Rather like transference during psychoanalysis, the ascription of roles to anthropologists working within institutions is a good indicator of organizational structure..

behavior. (Reneker 1993: 488)

After all, if we believe evolutionary information theorists like Susantha Goona-tilake, "information-seeking behavior" is implicit in even the most instinctive reflexes of *conatus*: the recognition of which aspects of the environment to incorporate into self (food) and which ones to keep out (danger) (Kolenda 1987:4). If life could be characterized as a continuous interaction with varied information environments, how useful is it, e.g. in Reneker's study, to give 31 respondents tape recorders and ask them to record instances of information-seeking behavior over a two-week period at Stanford University? Does such a study tell us something about the dynamics of information society or merely confirm the logomachy of information as a vague association of spurious eti-ologies and objectified social relations?

As a last-ditch effort to stimulate more philosophical interlocutors among the online community, I "seeded" an issue of *Wired* magazine with a letter to the editor complaining about the rampant technological determinism of an article in their June 1995 issue in an example of what newsgroup aficionados used to call "trolling."

> Technology is one part of the complex relationships that people form with each other and the world around them; it simply cannot be understood outside of that context. With this understanding, the simpleton's bipolar argument crumbles and the world is revealed— taa daa!—as a pretty complicated place. (*Wired* 3.09: 36)

Despite several supportive replies from *Wired* readers, I was unable to interview the "digital community" about the place of the information in the context of their lives, and eventually dropped that dimension of my study altogether. Although there have since been numerous ethnographies of self-described In-ternet communities since then, none to my knowledge have followed an "in-formation-seeking" thread.[73] As a telling postscript, part of that letter ("Tech-nology is one part of the complex relationships that people form with each other and the world around them; it simply cannot be understood outside of that context") was picked up by a variety of web sites collating variously inspirational quotations (e.g., www.saidwhat.co.uk), all attributed to "Samuel Collins," but, most likely, to the famous nuclear scientist "Samuel Collins" rather than to me. Ironically, "context" has been changed in these quotations to "concept."

The notion that "information society" primarily involves changes in so-cial relationships, while hardly an original insight, nevertheless shifts focus

---

73  This in itself is interesting. If we consider the genesis of the "network of networks" in AR-PANET and NSFNET, its explicit purpose was sharing information (originally military informa-tion). Anthropologists have tended, on the other hand, to treat online environments as if their sole purpose was to challenge hierarchies of self and subjectivity, i.e. to privilege the community over the community's work.

away from "information behavior" as a nodal contact of a "user" with her "data."[74] Studying the information age as a shift in *representation* already anticipates the reification of *social* knowledge into reified information. Information society signals the recombinatory transformation of social relationships—what Paul Virilio terms "mediatizing"—bringing us closer to certain loci of objects and people while distancing us from others (Virilio 1996). Studying *that* shift takes us beyond the ideologically delimited field of "information seeking behavior" into the nature of work itself.

As critics of the technological sublime have pointed out, information society cannot be reduced to the imposition of computers or automation on the factory floor or even the relative shift from Fordism to a "post-Fordist" service economy (Harvey 1989; Segal 1994). Instead, what differentiates this present stage of capitalism from earlier epochs is its unprecedented ability to transform the world into *information*, the commodified, labile knowledge-value that has, in some cases, superseded money as a medium of exchange. It is information that holds together corporate hegemony in the age of disorganized capitalism and it is the logic of *informatics* that has replaced nineteenth-century paternalism as the primary legitimation for capitalism's creative destruction. But, as I suggested in Chapter 1, information is no one thing; like a supremely viral meme, information combines with worlds of things, peoples, knowledges and cultures. Tracing information's deictic shifts—now denoting communicative changes in a corporation, now referencing political empowerment—is the true measure of information society. The "information object" is simply the event horizon of late capitalism, the point at which social relations, relations of production, imperialism, racism and gender inequality disappear into the gravimetric well of hyper-consumerism.

In fact, "information seeking behavior" already presupposes those relationships, already anticipates their shift. When we come to recognize shifts in government, business and academia as stemming primarily from a revolution in *information*, we are already locked into the inexorable logic of *informatics*; the complexities of our everyday life have already been trammeled under penetrating, telematic networks (Kroker and Weinstein 1994). From this standpoint, computropian critiques of the Internet and the coming information society are better understood less as serious polemics than as maudlin confirmations of cybernetic, totalizing frameworks.

Understanding information society as an organization and practice of people means, if nothing else, refusing to describe social life as primarily a *relation to information systems*, since that already anticipates digitized interpretations.[75] Rather than concentrate on this world of reified objectifications, I began to concentrate on the way people at the Library positioned themselves in terms

---

74  David Hess neatly traces such ideas in his 1995 summation of the field of science and technology studies (Hess 1995).

75  It is worthwhile asking if confining my ethnography to the Library of Congress doesn't also anticipate a certain reading of information society.

of policy, technology and organizational changes that were transforming the Library during my fieldwork tenure (1994-1997). How did they talk about the past? How did they imagine the future? How did they evaluate their position at the Library? How did they hope (or fear) it would change? By concentrating less on the mystagogical apprehension of technological marvels and more on the information society as an imagined scape fraught with conflicting ideological positions, I hoped to learn more about "information society" in its heterogeneity, i.e. information society as a cultural practice rather than as the smug afterglow of a technological revolution.[76] In the end, it tells us nothing of culture to examine technology *qua* technology; culture, as I suggested in Chapter 2, derives its force from linking disparate areas of social life and meaning into that Geertzian "web" (Hall 1994:523). Moreover, tracing the ideological force of information society means—by definition—employing varied scansion. Since it is always imbricated by power and politics, ideology cannot be located in the *object*. To elucidate the Library's information society is to trace contending appropriations and expropriations across a spectrum of discourses and positions.

What I've tried to do is understand information society as an institutional (and hence social and cultural) phenomena, and only in the last instance concerned with an "information explosion." Rather, I understand "information" in this chapter as a metaphoric touchstone telescoping real and imagined relationships in work and scholarship, both present and future. Not only are both utopian and dystopian dimensions part of these processes restructuring work and knowledge, but both the "age of information" and its antinomy inform varying positions people take in relation to their changing world. After all, "information society" and the "information age" do not necessarily mean that the world is awash with a surfeit of information. Rather, in a world of informatics, people define themselves vis-à-vis their propinquity to hypothesized bodies of information, i.e. a whole spectrum of relationships that can include scarcity as well as surplus.

What helps me to understand these (apparent) paralogisms is the *social drama*, a method of explicating social life from the standpoint of stagial crisis. Developed by Victor Turner is his studies of Ndembu social life, "social dramas" allow for what he called a "limited area of transparency on the otherwise opaque surfaces of regular, uneventful social life" (Turner 1957:93). The dramatic re-structurings of village life in either the historical space of *Schism and Continuity in an African Society* or the ritual space of *The Forest of Symbols* highlight key contradictions and inequalities in social organization and culture that would have otherwise gone unnoticed, consigned to the vast torpor of the

---

76 This is more difficult then it sounds. Even the Library's subject tracing are against me: "Information technology—Social aspects"; "Internet (Computer network)—Social aspects"; "Information technology—Political aspects." In each case, the free-floating subdivision is subordinated to the technological artifact. Really, the opposite is true; technology is the afterthought of contending social heterologies.

"imponderabilia of everyday life." It is for this reason, certainly, that Turner engages in the study of ritual in the first place; he is not so much interested in the character of social, political or religious institutions for their own sake as the ways in which these form the shifting contexts through which social relations are re-worked (Turner 1974). Of course, a bureaucracy is all about constancy and predictable productions of meaning and society; its function is maintenance, whether we mean by that maintenance of the nation (Herzfeld 1992) or the maintenance of racial or ethnic categories (Handler 1988).

> This results from the characteristic principle of bureaucracy: the abstract regularity of the execution of authority, which is a result of the demand for 'equality before the law' in the personal and functional sense—hence, of the horror of 'privilege' and the principled rejection of doing business from 'case to case.' (Weber 1946:224)

From the perspective of bureaucracy's functionalized operations, it may seem particularly specious to concentrate on the occasional eruptions of the exceptional and the sensational over the quotidian. Nevertheless, even the most earthshaking events must somehow be operationalized into the machinery of the bureaucratic apparatus. Literally, the bureaucracy must 'make sense' out of any phenomena it encounters or cease to function as a bureaucracy. The process of that rationalization—along with its characteristic condensations, displacements and lacunae—says much about the character of the organization, just as the argument over who will act as "Head Circumciser" in the ritual Turner describes tells us much about the inherent instability of Ndembu matrilineage.

## "INFORMATION WANTS TO BE FREE"[77]

> We will not comprehend why and how information becomes economically valuable by beginning with its own supposedly intrinsically attributes; we cannot uncover its real social framework in this fashion. What if, however, quite the contrary, we suppose that information is *not* inherently valuable? What if, that is, only a profound social reorganization can permit information to become valuable? (Schiller 1988:32)

> Government control over the amount and substance of information available about matters of widespread interest has been employed to deprive people of necessities, including disability benefits and health care, and to evade constitutional freedoms. (Demac 1988:143)

---

77 An old hacker maxim, invoked by libertarians, leftists and liberals alike (but for very different reasons). The inevitable question, "free from what?," seems not to have occurred to proponents of information transparency.

Looking back over the changes he'd help initiate during his first seven years as Head Librarian, James Billington utilized the now-familiar trope of steering a large, somewhat atavistic, organization away from a moribund past into a promising future.

> When I first became Librarian, I realized that preparing the Library for the 21st century depended on coming to grips with a number of basic problems that had not been dealt with adequately in the 20th century. It was evident that, for a variety of reasons, the Library had fallen seriously behind in several key areas: human resource management, financial systems, and clearing up the vast backlog of uncataloged materials in the Library's collections and insuring that those collections were under bibliographic control. These were basic practical matters that had to be addressed—and resolved over the long term—even as we explored new technology and new ways to bring the Library's resources and services into the 21st century. (Billington 12/1/95: 10)

Billington's millenarian narrative on the LC's future owes much to science fictions of American progress that propose technological palliatives that will "do more with less," providing better and more democratic services to greater numbers of people while cutting labor costs and overhead. What's interesting about Billington's statement, however, is the way it combines a vision of technological "fixes" with other, more subfuscous changes to human resources and basic accounting.

However, Billington's revisionist interpretations of the LC in 1987 still stress its *processual* problems, its organizational bottlenecks that contribute to arrearage growth and budget uncertainty. His Library of Congress is a *structure* rather than a community of people. What struck me upon interning at the Library in 1992, on the other hand, were the deep disagreements that seemed to fragment staff and users into competing, frequently acrimonious camps. It was not particularly difficult to prompt discussion of the Library's social problems; many people I interviewed volunteered unsolicited commentary.

For example, there was much talk of the deep racial conflicts that seemed to divide the staff into black and white.[78] These were made all the more poignant by the Library's parochial hiring practices. The majority of LC employees—particularly technical and paraprofessional employees—are recruited locally and regionally and the manifest racism that I saw at the Library seemed to mirror similar exchanges in D.C. as a whole.

Anticipating the "white man's rage" backlash that would cripple affirmative action programs in the mid-90s, many white employees in professional or administrative positions along with many white users suggested that the Library's

---

78  It would be a mistake, however, as I shall argue below, to reduce the Library's problems to racial problems alone. Instead, it is the invidious combination of racial and class divisions that earned the LC its reputation (in 1995-96) of having the worst labor relations of any Federal agency.

black employees were lazy and that still-extant affirmative action programs rewarded torpor rather than merit. Frequent, and generally apocryphal, anecdotes concerned black employees sleeping in lavatories and in stacks or telling their fellow, white employees not to work too hard. As one user off-handedly commented towards the end of our interview session:

> You wouldn't believe the number of convicts that were here [working] 20-25 years ago. Men with dew-rags on their heads and big, muscular arms. (interview, Scholar, Main Reading Room)

I was struck by the frequency and barely concealed belligerence of these comments, although most were presented to me as "unofficial" asides after I'd put down my pen and pad. Why should conversations about work, research and technology at the Library elicit such acid comments on race? These performances of race, I suggest, signal the sharp division of race and class that exists at the Library, a division that's become particularly prominent with the "re-invention" of government. Upper-level managers, senior staff, administrators and users are mostly white while the technical and paraprofessional staffers that form the bulk of the Library's workforce are mostly black. During my approximately 130 interviews with users and staff from all over the Library, I only heard one disparaging anecdote (union activists aside) about a senior-level staffer (apparently an alcoholic). No one I talked with suggested that these (mostly white) people were anything less than absolutely committed to their jobs, while technical and paraprofessional staffer were frequently castigated for their lackadaisical work ethic and their propensity to file grievances when their jobs became challenging.[79] Complaints about Library productivity, different (organizational) divisions or even not-on-shelf rates often devolve into the familiar language of race and racism. Perhaps the people I spoke with were trying to tell me something about race in the United States: that, despite frequent media productions of race and racism and the periodic activity of a few "bad apples" whose hate can be neatly exorcised in the space of a half-hour situation comedy, race and racism are institutionalized in every instantiation of social life and that those heterogeneous (racial) technologies are not alien intrusions into the otherwise benign organization of the Library, but are part and parcel of its fabric, its *habitus*. The emphasis on essentially *Parsonian* studies of organizational hierarchies, gatekeeping and power elides the centrality of race by replacing actual employees with autochthonous systems. I, on the contrary, believe that the eruption of racial and labor conflict at the Library is key to understanding an "information society" that is ordinarily understood as an essentially cybernetic—i.e. systemic and organizational—revolution.

It is interesting and, I think, quite telling, that anthropologists readily admit the orientalism implicit in classic ethnographies and Victorian anthropometry,

---

79   I should point out that I never observed anything less than exemplary work from staffers at all levels of the LC's organization.

but are less likely to spotlight the oftentimes implicit institutional racism that supports regimes of power/knowledge in their own work. Indeed, it is only comparatively recently that anthropologists have begun to un-pack the racial and ethnic inequalities that have, in many ways, fuelled the growth of today's information society (English-Lueck 2002; Freeman 2000; Xiang 2007).

Key to understanding the ways in which race and class conflict combine with organizational and technological changes in the information society is making links between areas of social life normally held apart by institutional fractionation. The following, then, is an attempt to trace the instances of social conflict that accompanied the sweeping technological and spatial shifts in the Library from the 1980s to the late 1990s, changes that—quite literally—brought the LC to the brink. Whatever the LC's future, much groundwork has already been laid in the policy and organizational decisions of the last decades. These decisions, mostly initiated by Head Librarian James Billington over the last twenty years, have little (ostensibly) to do with the paradigmatic revolution of technologies. It is my argument, however, that these incidents must be seen as inextricably linked to the technological changes that coexist with them.[80] I will examine three such incidents that transpired during the first years of James Billington's tenure as Head Librarian: the *Cook v. Billington* class action suit brought against the LC by its black employees, the closing of the LC's stacks to staff and users after the disclosure of widespread vandalism in 1993 and the continuing acrimony between management and labor, particularly between senior levels of management and the Library's three unions: AFSCME 2477 (the Union), AFSCME 2910 (the Guild) and CREA (the Congressional Research Employees Association).

## TROUBLES AND TREASURES AT THE LIBRARY OF CONGRESS

When Ronald Reagan appointed James Billington to the office of Head Librarian in 1987, the LC was divided by a number of serious problems that had developed during Head Librarian Boorstin's benign, if somewhat quiescent, stewardship.[81] Those problems were played out in a succession of dramas over

---

80  This is not to say that these emergent inequalities are in any way inevitably by-products of the "informational mode of development," as Castells calls it (Castells 1989). That they seem characteristic of much information age change is, in my opinion, less an effect of technological determinism than an indication of the pervasive effects of (historical) gender, class and racial inequalities in the United States.

81  Much of the information for this section is taken from the Library's two in-house newsletters, The Gazette and the Library of Congress Information Bulletin. I've found The Gazette particularly suggestive, since it was started in 1990 as a palliative for strained management-labor relations and (at least ostensibly) was meant to provide employees with a forum to raise their concerns. Over the years, the "town meeting" function of The Gazette has dwindled and, at present, it is thought of by most staffers as little more than a management mouthpiece. Nevertheless, angry exchanges do occasionally appear there, as in AFSCME 2477's and Lloyd Paul's letters in late June, 1995 (The Gazette, 6/23/95). More often, though, labor-management "consultation"

the relationship of labor to management and the relationship of scholars and staff to library materials.

The Library's labor force can be loosely divided into labor and management, although some people occupying technically managerial positions do not, in fact, supervise staff. The LC's *labor* can be further subdivided into *technical* and *professional*, terms that do not describe so much job descriptions as employee pay levels (GS levels).[82] For example, the distinction between technical (or paraprofessional) lies between GS-6 and GS-7, although here the Library has a tendency to exploit the ambiguity. As one "technical" employee explained,

> When I first came to the Library they had cross-over positions: when you could start in a technical position and move up to a professional position. Over in manuscripts they had people in to catalog manuscripts but they were stuck in G-6. Management chose to keep a gap between G-6 and G-7 (interview, Cataloging Directorate).

Cataloging, of course, can be a particularly recondite task, and is normally undertaken by the Library's *professional* staff. However: with the advent of "downsizing" and cost-cutting measures like copy cataloging (the utilization of cataloging originating at some institution other than the LC), management has been able to effectively "de-skill" some cataloging positions to technical positions.[83]

While the division of the LC's employees into "technical," "professional" and "managerial" positions may seem more or less arbitrary, their racial distribution follows a remarkably consistent pattern. When the Joint Committee on the Library reviewed the LC's "Multi-Year Affirmative Action Plan" and "Change in Employment Profiles from 1988 to 1992," they were struck by the overwhelming skewing of black employees into technical positions.

> Despite this fact, minorities comprise more than 43 percent of the Library's work force and they are disproportionately employed in low-wage, semi- skilled and unskilled [sic] and are grossly under-represented in occupations that require relatively more skills, education and experience. (U.S. Congress 1994b:19)[84]

And:

---

seems more contretemps than controversial, as in the month-long exchange of letters and accusations over the pricing of cafeteria salads in July of 1992 (Cf. The Gazette 7/24/92 and 7/31/92).

82 This is why employees sometimes describe their jobs as "paraprofessional" rather than technical, which implies a world of mechanistic labor rather than some of the abstruse and intellectual tasks that so-called "technical" staff undertake.

83 Although the union argues that these jobs have not been "de-skilled" at all. Rather, the same work is being expected of employees for less pay and little chance of promotion up the GS ladder.

84 Notice the interesting lexical shifts from named races and ethnicities to the imminently faceless "minorities," the overwhelming number (36.9 percent of the total workforce) of whom are black (Fineberg 7/26/91:10).

By contrast, the overall distribution of white employees is skewed toward the higher grade with more than 80% of all white employees at the Library of Congress in the two highest pay levels. (U.S. Congress 1994b:5)

A pattern of discrimination and rigidly maintained glass ceilings has been the rule at the LC almost from its inception, when, in the days following reconstruction, African American salaries generally fell in the $360-$600 range. When Daniel Boorstin was appointed Head Librarian by Gerald Ford in 1975, he inherited decades of invidious labor practices that systematically discriminated against black employees, a condition he did little to ameliorate in spite of his mild bureaucratic reorganization in 1978 ("Change at the Library of Congress":223; U.S. Congress 1979). Previous protests against Library employment, promotions and even cataloging policy in 1968 following Martin Luther King, Jr.'s assassination and again in a 1971 sit-down protest in the Main Reading Room had yielded few noticeable changes in LC policy and regulations, although scholars in other institutions published subsequent critiques of LC cataloging (Branan 6/21/96:10; Berman 1971).

Although employees filed a fusillade of grievances, promotions and hiring remained essentially unchanged until two related sets of grievances to the Library's Equal Employment Opportunity Compliance Office—one filed by David Andrews and Howard Cook in 1975 and the other by Tommy Shaw in 1980—were brought to the U.S. District Court as a combined, class-action lawsuit in 1982 (Fineberg 10/9/92:10-11). The suit was composed of two parts charging: 1). that the Library had discriminated against all black employees in competitive hiring and promotions; and 2). that the Library had discriminated against black employees in noncompetitive hiring and promotions using a "Section 4a" exception to the federal laws governing other parts of governments other than the legislative branch.

Library of Congress Regulation 2010-14, Section 4, provides that all employment positions are to be announced for competition with certain exceptions. One exception, Section 4a, gave the Librarian discretion to fill some positions without competitive postings. (Fineberg 10/16/92:1)

These "exceptions" fueled decades of more-or-less blatant crony-ism and, reputedly, continues today through the use of "custom-made" job descriptions applicable to only one candidate. That is, favored candidates will be "primed" for promotion through a series of special projects designed to increase that person's "quality points" and, in effect, delimit the eligible candidates to exactly one (interview, Collections Services, Acquisitions and Support Services Directorate).[85] Although the Library stalled the judicial process for over ten years, it finally admitted liability in 1987 to the Section 4(a) portion of the suit, but was still filing motions on the other parts. It was not until 1992 that

---

85  Quality Points" are a way of "objectively" assessing an application for federal employment.

the U.S. District Court issued an opinion on the competitive discrimination portion of the suit.

> Based on the disparate impact of statistical analysis of data from 1979-1988, the court found that each stage of the Library's process was too subjective and adversely affects black applicants [sic] than could be expected to happen by chance. (U.S. Congress 1994b: 32)

The Library was ordered by Judge Norma Holloway Johnson to pay an eight million dollar settlement to the plaintiffs in the class action and to eliminate the "subjective" elements in its hiring and promotions practices that were purported to have contributed to the discrimination.

> On 2 August 1994, U.S. District Court Judge Norma Holloway approved a preliminary settlement agreement to resolve a longstanding class action lawsuit concerning the Library's former personnel practices with regard to African American employees, *Howard R.L. Cook et al. v. James H. Billington*. The settlement would award past and present African American employees of the Library $8.5 million in back pay and forty promotions, with present employees only also eligible for ten reassignments. (Library of Congress 1995:75)

However, the *Cook* case decision came down in the midst of workforce reductions that impacted technical staff disproportionately, resulting in numerous RIF'd (reduction-in-force) positions and in the loss of important technical/professional cross-over jobs. In particular, the passage of the Balanced Budget and Emergency Deficit Control Act (aka the Gramm-Rudman-Hollings Act) in December of 1985 resulted in cuts in both essential library personnel and services that were to essentially freeze hiring up until my fieldwork in the mid-1990s. By the end of the 1980s, the Library had lost almost 500 staff positions (largely through attrition).

> During the decade, as the Library absorbed mandatory pay raises and sequestrations, the staff shrank more than 11 percent, from a total of 4,916 positions in 1980 to 4,348 at the end of fiscal 1990. (Library of Congress 1991:3)[86]

Hitting technical and paraprofessional positions particularly hard, the budget cuts exacerbated an already acrimonious relationship between library management and labor, prompting Congressional calls for sweeping reforms that anticipated the drive to "reinvent government" a few years later in the 104th Congress.

As a result of the 1986 budget cuts, hiring slowed to a virtual standstill, a freeze compounded by the Library's sluggish reform of its human resources

---

86  At the time, of course, Library management had embarked on a program of aggressive contracting; hence the number of staff positions actually cut may be much more difficult to calculate. In addition, since employment figures are given in FTEs (Full-Time Equivalent), the number of actual people at the LC may have increased over the intervening period.

policies in the wake of the *Cook* decision. Unions charged that appropriations for new positions were mismanaged or underutilized.

> For example, we reported to Congress that $3 million dollars specifically appropriated for the hiring of 163 new catalogers had apparently been used for other purposes. By the library's own admission, only 57 new catalogers were hired from the outside. (Stern and Moore 6/9/95:A26)[87]

The resulting workforce in the 1990s was highly stratified between an aging stratum of senior-level managers and section heads, on the one hand, and a pool of entry level employees occupying either lower G levels or temporary, contractual positions outside of the federal ladder of hiring and promotions altogether. As one Congressional Research Service staffer complained,

> Something like two-thirds of us will be eligible for retirement in 5 to 6 years. Not everyone will. You can see we're a pretty old operation—it could be a major gap. (interview, Congressional Research Service)

This coincides with a general trend in employment during the 1980s that saw the rise of what Manuel Castells calls the "dual city": the simultaneous growth of a technocratic elite and a moribund, largely de-skilled pool of entry-level workers (Castells 1989:227). And, at the LC, these post-Fordist strategies show little sign of abating. Ten years after the initial *Cook* settlement, black employees filed another class action suit, accusing the Library of, among other things, utilizing contract labor to get around Equal Employment Opportunity (EEO) regulations (Oder 2004).

All three conditions—the lack of closure on the *Cook* suit, the hiring and promotions freeze and the rapidly aging workforce—resulted in a notoriously low morale that reached a certain apogee with the "early outs" of autumn 1993, when older staffers lined up outside the Madison Building for the opportunity to take advantage of an early retirement buy-out from the Library's human resources department ("Library Offers 'Early Out' to Staff": 1). The sight of so many older LC employees herded through the early-out process struck many as extremely impersonal and indicative of the wide gulf separating the Library's management from its rank-and-file employees. As one of AFSCME's officers told me,

> I've seen buy-outs at other institutions, but nothing like the midnight buy-outs over at LC. (interview, AFSCME)

By the time I began my field research in 1994, staff morale had reached all-time low and the LC's labor-management relations were acknowledged by manage-

---

87 The utilization of appropriated money, along with other labor issues like the ratio of managers to employees, was the subject of a particularly vitriolic exchange of op-ed letters between representatives of AFSCME 2477 and Lloyd Pauls, then the Associate Librarian for Human Resources. As may be already obvious to the reader, I have taken the union position.

ment and labor alike to be the worst of any federal agency in Washington.

The Head Librarian's reaction to these ongoing conflicts is instructive. After his appointment in 1987, Billington's first actions were to 1); institute training seminars designed to "change the culture" of the LC and 2); reorganize Library management according to "teams." In this, the Librarian followed the time-honored practice of aping the language (though not necessarily the organization) of corporate America, a trend that ballooned in the 1980s and 90s with the hyperbolic growth of corporate revenues and the perceived failure of "big government."

Beginning in the 1980s, labor-management disputes, glass ceilings, pay disparities and other forms of inequality on the job were reconceptualized by corporations as "cultural differences." In this, business was following on the tails of a public policy world that preferred to think of all manner of urban dilemmas as the products of the "dysfunctional" culture of the "underclass" (Williams 1992). "Corporate culture" became a way of co-opting many of the 1970s and 1980s triumphs of an identity politics centered on race, ethnicity, gender and sexual orientation into a reinvigoration of ideologies of meritocracy.

> Although it is relatively easy to state that corporate ideals of "progress" differ substantially from socialist or feminist or antiracist ones, it is precisely the liberalism of diversity management that has serious consequences and which invites our consideration. As I will suggest below, corporate culture as diversity management is a monitory and influential example of liberal racism, a form of racism which, as many of us know, is far more subtle and difficult to expose, and yet typically characterizes life in complex institutions, like universities. (Gordon 1995:4)

At the LC, labor disputes and deep-seated racial conflicts arising from decades of institutional inequality were dramatically reinterpreted as communicative failures to be addressed with a "climate of trust and honesty by integrating, at all levels, the values in the mission statement into staff orientation, training, and performance appraisal" (Library of Congress 1988b:488).

While *affirmative action*, in its best sense, means actively challenging the status quo of organizations, there's little sense that the valuation of something called "diversity" in corporate culture results in any commensurate critique. Rather, much of "diversity management" involves the frank *preservation* of hierarchy. As one employee suggested,

> I think affirmative action and diversity are two poles. The concept of diversity is asking us to be complacent. (interview, Public Service and Collection Management I Directorate)

One of the outcomes of these recommendations was *The Gazette*, the LC's newsletter for its employees. The other outcome was a period of obligatory "vision training" initiated by Rhoda Canter, then the Associate Librarian for Special Projects. Emily Martin describes the goals of these seminars:

In addition to gender barriers, the events are also meant to break down hierarchical barriers between management and labor. Groups that go through the exercises together are usually composed of both management and labor, and a boss might well be depending on his secretary or an assembly line worker to belay him with a rope when he jumps off a tower or vice versa. (Martin 1994:213)

Although I never attended these sessions (nor would I have been permitted to), staff members I spoke with reported various, oftentimes comedic, strategies of resistance to the "feelgood" messages of cooperation, understanding and shared values. Some would refuse to speak at all, while others interrupted meetings with boorish comments and annoying questions. While adopting the stereotype of the misanthrope-librarian allowed staffers to resist this patronizing, corporate programming, it also revealed a considerable level of cynicism and pessimism over the Library's future. Although my "sample" was hardly representative, none of the employees I spoke with thought that these exercises were worthwhile or, indeed, even planned with the interests of employees in mind.

We've lost ground after the Rhoda Canter debacle. There was at least a fake attempt to listen and to speak for informally. At the time I think it was a ruse. (interview, Collections Services, Cataloging Directorate)

However hollow the "consultative management" program may have been, it allowed management to continue to make highly hierarchical organizational and policy decisions. The LC's rank-and-file were probably not comforted with such "team" approaches to management such as Head Librarian Billington's promise (threat?) in 1992:

I will be visiting parts of the Library over the next few weeks in an effort to talk to more of you. I will also be drawing a few names at random from a total list of our staff for a series of informal, off-the-record meetings in my office during this important period of strategy formation. (Library of Congress 10/14/92)

This "enforcer approach" to consultative management seems less designed to elicit creative input from heretofore disempowered sections of the LC's staff than to legitimate existing authority.

The "team" approach to management was in part derived from a series of popular, private sector theories emphasizing flexible styles of management over what were considered outmoded, hierarchical approaches. Books like *The Vest Pocket CEO* and Peter Drucker's corporate manifestos all stress the importance of flexible forms of decision making and production over what they see as more vertical, "stove-pipe" arrangements of workers and managers (Haim 1990). In practice, however, few of the popular, managerial "styles" from the late 1970s to the present have been anything more than passing fads to be discarded with the next wave of popular literature.

Some people, including many managers, blame corporate problems on management deficiencies. If companies were only managed differently and better, they would thrive. But none of the management fads of the last twenty years—not management by objectives, diversification, theory Z, zero-based budgeting, value chain analysis, decentralization, quality circles, "excellence," restructuring, portfolio management, management by walking around, matrix management, intrapenering, or one-minute managing—has reversed the deterioration of America's corporate competitive performance. (Hammer and Campy 1993:25)

Whatever the effects of the reorganization on management's performance, it had the effect of creating a strained, almost contrapuntal, dissonance between highly specialized, more traditional civil service positions, on the one hand, and an almost impossibly fluid cadre of senior-level managers whose careers demonstrated a high degree of mobility from "team" to "team" and from division to division, on the other.[88]

Some of the organization is so entrenched that it takes a revolution to change; other parts seem so fluid that you can't hold onto it for a second. The part of the Library that is of interest to the Librarian are [sic] highly fluid [ . . .] It's the first environment I've ever worked in where people [at the top] aren't hired for specific jobs. You can be put on detail anywhere. At the Library of Congress if you're a certain grade level, you can go anyplace. The function takes precedence over the people. (interview, former manager in Collections Services)

The effect of this "team" approach, among other things, was to effectively buffer the Librarian from the bulk of the organization's service units with a hand-picked squad of "multiskilled" managers. As the Joint Committee on the Library admonished in 1994, this approach to senior-level appointments mystified—rather than illuminated—LC operations.

Moreover, since 1989, the institution has operated under the "management team" approach, which is analogous to a "senior staff" type operation. This approach, while providing managers a ready forum for information exchange, tends to mitigate responsibility for individual managers' actions. Management by "consensus," unchecked autonomy, and a lack of accountability for decisions made actions taken are among the negative characteristics of "team management." (U.S. Congress 1994b:7)

For their part, Library divisions were reorganized in 1991 into "service units": Collections Services, Congressional Services, Copyright, Cultural Affairs, Library Management Services and Special Projects, but were subsequently changed to Collections Services, Constituent Services, Congressional Research Services, Copyright Office, Cultural Affairs Human Resources Services and the Law Library (Library of Congress 1991a:7; Fineberg 10/23/92). Of course, or-

---

88  e.g., the various (re)appointments of Daniel Mullhollan, Rhoda Canter, Lloyd Pauls and Hiram Davis, just to name a few.

ganizational charts are highly ideological objects, artifacts expressing both the outward, public identity of the organization as well as its ideal relationship to itself; it is an essentially *communicative* technology (Hall 1993:181). So, while some employees felt their jobs really had changed with the reorganizations of the 1990s, others considered it little more than a name change undertaken to impress Congress. One of the areas that both management and staff felt had changed significantly was "Collection Services," particularly the areas of the formerly separated descriptive and subject cataloging, which were reorganized according to broad (and sometimes discontinuous) subject area "teams" composed of both descriptive and subject catalogers engaged in "whole book" cataloging, i.e., doing descriptive and subject cataloging at the same time.

Whatever the effects of reorganizations and name changes, the Joint Committee on the Library was not impressed with this approach to management.

> For example, five major management reorganizations have been undertaken at the Library in the last five years; more has yet been completed [sic]. Each new reorganization has resulted in the Library's [sic] implementing a new and different body of personnel and rule changes, and consequently created, deliberately or not, an atmosphere of confusion and frustration, inadequate transmittal and exchange of information, and a lack of coordination among library departments. (U.S. Congress 1994b:13)

Were the many organizational changes initiated by Head Librarian Billington and his management team purposely obscurantist? Certainly, vague hierarchies and diffuse authority oftentimes served to limit the efficacy of employee grievances. One AFSCME negotiator I talked with wondered if the organization's fluidity wasn't part of the LC's overall strategy.

> Sometimes you wonder if it's just management disorganization or if they're trying to screw with unions: 'Oh, we're so disorganized, we haven't gotten to that grievance.' (interview, AFSCME)

Whatever the case, employees charge that the Library has worked to limit the effectiveness of horizontal communications. But this obscurantism has not stopped LC management from demanding concrete information from its employees, as in management's recent calls for AFSCME representatives to provide an exact accounting of their time spent in guild duties (Oder 2007). Nor have allegations stopped LC management from subsequent reorganizations, with cataloging, in particular, bouncing about the organizational chart, testament, perhaps, to the way the Head Librarian has construed that division as a problem (Library of Congress 2005:xi).

## UNIONS, BARGAINING AND THE RISE AND FALL OF CONSULTATIVE MANAGEMENT AT THE LC

The Library of Congress has two unions—AFSCME (American Federation of State, County and Municipal Employees) Local 2477 and AFSCME Local 2910—and one professional association, CREA (the Congressional Research Employees Association). AFSCME Local 2477 represents the Library's technical and paraprofessional staff, while AFSCME Local 2910 represents the professional staff. Both paraprofessional staff and professional staff were represented at one time by AFGE (American Federation of Government Employees) locals, but were summarily kicked out when Library members spoke out against the Vietnam War. AFSCME officials (at the Council level) seem to have a great deal of respect for the two Library locals, which they see as continuing an activist tradition up to the present.

> What I find unusual about the LC—usually, when you have long-term locals like 2477, you have a period where the unions stop fighting over everything. What the difference at the LC is the union's still stuck in the earlier stage. (interview, AFSCME)

Of course, many members of the locals believe that AFSCME continues their fight because, in part, management continues their effort to undermine union strength.

However, during the 1980s, unions suffered a series of debilitating setbacks through: 1). unprecedented downsizing in the parts of the labor force most often represented by unions (e.g., the manufacturing sector); and 2). an increasingly mobile capital that could elide union power based on the shop floor by moving part of production to "right to work" states or to other countries (Davis 1986). Indeed, labor conditions in general seemed (and seem) in many ways as abominable as they were in the late-nineteenth century (Sexton 1991).

In addition, Reagan's firing of air traffic controllers was in some ways a death-knell for even the modest labor activism of the 1980s.

> With conservative federal judges, with probusiness appointments to the National Labor Relations Board, judicial decisions and board findings weakened a labor movement already troubled by a decline in manufacturing. Workers who went out on strike found themselves with no legal protection. One of the first acts of the Reagan administration was to dismiss from their jobs, en masse, striking air traffic controllers. It was a warning to future strikers, and a sign of the weakness of a labor movement which in the thirties and forties had been a powerful force. (Zinn 1995:562)

In the midst of such reactionary conservatism, unions embraced a variety of strategies to recoup their losses, including the then-current corporate values of "flexibility" and "cooperation" over what were considered "outmoded" styles of adversarial bargaining, despite the fact that these selfsame refrains of "flexibility" were being used to legitimate unprecedented levels of downsizing and deskilling. Bluestone's and Bluestone's *Negotiating the Future* iterates a fairly widespread sentiment (among corporate management, politicians and policy-makers) that unions had heretofore engaged in "needless" bickering but should now cooperate with management in order to usher in an era of prosperity and munificence.

> In unionized industries, management's otherwise unfettered right to rule the workforce continues to be circumscribed by union contract, and the workplace itself is run more democratically. Yet even here, in most instances the present demarcations between the rights and responsibilities of employers and employees is drawn sharply in hundreds of pages of fine print and enforced rigorously within a structured adversarial environment. If not exactly class warfare, the present framework of labor-management relations in shops, offices, and factories throughout the nation remains largely antithetical to what America needs most: much higher productivity, much better quality, more innovation, and far more employment security and job satisfaction. (Bluestone and Bluestone 1992:13)

It would be difficult to exaggerate the wide currency such "cooperative" metaphors held in the 1980s and 1990s, metaphors grounded in the fluidity (and anomie) of information society.

By the close of the twentieth century, these ideas had reached the status of "common sense," i.e. a level of uncontestable hegemony over the managerial psyche. Even more militant unions adopted the language and techniques of the managerial class, incorporating information technologies and "flexible" styles of communication into their day-to-day operations (Piore 1993).

The LC's AFSCME locals, beaten down by a succession of debilitating budget cuts and hostile administrations in the 1980s, were no exception.[89] They, too, capitulated to a more "cooperative" relationship in their 1991 collective bargaining agreement.

> The Parties agree that cooperative efforts embody the principles of open dialogue, responsiveness, timely action and the sharing of information. Cooperative efforts require shared responsibilities, mutual respect and courtesy between individuals, and problem solving which focuses on issues rather than personalities. We agree that cooperative efforts shall encompass all aspects of the union-management relationship (i.e., collective bargaining, grievance handling, dispute resolution, problem solving, committee work). (AFSCME Local 2477 and Library of Congress 1991:2)

The bargaining agreement was framed as a transcendence of the adversarial relationships of the past and a new beginning for the Library's unions as partners to the administration in "consultative management." However, it wasn't long before the Locals began to regret what they later described as "giving in." When

---

89 This was probably not helped by the conciliatory tone AFSCME Councils were sounding in the late 1980s and early 1990s. In our interviews, for example, I found much of the same language of "partnering" and "cooperation" that the UAW was using during the same period.

I interviewed AFSCME locals in 1995, their collective bargaining contract was again up for renewal and members were anxious not to repeat what they saw as the mistakes of 1991.

> We may have to open up everything [on contract renewal] because we were told on our last contract we had. A lot of it was fuzzy. It was struck on trust and consultative management. We agreed to that it would not be precise because we were going to be so trusting. When they came back to us with a reply to a grievance [after a contract was signed] they replied with very formal language. (interview, AFSCME 2910)

The "team approach" to Library management was supposed to emphasize open communication and the free exchange of information. However, just the opposite seems to have happened; unions reported an organizational murkiness that worked to weaken the ability of employees to bargain with management. In particular, aspects that Library employees felt particularly insecure about—promotions and contracting out to temporary staff—grew steadily more opaque, even as the Information Technology Services Division grew more central to the Library's day-to-day operations.

> We've got contractors all over the place. You hear, through word of mouth, 'Who are the people in the basement?' You go over to human resources, they don't know who's contracted. You have to go over to Landover to Contracts and Logistics; they're not even automated. We file unfair labor practices, we file grievances: it's very hard to get a handle on contracts. (interview, AFSCME 2910)

Many employees were terribly anxious about their positions and their future careers at the LC; rank-and-file employees I talked with wondered if they'd be RIF'd out of a job in the next fiscal year or assigned to another department. One "paraprofessional" cataloger had applied to the Leadership Development Intern Program, one of two or three "career enhancement" programs available for technical staff hoping to advance to a managerial track, but found her application lost in a fustian cloud of diffuse authority.

> I went through up to the reference part of the application. I don't know what happened. Initially, I was reluctant to apply to the program but you can enter the program and end up out of the Library altogether in a different department. [Now] I want to know what my ratings are. I only asked after I met with the woman who interviewed me who said she'd lost control [of the hiring process]. Communication sucks around here. (interview, Collections Services, Cataloging Directorate)

I cannot over-emphasize the extent of job-paranoia at the Library, at least during the height of my fieldwork in '94-'95. People's fears about their jobs were only made worse by the almost complete mystification of managerial decision-making.

That uncertainty was made even more difficult by the almost decade-long absence of a chief of labor relations at the LC, a position finally filled in 1995 (Library of Congress 1996:95). Few people had any clear idea of the LC's priorities in the coming future and this worried them. As a result, much of the material I recorded over this time was unsubstantiated rumor about the looming liquidation of this or that division.

> The most important means of communication is verbal. The rumor mill is still alive and well—It's not controllable and it's not an overt means of communication. (interview, AFSCME 2477)

This last part seems especially important. The LC's two newsletters—*The Gazette* and the *Information Bulletin*—as well as memoranda, e-mails and servers, are management-controlled; the "rumor mill," however inaccurate, is not. It is telling that many people I spoke with expressed unease with e-mailing me later with follow-up comments. They feared that management would exercise what were, after all, its proprietary rights and monitor outgoing communications.[90]

All of the creeping uncertainty, blatant misinformation and deliberate ignorance made some employees wonder if they were working in "information society" at all.

> The information highway is going out but there's no sense of it coming from people on the inside. This is coming from the sixth floor.[91] (interview, AFSCME 2477)

But this coexistence of new technologies with near "information blackouts" is, I believe, symptomatic of an information age *flexibility* that centralizes both knowledge and control. At the LC, this has been most evident in "SWAT teams," highly fluid organizations of catalogers and technicians who were organized to process arrearages and were disbanded after some short period of time, limiting the control employees felt they had over both their work, the conditions under which they worked and their ability to organize collectively against supervisors, chiefs and managers.

> More and more we have things like SWAT teams which form for a while and go out of existence. A great deal happens on the level of temporary teams in divisions. (interview, AFSCME 2910)

Those shifting organizations worked on a principle of centralized, managerial control and a "flexible" labor force that could be moved to any division in the Library. That is, it depended on the maintenance of an information asym-

---

90  This is a very real concern. There's ample evidence that institutions in both public and private sectors regularly monitor e-mail, tap phones and surreptitiously videotape employees.

91  The "sixth floor" refers to the sixth floor of the Madison Buildings where the Head Librarian's office is.

metry: flexible workers went where they were told without the bargaining or negotiations that would come with "information equality." As Martin writes of Total Quality Management (TQM) training exercises:

> The experience models physically the nature of the new workers that corporations desire: individuals—men and women—able to risk the unknown and tolerate fear, willing to explore unknown territories, but simultaneously able to accept their dependence on the help and support of their coworkers. In a word, *flexibility*. (Martin 1994:214)

But, importantly, only labor needed to face the unknown; for management, "flexibility" lay in the perfect control of information—perfect knowledge. It was, therefore, entirely consistent that information society at the Library of Congress involved the imposition of what can only be described as *willful ignorance*.

> They had some positions—GS-7s—They decided they would      put it at GS-4 and call it a professional position [ . . .] I wanted to talk about the technology part of it now. All they really want us to be is key-punchers. We've seen bits and pieces of our jobs taken out in order to justify their continued existence. They've taken our positions, our responsibilities. (interview, Constituent Services, Public Service and Collection Management II Directorate)

And:

> Information is accessed for information and there's always a danger. Even when I was in my work unit we had several systems. I used to access all of them and get the information. One day she [supervisor] came and said OCLC may make us confused. She forbid us to use all the systems that we had there. (interview, Collections Services, Acquisitions and Support Services Directorate)

Can the super-flexible, telematic world of the digerati only exist at the expense of the worker? Does an "information age" always signal an authoritarian control over knowledge? While I would resist the notion that "information society" unavoidably brings with it an intensified hierarchy, I nevertheless believe that, to understand changes at the LC or at other institutions, we must look to the contraction and sublation of information in addition to its supposed explosion.

## SECURING THE COLLECTIONS

The theft and evisceration of library materials has long been a sore spot for libraries, public, academic and private. Although the Library of Congress had pursued a policy of locking up valuable, pre-1800 imprints since Putnam's tenure, the bulk of its 19th century collections—including folios and valuable prints and sketches—were still in the general stacks, stacks to which some researchers could gain access. Also, the Library's survey of its collections for vandalism and theft had been sporadic at best. It is probably not exaggerating to suggest that there had *never* been a complete, systematic inventory of all of the Library's holdings since its accession of Jefferson's book collection in 1815, and then only because Jefferson had provided the complete catalog.

There had been a count of materials "by estimate" only in 1898 and a "new count of printed books and manuscripts" in 1902. Thereafter there had been a single inventory of the classified collections which began in 1928 (June) and ended in 1934 (May), showing 170,692 volumes missing from their places. (MacLeish 1945:111)

While that inventory may sound complete, remember that there were some 400,000 volumes in arrearage at the time!

As at the New York Public Library, the Library of Congress never had an open-stack policy; however, under some circumstances that were, apparently, at least somewhat open to the discretion of individual staffers, users could gain limited, short-term access. Most long-term readers considered it easier to get a stack-pass during Daniel Boorstin's tenure as Head Librarian, which may be a reflection of Billington's policies, the staff-cuts from the Gramm-Rudman Hollings act, or both.

Up until he was named Librarian of Congress I felt as if the policy of the Library was to keep people from getting their hands on the material. It wasn't as if the staff weren't wonderful because they were; they were absolutely fabulous! But—as a policy—I felt like the place was trying to keep people away from it. (interview, Scholar, Main Reading Room)

And:

There was a time in Prints and Photographs when we used to go back into the stacks to get our own photographs. It was marvelous because what you could do is browse. The Paris edition of the New York Times is a very rich collection. They have finding aids for the archives but the Library has become more and more restrictive. (interview, Scholar, Prints and Photographs)

Likewise, there was little reason for deck attendants to check stacks passes. As one former deck attendant told me:

I think you could probably get back there even if you didn't have a pass before, you know, because frankly nobody checked and nobody really cared. (interview, Constituent Services, Public Service and Collection Management II Directorate)

However, this benign complacency ended in the early 1990s.

Between May of 1991 and June of 1992, Library of Congress police apprehended seven people for the theft of library materials (U.S. Congress 1994a:42-43). Although reported instances dated back to 1986, the most well-publicized arrest was in Spring of 1992 and involved Fitzhugh Opie, an Alexandria, Virginia book dealer who had been a Library patron for over a decade but who had been finally caught in a "sting operation" carried out by Library police and certain Manuscripts Reading Room librarians (Streitfeld 1992).[92]

In response to the theft and to a previous internal report, the Head Librarian closed the general collections to users on March 30 of 1992 and to most employees on May 4, 1992. It was, by Billington's own admission, an emergency security measure.

It is probably difficult for people outside of the Library to understand researcher and staffer outrage at the closings; really, it goes beyond mere bibliomania to, I believe, the nature of research itself. In fact, one encounters an interesting lacunae in writing about the relationship of a researcher to her material. To be sure, there's much written on *archival method* and on *historiography*, but nothing on the *habitus* of historical or archival research, why something catches someone's eye while something else does not. Indeed, as I have suggested above, library user studies, with their reduction of agency to information-seeking behavior, seem to have little grasp of what might differentiate the work of a scholar from, say, that of a high-school student preparing a paper for class (Mann 2006). I am not of the opinion that this inchoate relationship needs to be explicated. It seems to me very personal, a relation that goes well beyond the "hermeneutic circle." I submit that much of it has to do with the "democratic interpellation" of being at the center of the Library's collections, in the middle of the Main Reading Room and at the center of the world's largest library. For researchers and for much of the staff involved in processing or cataloging, the *material* of the Library collection has a great deal of meaning and the stacks are a great source of personal pride for Library users and staffers alike. It would be safe to say that the stack closings caused many people to question both the institution of the Library as well as their own relationship to it.[93]

Nevertheless, the tacit and eminently personal relationship researchers had with collections at the LC made public debate problematic. The debate in Congress, such as it was, and the debate in library and information science publications, hinged on the efficacy of "serendipitous discovery" versus what Thomas Mann would call more predictable information systems. There were points on both sides. Clearly, the Library Classification is designed to support (and repay) a certain amount of browsing; otherwise, materials could be just assigned accession numbers (as they are presently at many high-density storage facilities). But it is also true that browsing the shelf is not a particularly good way to access materials. Take any anthropology book, for example. The LC

---

92 Although staff members I talked with suggested that Opie was apprehended less through the alacrity of criminal investigators than through his own brazen stupidity. For example, even though he was a regular patron in the Manuscripts Reading Room and almost all of the staff knew his name, he used aliases when filling out call slips for materials.

93 The reason this discussion appears here in Chapter 6, in fact, is because staffers I interviewed considered stack closings every bit as serious a grievance as RIF's, stagnant wages and lack of job training.

Classification for Sharon Traweek's *Beamtimes and Lifetimes* is QC774.A2T73 while Hugh Gusterson's *Nuclear Rites* is U264.C2G87. Not only are these two ethnographies of science not shelved together, but neither are associated with the portion of the classification set aside for anthropology and ethnology in the "G" schedule! That said, my own experience, part of which stems from having browsed the stacks myself (with a staffer), is that, for much of the research that might actually bring a scholar, Congressional researcher or whomever to the Library of Congress ("the Library of last resort"), browsing is probably the most effective way to find things. In other words, given that a trip the LC is not supposed to be one's initial effort at "information seeking," it follows that the LC's best resources are precisely those that differentiate it from those of, say, a local, public library. While a *monograph*—i.e., a secondary source—is readily accessible through the Library's systems, other sources are more difficult to find. Pamphlets, periodic (i.e., non-serial) reports, catalogs (particularly old catalogs), may be *cataloged* in the system with full Classification schedules, but, because they are typically quite thin and do not have a spine "face-out," they're frequently passed over by deck attendants.

Characteristically, the Librarian recommended a technological fix for the problem, ordering the development of a cataloging application in order to "simulate" the serendipity of stack browsing. But the contention that the resulting product—ACCESS—would replace direct browsing seemed, to many, spurious at best.

> After I ordered the book stacks closed in 1992, the Library began training visiting researchers to use our new and user-friendly computerized catalog to access our collections and to compile bibliographies without direct access to the stacks. (Billington 12/1/95:11)

The ACCESS application was a front-end program that allowed researchers to use the same syntax for a number of different catalog files that would ordinarily take a complex lexicon of commands and file delimiters. What it was not, of course, was a new *catalog*; there was no advantage (from a numerical standpoint) in using ACCESS over the Library's main catalog (which ACCESS merely searched through the LOCIS "bow-tie" program). It is unlikely, therefore, that researchers who found the old catalogs inadequate for their research would have been satisfied with ACCESS.

Reader and staff reaction to the stack closings was, predictably, extremely critical.

> The staffers barred from the stacks are more than merely "irked." We resent being sacrificed to a dog and pony show. (Burnwasser 5/15/92:2)

And:

> I, for one, am not just "irked," but am angry and insulted that the one fringe benefit of working at this institution is to be summarily canceled. I am not a

thief. I have a Johns Hopkins doctorate in a  specific area of study, but have spent many pleasurable lunch periods browsing among L.C. holdings in a field new to me, taking advantage of the stupendous amount of knowledge which sits there shelved and waiting to be absorbed. While one could make a case for any increased knowledge being of value to a LC employee, this is not, to use the now-endemic bureaucratic language, a "job-related function." (Simon 5/29/92:2)

In the months surrounding a hearing before the Joint Committee, employees and users worked to clarify their relationships to the Library's collections and to make their case that stack access was no mere "fringe benefit" of their work at the LC, but an endemic part of their professional lives. In particular, much of this was because the Librarian had suggested, on several occasions, that limited access might be reinstated for some of the people who had been denied access during the security clamp-down (Fineberg 5/15/92). In addition, several articles from labor historian Grace Palladino in the *Chronicle of Higher Education* and the *Washington Post* and a "Resolution on the Library of Congress" adopted by the American Historical Association in December of 1992 publicized the stack closings and motivated researchers to think about their relation to Library materials so that, when I posed questions in the course of interviews two years later, it was evident they'd given the matter some thought (Palladino 1993). Who was the Library for? What responsibility did it owe them? The depth and variety of people's answers to these questions is worth mentioning. I have listed several here, both from interviews and from published sources and Congressional hearings.

> The serendipitous discovery when browsing the stacks not only benefits the researcher or employee personally but it often has great value for the Library. Because of the vastness of the Library's collection, the Library really doesn't know what is the current value of every item in its collection. Two employees who  are no longer allowed access to the collections have, in the past, discovered priceless treasures which were in the general collections. (U.S. Congress 1994a: 15)

And:

> Why do scholars need access to the stacks? This is a question which really has not been addressed. It is not serendipity. It is because no matter how well cataloged the Library's holdings are, there is no way of knowing all the materials that exist relevant to particular research interests. Many of them are old; many of them are unindexed, and some are not effectively cataloged, as I myself have found in doing research at the Library. (Eric Foner, in U.S. Congress 1994a:36)

And:

> I would like to focus on the access to and within the stacks, because this is the morale buster at the Library. It took the intervention of a Federal mediator to get the Library to acknowledge that access was necessary for employees who are

fulfilling training requirements, requirements necessary to achieve the next highest grade level in the promotion plan and also for those participating in Library sponsored career development program [sic]. (Dennis Roth, in U.S. Congress 1994a:18)

And:

It's affected the graduate-level work that you've seen. The young ones, they have no idea what they're missing. Any in-depth research is stymied. You really have to know the material. I can spot these things, where they've gotten the material. Either it's stuff not in the catalog or there's no cross-reference. The upshot of the whole thing is the quality. I label these people (probably unjustly) the know-nothings. Let's be realistic. So the History books written in the future probably won't be as detailed. (Interview, Scholar, Main Reading Room)

And:

The closing of the stacks—it has changed research.   not only that they closed the stacks; they've also stopped the card catalog. (Interview, Scholar, Main Reading Room)

And:

Well, it turns out that the very best way to survey fiction actually turns out to be going back to the stacks and walking the stacks. I mean that's the way you do it. And so, to see what the books look like. I mean, mysteries, if there's a cover on them, have a  distinct style and if you see what the books look like you can find the books. (Interview, Scholar, Main Reading Room)[94]

The relationships people form to the materials they use are highly individuated. Blanket terms like "information seeking behavior," it seems to me, work to obscure these differences under narrow ideas of access. Of course, much of these experiences lie outside the purview of reference staff. Library and information science professionals are typically consulted during either the initial stages of research or by people whose research needs are more *denotative*—i.e., fact finding versus thematic or idea-oriented. For example, reference librarians typically conceive of "information seeking" as a rather narrow band of reference questions and answers.

For example, I once helped a woman who wanted  information on "managing sociotechnical change." She had already been referred to one of the best indexes to journal in the management field, *Business Index*; but she'd had no success with it. The reason for its failure is that it uses *LCSH* category terms, and there is

---

94  Of course, these paper-back books would have to be in special collections, since books shelved in the Library's general collections are re-bound. This has caused some concern, since, oftentimes, cover art is itself a worthwhile collectible.

no category term for what she wanted. (Its "Management" subject heading was much too broad.) (Mann 1993:71)

Compare Mann's "question and answer" reference example with a more in-depth description from one of the Library's more established scholars.

> I'm still reading through arcane books by chemists who sort of are journalists at the same time and catching their vision of the future. I've been reading a lot of neo-Malthusian fears about over- population and future-famine and what can be done about that. The thing, you know—you work here and it's very hard to stay disciplined because you get one thing and it leads to another and I've just un-earthed the whole literature on Malthus and population and birth control and then that leads to racism and then there's no end. (interview, Scholar, Science Reading Room)

While Mann's example is a fairly clear cut example of "information sought" and "information received," it is patently more difficult to place a label on the above researcher. Is it a "hermeneutic circle"? A postmodern metonymy? It is not the scope of this chapter to parse the ethnomethodology of scholars, but simply to point to the gap between two courses of "information-seeking behavior."[95]

After the 1993 Congressional hearing, it became plain that the Library was not going to rescind its closed stack policies and re-open to a limited number of library users.

At the same time, some staff attempted to foist the blame for thefts and vandalism onto users.

> Another staffer said he "had no proof, but a gut feeling" that people from outside the Library are the problem. "I think people working in the stacks don't have the motivation. But people coming here know exactly what they want." (Fineberg 11/24/95:7)

And:

> "By closing the stacks, you are by implication saying that staff are responsible. I have not seen any evidence of staff destroying a book," said Rosemary Plakas, American history specialist, Rare Book and Special Collections Division, at the first forum. (Fineberg 5/15/92:9)

In 1995, after the stacks had been closed to researchers for almost three years, another "scandal" broke about a fresh wave of thefts and mutilations in the Library stacks. Deborah Maceda, a member of the LC Police force, had been reporting additional mutilations to the Library collections after the 1992 stack closings. Her memos, however, seemed to anger her superiors in Protective Services and she was demoted to a non-police job in the Law Library pending

---

95 Many primers on reference work are, in fact, exclusively concerned with these more "pyramidal" reference interviews.

disciplinary proceedings. Luckily for Maceda, a letter to Connie Mack, the Chairman of the Joint Committee of the Library, resulted in a full-scale investigation of Library practices and another round of unflattering media coverage (Gleick 1995). Confronted by allegations from the Joint Committee and the press, Billington "stripped the library's police force of its investigative authority" and undertook another review of Library of Congress security (Streitfeld 1995:C1).

Billington's office responded to the scandal by intimating that library employees were behind the recent thefts.

> When asked to evaluate the Library's security plan, he stated that it was more a list of problems than an integrated plan. Also in response to questions, he stated that the greatest security threat was internal and not external. (Miller 1995)

Not only were certain unscrupulous employees responsible for the thefts, he suggested, but the organization itself was culpable; by extension, the entire staff was indicted.

> Regrettably, I have received in recent days strong indications that our book collections are again being pillaged. Even more regrettably, the Library has let its vigilance slip by allowing bureaucracy to hamper the best efforts of our staff. (Billington 8/17/95)

And:

> "We cannot relax," he said Tuesday, "since there will always be those who will attempt to plunder the nation's heritage for private gain. We can't afford to let bureaucracy hinder our continuing efforts to deal with the threat." ("JHB Asks Staff to Help Tighten Security":1)

The media exposure resulted in increased levels of security and the investigation of, at least, some staff. It's important to note that Library security was felt to be highly variable in its effects on different groups, centered mostly on the technical and para-professional staff.

> We all remember the staff meetings where Dr. B. left us feeling that Library staff were the main threat to the collections, especially the African Americans who work in the stacks. The ugly turn may be that someone higher up on the organizational food chain is responsible for not halting the pilfering in the collections and now the witch hunt is on. (AFSCME Local 2477 1995a)

This was compounded by the LC's pointed observation that the African American literature section of the stacks was the most vandalized (Library of Congress 1995). Right away, after the initial scandal broke in 1992, staff mail was scrutinized for stolen documents while Library management initiated surveillance of the rank-and-file (Heiss 1993:2).

Cameras (hidden and open) and electronic tracking enable the Library to watch your comings and goings. They give the agency the capability to generate records on you that you are unaware of. Based upon these records you can be charged with any number of violations of LCRs [Library of Congress Regulations], without ever knowing that you ever did anything wrong or that anyone was watching. Don't believe us? Just ask the chief who, after complaining about the unauthorized use of his office after hours, found himself the unintended star in an X rated movie. All the juicy tidbits caught by a camera hidden in his office in response to his complaint. (AFSCME Local 2477 1995b).

This extends to electronic communications. Certainly, over my term of fieldwork at the Library, employees were careful not to e-mail me with overly-critical comments and many of them expressed the belief that their e-mails were being monitored. This impression—whether true or not—was not exactly belied by the Library's policies. Since security measures placed the LC in a state of continued alert, all employee communiqués could be considered open to repressive invigilation.

The post-2001 era (including the anthrax scares of 2001-2002) has only heightened the citadel instincts of LC management. Now, ubiquitous surveillance can be additionally legitimated as the patriotic defense of the nation's knowledge.

## INFORMATION AND POWER AT THE BIG HOUSE

On December 18 of 1995, the Library's Interpretive Programs Office put up a new exhibition near the cafeteria on the 6th floor of the Madison Building. It was called "Back of the Big House: The Cultural Landscape of the Plantation" and focused on the social and cultural life of slaves in the American South through a selection of photographs and slave narrative/life histories. Its purpose was to redress an often overlooked side of plantation life, namely "the slaves' side of the plantation."

> As we look over these images and attend to the testimonies, we would do well to recall that plantations were contested territories. We must remember that back of the Big House the views held by slaves were very different from those espoused by plantation owners. The history of plantation life cannot be fully understood unless the slave perspective is acknowledged and the plantation landscape is viewed as a slave might have viewed it: that is, from the inside looking out. ("The Cultural Landscape of the Plantation," unpublished exhibit brochure)[96]

The exhibit, redolent with the language of "resistance," joined similar studies undertaken in history, anthropology, archaeology and other disciplines seeking to explore not only African American lifeways and culture under slavery, but

---

96  Cf. Vlach 1993.

also to document African and Caribbean continuities in black life (Orser 1990; Singleton 1985). It was curated, in fact, by John Michael Vlach, an anthropologist and American Studies professor at George Washington University.

Nevertheless, the exhibit was pulled by orders of Winston Tabb, Associate Librarian for Library Services, three hours after it went up, reportedly because additional materials and seminars contextualizing the exhibit were not yet available (Tabb 1996).

> They took the exhibit down immediately, without being asked, because it should not have opened at LC without more careful thought given to its location or preparation, such as a seminar or symposium on the exhibit's content and purpose. (Fineberg 1996c:3)

But the LC's official explanation seemed particularly feeble. After all, other institutions like Washington, D.C.'s Martin Luther King Library put up the exhibition without the exhaustive seminar or symposium series and, apparently, without noteworthy protest.[97] It seems more likely that the Library canceled "Back of the Big House" because offended employees threatened to turn the exhibit into another public relations disaster, following on the recent cancellation of a contentious Freud exhibit and a Congressional investigation of lax Library security ("Library Postpones Freud Exhibition"; Gleick 1995).[98]

It is true that the celebratory quality of the exhibit, like other studies showing "counterhegemony" in slave art, music and culture, underplayed the violence and trauma of plantation life. Is it really accurate—or even particularly helpful—to reconfigure slave quarters into "African-American villages" ("The Cultural Landscape of the Plantation," unpublished brochure)? Does the insistence on a genuine African American culture decontextualize slave life from its manifest inequality? Perhaps: but the opposition to "Back of the Big House" was more an indictment of Library labor and race relations than a critique of historiography. "The Big House," after all, is a name many employees found appropriate for the Library of Congress itself, a reference to its absolute, oftentimes draconian, authority to move employees and delegate work assignments, a hierarchy that bears down heavily on black employees. Pictures of slaves picking cotton under the watchful eye of the white overseer reminded many employees of the desultory ratio of white supervisors to black paraprofessionals, an imbalance that continues to plague the LC (Smith 1996; Oder 2004). In addition, some staffers charged that the exhibit's placement by the elevators and the cafeteria seemed calculated to "remind black employees of their place."

What particularly interested me were the letters that followed in the wake of

---

97  The exhibit re-opened at the Martin Luther King Library under a new name: "The Cultural Landscape of the Plantation.".

98  Most newspapers covering the exhibit cancellation were also skeptical of its purported "spontaneity" and cited critiques from outraged staffers (Weeks 1995a; De Witt 1995).

the Library decision, letters condemning the LC for its capitulation to "political correctness" and for its sacrifice of history to politicized radicals.

> What chance, then, do the American people have to experience a "Library without walls?" We have become just like the Smithsonian Institution, which pandered to a vocal minority and scrapped the *Enola Gay* exhibit. Young Americans are being distanced from the unpleasant—yet true—realities of their own history because of tender and presumptuous sensibilities of an inappropriate "political correctness." (Orr 1996:3)

Without commenting on the appropriateness of lumping Library of Congress employees with conservative groups critical of the Smithsonian's portrayal of the bombing of Japan, I nevertheless believe that Orr raised—in spite of himself—an important point. In the "library without walls," the very pinnacle of an enlightened information society and the purported renaissance of the public sphere, *every* aspect of information should be culpable to a public's gaze. This would include both the plantation exhibit *and* the controversy surrounding it. Aren't the social relations and discourses framing "Back to the Big House" also important to our understanding of slavery as an American past structuring an American present? Whether or not "Back to the Big House" was marred by slipshod scholarship subordinated to a hackneyed language of subaltern resistance is not necessarily germane to this discussion. In canceling the exhibition, the LC squelched what amounted to critical, public discourse on the meaning of history for the present. It's ironic, I believe, that journalists would construe employee protests as antithetical to the free flow of information.

> If, as some have suggested, the problem is not fear of these exhibits per se but fear of internal staff dissension in a period of precarious morale, then that precariousness ill serves the library's ability to stand up for the values it would seem obliged to represent. A Library of Congress that cannot see any reason to weigh carefully the withdrawal of information from circulation is in a strange position to act as guardian of the nation's intellectual patrimony. ("A Library on Tiptoe": A,18:1)

But were LC employees offended by the *information* or its *obstruction*? I would argue that employee's reactions to the exhibit provide a better window onto the politics of race than the exhibit itself, or that, at least, they augment the exhibit, *historicizing* race rather than merely producing historical *product*.

Or, perhaps, the "library without walls" is, in its potentiality, *too* transparent. If, on the one hand, the information age promises an ultimate transparency of government, knowledge and power to the skeptical gaze of a critical public than, on the other, it provokes an equally potent obfuscatory reaction simply by virtue of its reduction of knowledge to its purest essence in "information." The "real information"—those traces of knowledge and power embedded in social life—falls by the wayside.

Take your browser and point it to "www.loc.gov," the LC's monolithic Web site. Search for "Back of the Big House" or "The Cultural Landscape of the Plantation." You won't find it. Would it have been appropriate to include the exhibit on the Library's server? Maybe so, but I'm certain LC management never considered it. By itself, I suppose, a digitized "Back to the Big House" would have stimulated the same hue and cry that marked the December opening of the physical exhibit. But that controversy would have been a more honest and "informative" window on the enduring inequalities of race and work in the United States. I submit that Library employees, angry over Library management's continued stonewalling on the Cook class action suit, despairing over a labor policy of "doing more with less" that effectively limited opportunity for black employees to low-level technical jobs by eliminating "cross-over" positions, used one of the only tactics available to them: the "ownership" of the history of American slavery in an era of sometimes dubious identity politics.[99] However: it is, evidently, acceptable to carefully—and even critically—examine America's racist past as long as those events, photographs and texts stay safely locked in the past. They should not, at any rate, intrude into the present, with its perfectly "level playing field." It is ironic that the exhibitor's planners would celebrate the myriad acts of quotidian insubordination and resistance that marked slave life while purposely quelling similar displays at the Library.

## INFORMATION SOCIETY=INFORMATION ANXIETY

Along with countless articles and monographs vaunting the varied pleasures of the information age, the 1990s witnessed a number of publications warning readers of "information overflow" and advising them on the effective management of the information in their lives.

> As your own smart agent, you are responsible for managing your own personal signal-to-noise ratio, enhancing the signal—information that is accurate, relevant, economical, articulate, and evocative— and eliminating anything that blocks out or distracts meaning. (Shenk 1997:188)

Thus, information became not only a *value* to be produced and exchanged, but a *problem* to be managed. Information makes all of us implicit *managers*, what Donald Brenneis has called the "nonce bureaucrat." And like a manager, information forces us to do the difficult work of "downsizing" our information organizations and "streamlining" operations to increase the efficiency of the whole.

> The secret to processing information is narrowing your field of information to that which is relevant in your life, i.e. making careful choices about what kind of information merits your time and attention. Decision making becomes more

---

99  The pitfalls of an "identity politics"—e.g. its ignorance of class and its limited potential for concerted political action—are both myriad and well-discussed in the left press (Cf. di Leonardo 1994).

critical as the amount increases. (Wurman 1989:317)

While information society signifies, reportedly, an "explosion" of meaning and text and a commensurate increase in access, it also seems to mandate an *attenuation* of information to areas of defined relevancy. When we consider information at more macro levels of political economy rather than our individual choice, that purposeful truncation takes on a more sinister quality. In this formulation, what we might call the drama of the information "Haves" and "Have-Nots" is hardly a sign of the failure of information society; from the perspective of ruling elites, information "black holes" might be counted as its greatest success.

In this Chapter, "information society" appears less as an epochal transformation wrought by technology than class, race and hierarchy carried on by other means. In an institutional climate of excessive fractionation, it behooved the Library to stress the "transparency" of information and portray its employees and even its users as an impasse to the free flow of information and a danger to the sanctity of its collections. Users and employees, on the other hand, stressed the social dimensions of "information," both in its human dimension as the product of a certain kind of relationship and indeed, a labor, as well as something that can be used to manipulate staff, users and Congress by managers eager to maximize budget appropriations while minimizing social discord.

In this case, the "management" of the "free flow" of information takes on a sinister tone, since it amounts to the provision of information in some areas (e.g., on the National Digital Library) at the expense of other areas (e.g., management accountability). Above all else, "information" becomes something to be controlled, allotted, withheld and hidden.

CHAPTER 7

## Conclusion: The American
## Pastoral Revisited

This has neither been an argument for nor an elenctic rant against the purported "information age." It is just as futile to hearken back to an irretrievable (and largely illusory) past as it is to naively exculpate our shiny, new worlds of information technologies. Instead, I have tried to trace the *limits* of information society: those places and dramas where brilliant fictions of a progressive, autogenetic information society give way to power politics, class war and egregious racism. In short, I have tried to evoke the cultural attributes of what some theorists call "information society." I suggest that virtual libraries and digital futures involve shifts in *lived* and *practiced meaning*, i.e. a way for organizations, employees and users to understand, negotiate, rationalize and castigate the world around them. These shifts reflect and reproduce the progressive alienation and commodification of knowledge also central to information society. While the folding of knowledge into value-laden information may be a dream (and nightmare) for LC users and staff, the *cultural* aspects of information society are already well represented in the hierarchy, structure and practice of the Library's world. I have tried to demonstrate this through the *structure* of this book as well as its contents, a structure that begins as a "book about books" but that ends with the people whose work and lives buttress that bibliomantic order. In Chapter 3, I traced the Library's persistent spatial problems, problems that are a consequence of the same, nationalist genius behind the LC's nineteenth-century origins. In the construction of what is now called the Jefferson Building, readers were placed at the center of a nationalist machine representing the perfect synergy of knowledge, nation and technology. Sitting at a desk at the center of the great Library, the nineteenth century reader could reach out into universal collections, courtesy of the pneumatic tube and the automatic book conveyor. But that "perfect" order, implying "perfect" knowledge and "perfect" access, is impossible to sustain. After all, the reverse of "universal collections" is "universal chaos," a fecund, entropic disorder that the LC has fought for much of its existence. The Library's many spaces

reflect the shifting, compensatory strategies of its management and its planners. But those strategies are by no means coherently articulated; their varied
practice, like the twisting corridors of books themselves, suggest an institution
fundamentally at odds with itself. The history of the LC is, in this sense, the
history of the development of new technologies to keep readers at the center
of the "knowledge machine." In Chapters 4 and 5, therefore, I looked to the
Library's many machines as synecdoches for different visions of "information"
and "information society," visions that uneasily coexist in the Library's organization. If we consider that information science at the LC and beyond begins
with the idea that "perfect" information implies "perfect" presence (a decidedly
Cartesian precept), than there is from the very outset a fundamental tension in
information technologies. I argue that the card catalog and, after it, the MARC
record, already imply a certain distance from the materials these technologies
represent. For the LC, this distance was compounded by the budgetary crises
of the 1980s. In this respect, I suggest that the digital library should be seen
less as the next step on a chronology of progress than as an attempt to (ideologically) close the distance between reader and read through a technological
palliative that delivers an image of the LC that is only indirectly related to its
collections and organization, decidedly problematic areas that turn transparent
in the "library without walls." Finally, in Chapter 6, I turned towards the *labor*
of the Library to examine the multifarious problems of an institution that figures itself on the cusp of "information society." It is, perhaps, a truism that the
varied labors of employees and scholars make up the world of "information."
Yet LC management, following the initiatives of corporations in the 1980s and
90s, has grown increasingly intolerant of these laborers, portraying them as
*enemies* rather than *engines* of knowledge.

All in all, I describe many "Library of Congresses" in these pages. It is a function of what I am calling "ideas of information society" that certain visions of
the Library are privileged over others and that the digital library at the Library
of Congress has as much to do with what went before as it does with advances
in this or that technology (narrowly conceived).

It has been the implicit argument here, however, that the *machines* and
*spaces* of the information age—those touchstones of our shiny, new, telematic world—are less important than the people who enable and interpret the
objects in our life. Hence, the last word has been left to those who *labor* at
the Library. It is the Library's users and staff who stand to lose the most in
the fractious battles of the twenty-first century. For them, the beginning of
this or that pilot program or the adoption of this or that software represent
nothing so much as a widening gap between management and workers, users and collections. For these people, perhaps, "information society" means
nothing more than the glib, lexical shift from "efficiency" and "automation"
to "flexibility" and "digitization." The results—widening gaps between GS-6
and GS-7, ruinous consultative management and less access to rare, underutilized collections—are the same.

All of these things, these spaces, machines and people, drag on the "information age," keeping us from an escape velocity that would slingshot us into our wildest science fictions of information transparency and information propinquity. But these troublesome bodies that multiply and fibrillate are also the same bodies that enable all of the advances and shifts characteristic of "information society." They are the dynamo generating the "information explosion." So why does the LC pit its resources, as it were, against itself?

## PUBLICITY AND TRUTH

I look in my pantry at the canned foods, the noodles, the cooking oil. It's not enough that I buy and eat these things. Now, I can (virtually) consume their representation on that publicist of publicists, the World Wide Web. Want to find some new recipes for those canned vegetables? Try www.delmonte.com. Wondering if there's any new flavors of "Ragu" spaghetti sauce coming out? Point your browser to www.ragu.com.

On the web, "information" is often coterminous with "publicity," and businesses hawking their product jostle alongside more altruistic information providers like universities and the Library of Congress. At a time when many heretofore public institutions (e.g. museums) have come to accept—grudgingly or not—some level of corporate sponsorship, we might see the proliferation of ".com" sites on the World Wide Web as a kind of private industry philanthropy. Or are these institutions inherently more altruistic than Pizza Hut? Is "information" innocent of the increasingly commercialized imperatives of information's production?

Following the widespread adoption of "Netscape" in 1995, countless discussions among digerati—on- and off-line—have centered around the effects of commercialization on the growth of the Internet. Would the presence of advertising have a belligerent effect on the freedoms enjoyed by "Internet communities"? Would the federal government step in to regulate what had become, by 1996, an important source of revenue? The passage of the 1996 Telecommunications Act signaled something, whether a death-knell to free speech or a wake-up call to liberal capitalism (or both) is still a matter of endless peroration.

That the National Digital Library is a proprietary collection of documents is, on the one hand, an inevitable product of archival necessity. But it is also the conscious effort to elevate publicity over debate and the consumption of information over the rational apperception of knowledge. In the bad, new world of "TQM" government, the image of the institution takes precedence over the institution's function. To those on the inside, it is quite expected: in a federal government in a state of tumultuous retrenchment (at least in education and social services), every publication, every product, every report must be bent towards self-preservation. To put it bluntly, "selling" the LC has never been more important.

## ATTACK OF THE PO-MO "IMAGE SLUTS": THE RISE OF INFOTREPENEURING

> Where once information was perceived as a public resource which ought to be shared and free, now and increasingly it is regarded as a commodity which is tradable, something which can be bought and sold for private consumption, with access dependent on payment. (Webster 1995:115)

The Library has had "for-fee" services for many years. For example, cataloging distribution was, from the outset, supposed to be a self-sustaining operation, its products supplied at cost with a small mark-up for infrastructure (Rosenberg 1993). Of course, it was heavily subsidized with staff, equipment and space in the LC's increasingly crowded physical plant.[100] Consultants like Booz-Allen and Hamilton have urged the LC to adopt to more fee-based services, an idea that most people in the LC—regardless of their politics—have furiously resisted. But despite the principled rejection of fees for basic library services, the LC under Head Librarian Billington has cultivated the patronage of an increasing number of corporations, among them Xerox, Ameritech, Microsoft, Google and a host of other private concerns represented by the Madison Council, an elite group of "advisors" to the Head Librarian. Many at the LC fear that the introduction of corporate sponsorship will turn the institution's mission away from the work of cataloging and bibliography and towards flashy exhibitions and tourism or, worse yet, that basic publications and services will be absorbed into the ballooning corporate sphere.[101]

I worked at the cusp of this process of privatization as a contract researcher. In most contract research at the Library of Congress, one undertakes the retrieval of otherwise free information for a *price*, utilizing the LC's free databases, reference materials and collections for a client too busy to do the research herself. Building a bibliography of, say, *Ursus maritimus* was made immeasurably easier by several CD-ROM databases on natural science and conservation, together with the LC's many journals, abstracts, conference proceedings and reference works. I was joined by other researchers pursuing Congressional Committee reports, genealogies, treasure maps, biographies and marketing demographics. However, every division of the LC's collections has its concomitant contractors. While I did contract research in *print* materials and hence spent most of my time in the Main and Science Readings Rooms, I had the opportunity to meet and talk with several scholars doing film and picture research. Nowhere, it seems to me, was this process of *commercialization* more evident than in the Prints and Photographs and Motion Picture Reading Rooms. One scholar described a large, but by no means anomalous, project.

---

100 This, in contrast with the ostensibly for-profit services of OCLC (Ohio College Library Consortium), at one time the LC's main rival in cataloging.

101 This has certainly happened at a number of other federal agencies, notably the Department of Commerce, the Department of Labor and USAID.

Right now I'm working on a really fascinating project. They are CD-ROMs teaching history and archaeology. It's the best text-CD-ROM interactive I've seen. The one I'm working on is the Civil War and African Americans. They need 300, 400, 500 images. (interview, Scholar, Prints and Photographs)

Jean Baudrillard has probably best articulated (and sometimes celebrated) the notion of postmodern society as an *image-laden* one awash with empty, self-referential simulations (Baudrillard 1983). Much of Baudrillard's writing (and particularly his later writing) is concerned with the circulation of empty simulations, signifying nothing: a closed, telematic world (Cf. Best and Kellner 1991; Kroker and Weinstein 1994). The LC—along with other institutions like the National Archives and the National Library of Medicine—is a major player in this burgeoning economy of signs, supplying textbook companies and other publishers with an almost endless supply of public domain images that can be reproduced without fear of copyright infringement.[102]

Picture researchers are oftentimes scholars with advanced degrees in art history or history who possess both an aesthetic and technical knowledge of photographs and motion pictures. For them, contract work is a way to remain close to historically important, aesthetically complex collections while managing to make a living. But the chief concerns of clients—high quality, never-before-seen, topic-specific photographs—are not always shared by the researchers.

A year and a half ago, a lot of people were getting scanners. There were a lot of people who were just starting—they're image sluts. They wanted a million images but they didn't know what the images were. It was this quantity thing: 'Our machine has the capacity to load one thousand images'. I suppose I fall into the artistic group. But working here I've developed a great respect that you should represent this stuff accurately. (interview, Scholar, Prints and Photographs)

Photographs, prints, motion pictures—images—are a part of the historical record, products of a specific time and place that are both socially and textually embedded. But they are also the *sine qua non* trophies of postmodernism, the self-reflexive, recombinatory signs that are the coin of advertising, propaganda, fashion and entertainment. But Matthew Brady's Civil War photographs aren't like the fashion spreads in *Vogue*. The Library's photographs are different, aren't they?

The Farm Security Administration collection vertical files occupy center stage in the LC's Prints and Photographs Reading Room. As a record of American life in the first part of the twentieth century, the FSA collection is without parallel. Talented documentary photographers set out to capture something of American life in all its diversity. They were—in the truest sense—visual

---

102 Although, it has to be admitted, this is not always the case. The LC collects some copyrighted photographs that publishers must be wary of using indiscriminately. The situation is even more precarious in motion pictures and researchers in both divisions sometimes take out copyright omissions insurance.

anthropologists, creating powerful, visual stories about groups of farmers, factory workers, children and so on: a remarkable achievement in a progressive age. However: the FSA files are arranged not by the integrated *stories* in which they were taken, but by subject and geography. Filing and cross-referencing the photographs under this system makes them immeasurably more useful to picture researchers whose needs are topical and thematic. This system, however, is open to certain abuses.

> There's a case in point. There's this wonderful picture of an African American family on a little strip of land. They're actually flood victims. It's from 1960 but it looks like it was from 1890. This picture of flood victims has been used for black people migrating. (interview, Scholar, Prints and Photographs)[103]

The photograph appears in at least one prominent history textbook, *The Enduring Vision*, edited by a number of famous historians, among them Clifford E. Clark and Paul S. Boyer. The caption relates the photograph to the for-profit homesteading associations that proliferated in the wake of Reconstruction.

> Forming a real estate company, Singleton traveled the South recruiting parties of freedmen who were disillusioned with the outcome of Reconstruction to settle for the "fine rolling Prairies" of Kansas. These emigrants, awaiting a Mississippi River boat, looked forward to Midwestern homesteads, freedom from violence, and political equality. (Boyer *et al* 1990:559)

Does the historical veracity of photographs outweigh the utility of an image in the circulation of information? Does it matter that these are victims of a flood and not itinerant migrants on their way to Chicago? Or is it only important that the photographed family is *black* and, as such, emit the *sign* of black, a fungible image suitable for the mediatized productions of a postmodern society? Despite a real concern for the historical context of its materials (manifest in the finding aids in its collections and the judicious subject cataloging of non-print collections with printed primary and secondary sources), the LC does cater—to some extent—to those interests that would utilize its materials as "empty signs," or, as I have argued, "information."

In 1989, presumably aware of growing importance of images (photographs, graphics, prints) to computer industry, Microsoft's celebrated *bête noir* Bill Gates founded Corbis (www.corbis.com), a privately held company selling prints and digitized images from its vast archive. During the 1990s, the company began to build its collections aggressively, buying the rights to commercial archives and reproducing countless public domain negatives. One by one it finagled the rights to historically (and commercially) important collections all over the world: the Bettmann Archives, Russia's State Hermitage Museum, the Robert Holmes and the Ansel Adams Collection. As its website boasted in

---

103 i.e., for the Great Migration of African Americans to urban areas in the North of the United States during the first part of the twentieth century.

the late 1990's,

> Corbis has built its collection from the ground up, according to a visionary busi-
> ness plan that takes advantage of new information management and distri-
> bution technologies. It currently contains more than 20 million images, with
> one million in high resolution digital format mapped against a sophisticated
> database, making it the largest collection of quality images in the world. (Corbis
> [online])

There are many critics of Corbis who charge that its online and CD-ROM
products are a circus of images without substance, pictures and graphics sun-
dered from their past and their context and presented for the dull amusement
(rather than the edification) of a jaded, image-saturated public (Goldberg
1997; Manes 1996).

In 1994-1995, Corbis was at the Library of Congress, copying files and
ordering negatives. For a while, many of the picture researchers working out
the LC were nervous, expecting Corbis to preempt their own services. This
seems not to have happened, with the aggregate number of advertised picture
researchers actually *growing* since 1994-1995.[104] Nevertheless, the existence of
a giant, image vendor like Corbis raises serious questions about the eclipse of
"democratic town-hall" information by proprietary information vendors.

> That's what Microsoft did: they came here and got a lot. I don't know how much
> they got. They needed people to xerox the index cards. There's 15 million items
> in Prints and Photographs. The negative cards don't represent the whole collec-
> tions. They're going to purchase this stuff. Why couldn't the Library have done
> this itself? (interview, Scholar, Prints and Photographs)

Why couldn't the LC have initiated a Corbis-like Web site and sold its collections at market prices? To begin with, they are a *library* and, as such, secure
much of their non-book collections from philanthropic donors who give their
papers, archives and recordings to the LC precisely because it is a pre-eminent,
public institution.[105] Also, as James Billington has suggested more than once,
the job of the Library may be to *facilitate* corporate profits, but not to initiate
them.

Are companies like Corbis a measure of our future "information society?"
Will the Library become another information vendor selling history to the
largest bidder? Clearly, staff and users were worried over this eventuality and
saw, for example, the appointment of a former Xerox executive to the Photodu-
plication Service or the underwriting of Library exhibits and online programs

---

104 I base this observation on a list of contract researchers that the Library of Congress freely
distributes to interested scholars.

105 Increasingly, there's a profit to be made by selling one's papers and manuscripts to better-
heeled archives and libraries. With its modest acquisitions budget, this is a growing concern for
the LC. For example, Kurt Vonnegut had papers at the Manuscripts Division on deposit (that is,
for safe-keeping), but took them back to sell them.

by corporate sponsors as harbingers of bad times to come. But it has been the argument here that, while the analysis of the ongoing process of the privatization of traditional, public-sphere functions is clearly important, it is also redundant. Whether or not the LC is taken over by corporate interests may be important, especially to the scholars and contract researchers who depend upon its accessible, public services, but it is not the only index of "information society." That is, I have argued that, while it is vitally important to agitate for free and accessible information in public and private institutions, the "culture" of the information age does not depend in any *a priori* way on whether or not we pay for book retrieval and reference questions. Instead, I have looked to the oftentimes contradictory ways people talk and write about information in the spaces, machines and organizations at the Library of Congress. The architecture of LC machines and buildings tells us something about the way some people believe information society should (or should not) work. In the same way, Congressional testimonies, newsletters and newspaper articles suggest which aspects of this information society Library management believe will resonate most with Congressional subcommittees and the voting public. Finally, fractious labor disputes and narratives on Library access say something about what hopes and fears people bring to this emergent formation. By looking at the development of these discourses during a period of particular crisis at the Library of Congress in the 1980s and 1990s, I have tried to evoke the cultural dimensions of the information age, that is, the range of consensus, debate and contradiction adhering to ideas of "information" at a particular moment in history. The Library may become another crass, information merchant churning out history for a price, or it may not. It is still, as I have demonstrated, as much a part of that "information society" as Microsoft, Corbis or Booz-Allen and Hamilton.

Information society is all part of the hype, a way of selling the Library to a Congress and a public ostensibly hostile to government spending and centralized bureaucracy. With a digital library, the LC can tout its manifold treasures to tourists and schoolchildren without the fuss and bother of acquisitions, cataloging control and archival work. In this context, a "Library Without Walls" is a library where the dross of the physical falls away to reveal valuable jewels of information: KGB letters, the Presidential papers of George Washington, photographs of Harry Houdini at the height of his power.

But that feeling of transparency is only purchased at a price: the oftentimes belligerent denuding of skills and scholarship for the rank-and-file scholars and workers whose lives have been bound up with the LC for decades. The Digital Library may broaden access to certain collections at the Library of Congress, but it also, in its organizational fractionation, serves to obscure decision-making and ossify hierarchies in such a way as to compound existing inequalities in race. That is to say, "information society" may be a bunch of hype trundled out for a petty, meretricious Congress, but it is still a singly *powerful* hype, legitimating firings, de-skilling and even racism, all in the name of "flexibility," "cooperation" and "consultation." Information society emerges here in the midst of power and culture, scanning the discursive space between ideology and commonsense.

## AMERICAN PASTORAL REDUX

A (January 1997) television advertisement for MCI's online service drones, "On the Internet, there is no race." What there is in these commercials is a curious, if entirely predictable, recidivistic scent about advertisements and articles hyping the "Internet" that echo almost Jeffersonian sentiments (and contradictions) about enduring inequalities and liberal pluralism in the United States. While enthusiastic literary critics trumpet the "death of the subject," I wonder if a "race-less" Internet doesn't just re-write the pastoralist myth of white, male autochthony on what has been widely construed as America's "electronic frontier" (Bukatman 1993; Poster 1990). As Henry Nash Smith, Leo Marx and others have demonstrated, the "pastoralist" mode popular in nineteenth-century thought creates an anhistorical, "virginal" space for the penetrations of white, male, manifest destiny.

However, the establishment of a middle ground between "savagery" and "civilization" is always already occulted by the driving force of the capitalist machine (Marx 1964). But the machines that inevitably interrupt American pastoral reverie are also agents of pastoral return, for if machines defile the pristine, Edenic spaces of the white middle-class, they also condition the possibility of its redemption. This is part of what many have termed the "American technological sublime" (Segal 1994). As Warren Belasco has written about the history of motoring:

> If the railroad—Frank Norris's encroaching "octopus" —was the conglomerate present, the car was the New Freedom. It promised a nostalgic return to a simpler age of benignly individualistic operators, an age set before the beginnings of the Industrial Revolution, and thus, before the railroad. Through the early 1930s, touring literature described automotive transport as a revival of stage-coach and carriage travel. Railroads had supplanted stagecoaches and now cars would replace railroads. (Belasco 1981:20)

That is to say, in the American technological sublime, the return to the past and the path to the future are (ideologically) inseparable, held together however fugaciously.

"The computer"—as a metaphor or a metonym—promises a return to the "garden," i.e., a virginal, isolated space from which one can launch a new existence apart from the sinful vicissitudes of the base world. With its customizable desktop, the PC in the Microsoft age is a particularly poignant example. That is, all of these "lively machines" possess the power to return "us" to mythopoetic places of purity before "the Fall" of politics, power, race and class. But, in effect, "there is no race" only because the bodies of those intractable Others have been neatly (or not so neatly) transcended. That is, race appears ancillary to our "virtual future" because to focus on race would be to consider the attendant inequalities of information society: not only the somewhat naive issue of who has Internet access, but also the social inequalities of a social order privileging a digital elite over increasingly disenfranchised minorities. Simply put, it would make bad advertising copy. The wired world sells a telematic future that doesn't so much "deconstruct" the subject as "white-wash" it in an orgiastic celebration of bourgeois values and bourgeois selves. In the 1990s, advertising moguls raced to clothe their Internet-based services and products in the rich, if hackneyed, language of the American pastoral, investing it with all of the regenerative and salutary properties of the great outdoors.

"Information society" is that cultural propensity to project a vision of consumers and products in ideal transcendence, sublimating social labor and institutional inequality to capitalism's unconscious. Construing "information" as a bounded, shiny surface without a past, without a production and, ultimately, without a context, is not only to fall into the classic, Burkean trap of the "paradox of purity," it is also to sunder the interconnections that make "information" possible in the first place (Burke 1969). The "pathetic fallacy" of the Internet is the misrecognition of the human and the social in the confines of the bounded, digitized text to the exclusion of the different relations of knowledge that condition its existence in the first place. We must see "information society" as part of a late-modernist penchant for sublimating the traces of power, social conflict and racial politics in order to attain a "consensual" corporate culture. This is another, more sinister, connotation of transparency—the elimination of those troublesome bodies that impede the image of progress and pastoral return.

It is not so easy to lose oneself in Calvino's reading utopia. On its way to the National Digital Library, the Library of Congress may downsize its workforce and restrict access to its collections, but it does so at the cost of its historical mission, still its primary source of legitimation. To delimit the LC's functions to self-referential publicity is to abnegate the Library's role in the national order. This "reading" can only be obtained at the untoward cost of social violence. That is, this information society is already a function of modernist political economy. Less than a stage that we have or have not attained, I see information society as another ideological noumenon in the fractious battles of late modernity, along with the mechanization of the first half of the twentieth century and the automation of the second. Information's future, whatever stories we choose to tell ourselves, will surely mean shifts in power and control. The romance of the Reader and the Other Reader, I fear, will remain a function of these varied, para-textual orders.

# REFERENCES

"A Bill of Writes."
   1995   Wired 3:224.

"A Library on Tiptoe."
   1995   Washington Post 12/22/95: A, 18:1.

AFSCME Local 2477.

   1995a"In Deep . ." AFSCME-GRAM 10/12/95,
          no. 19.

   1995b"Big Brother at the Library." AFSCME-
          GRAM 3/10/95.

   1996   Memo, 10/18/96.

AFSCME Local 2477 and Library of Congress.
   1991   Collective Bargaining Agreement Between
          the Library of Congress and the American
          Federation of State, County and Municipal
          Employees Local 2477. unpublished.

Alter, Robert.
   1989   The Pleasures of Reading in an Ideological Age.
          New York: Simon and Schuster.

Althusser, Louis.
   1971   Lenin and Philosophy and Other Essays.
          London: New Left Books.

American Historical Association.
  1993     "Resolution on the Library of Congress."
           Reprinted in Progressive Librarian 6/7.

Anderson, Benedict.
  1991     Imagined Communities. New York: Verso.

Anderson, Gregory T.
  1992     "Dimensions, Context, and Freedom: the Library
           in the Social Creation of Knowledge." In
           Sociomedia: Multimedia, Hypermedia, and the Social
           Construction of Knowledge, ed. by Edward Barrett,
           pp. 107-124. Cambridge: MIT Press.

Appadurai, Arjun.
  1990     "Disjuncture and Difference in the Global
           Cultural Economy." Public Culture 2(2):1-23.

  1991     "Global Ethnoscapes." In Recapturing
           Anthropology, ed. by Richard Fox. Sante Fe, NM:
           School of American Research Press.

Appadurai, Arjun and Carol A. Breckenridge.
  1988     "Why Public Culture?" Public Culture 1(1).

Applewhite, E.J.
  1981     Washington Itself. New York: Alfred A. Knopf.

Aranson, H.H.
  1986     History of Modern Art. New York: Harry N. Abrams, Inc.

Architect of the Capital.
           unpublished memoranda and reports from the
           Library of Congress building files, Archives of
           the Architect of the Capitol.

Aronowitz, Stanley and William DiFazio.
  1994     The Jobless Future. Minneapolis: University of
           Minnesota Press.

Asbell, Bernard.
  1965     The New Improved American. New York: McGraw-Hill.

Augé, Marc.
　　1995　　Non-Places. New York: Verso.

Avram, Henrietta.
　　1968　　The MARC Pilot Project. Washington, D.C.: Library
　　　　　　of Congress.

　　1975　　MARC: Its History and Implications. Washington,
　　　　　　D.C.: Library of Congress.

Banta, Martha.
　　1993　　Taylored Lives: Narrative Productions in the Age
　　　　　　of Taylor, Veblen, and Ford. Chicago: University
　　　　　　of Chicago Press.

Barthes, Roland.
　　1967　　Writing Degree Zero. London.

Bateson, Gregory.
　　1991　　A Sacred Unity. New York: HarperCollins.

Batteau, Alan.
　　1995　　"Constructing the Other in Narrowband
　　　　　　Environments." Paper presented at American
　　　　　　Anthropological Meeting, Washington, D.C.

Baudrillard, Jean.
　　1983a　　In the Shadow of the Silent Majorities, or,
　　　　　　the End of the Social and Other Essays.
　　　　　　New York: Semiotext(e).

　　1983b　　Simulations. New York: Semiotext(e).

Behar, Ruth.
　　1993　　Translated Woman. Boston: Beacon Press.

Belasco, Warren James.
　　1981　　Americans on the Road. Boston: MIT Press.

Benfer, Robert A., Louanna Furbee and Edward Brent, Jr.
　　1996　　"Expert Systems and the Representation of
　　　　　　Knowledge." american ethnologist 23(2):
　　　　　　416-420.

Berman, Marshall.
    1982    All That Is Solid Melts Into Air. New York:
             Penguin.

Berman, Sanford.
    1971    Prejudices and Antipathies: a tract on the LC
             subject heads concerning people. Metuchen, NJ:
             Scarecrow Press.

Best, Steven and Douglas Kellner.
    1991    Postmodern Theory. New York: The Guilford
             Press.

Bial, Raymond and Linda LaPuma Bial.
    1991    The Carnegie Library in Illinois. Urbana, Ill.:
             University of Illinois Press.

Billington, James.
    1995    "The Mission and Strategic Priorities of
             the Library of Congress." The Gazette 6(40):7-9.

    8/17/95
             "Office of the Librarian Special Announcement."
             No. 95-11; unpublished memo.

    1995    "JHB Tells Congress of LC Efforts." The
             Gazette 12/1/95:1,9-15.

    1996    "Libraries, the Library of Congress, and the
             Information Age." Daedalus 125(4):35-54.

Bluestone, Barry and Irving Bluestone.
    1992    Negotiating the Future. New York:BasicBooks.

Boddy, Julie and Stanley Goldberg.
    1995    "The Age of Information & the Library of
             Congress." Z Magazine, September.

Borges, Jorge Luis.
    1964    "The Library of Babel." In Labyrinths.
             New York: New Directions Publishing.

Boswell, Paul.
    1994    No Anchovies on the Moon. Washington, D.C.: Seven
               Locks Press.

Bottomore, Tom.
    1993    Elites and Society. New York: Routledge.

Bourdieu, Pierre.
    1977    Outline of a Theory of Practice. New York:
               Cambridge University Press.

Bova, Ben.
    1989    Cyberbooks. New York: Tor.

Boyarin, Jonathan.
    1994    "Death and the *Minyan.*" Cultural Anthropology
               9(1):3-22.

Boyarin, Jonathan (ed.).
    1993    The Ethnography of Reading. Berkeley: University
               of California Press.

Boyer, Paul S., Clifford E. Clark, Jr., Joseph F. Kett, Thomas L. Purvis, Hard
Sitkoff and Nancy Woloch.
    1990    The Enduring Vision: A History of the
               American People. Lexington, Mass.: D.C. Heath
               and Company.

Branan, Brad.
    1996    "White Makes Right." Washington City Paper
               6/21/96:10.

Braverman, Harry.
    1975    Labor and Monopoly Capital. New York: Monthly
               Review Press.

Buckland, Lawrence E. and William L. Basinski.
    1978    The Role of the Library of Congress in the
               Evolving National Network. Washington, D.C.:
               Library of Congress.

Bukatman, Scott.
    1993    Terminal Identity. Durham, NC: Duke University
            Press.

Burke, Kenneth.
    1969    A Grammar of Motives. Berkeley: University of
            California Press.

Burnwasser, Lee.
    1992    "Barring Staffers from the Stacks" (op-ed).
            The Gazette 5/15/92:2.

Calhoun, Karen.
    2006    "The Changing Nature of the Catalog and Its
            Integration with Other Discovery Tools." Report
            Prepared for the Library of Congress.
            [www.guild2910.org]

Calvino, Italo.
    1981    if on a winter's night a traveler. New York:
            Harcourt Brace Jovanovich.

Case, Donald O.
    2002    Looking for Information. San Diego, CA: Academic Press.

Castells, Manuel.
    1989    The Informational City. Cambridge: Basil
            Blackwell.

Castillo, Debra Ann.
    1982    Librarians in Babel. Doctoral Dissertation,
            University of Wisconsin at Milwaukee.

Caulfield, Brian.
    1997    "Morphing the Librarians." Wired 5.08:64.

Chambers, Iain.

    1994    migrancy, culture, identity. New York: Routledge.

"Change at the Library of Congress."
    1978    LC Information Bulletin 37(13).

Chartier, Roger.
1994    The Order of Books. Palo Alto, CA: Stanford
        University Press.

Claeson, Bjorn, Emily Martin, Wendy Richardson, Monica Schoch-Spana
and Karen-Sue Taussig.
1996    "Scientific Literacy, What It Is, Why It's
        Important, and Why Scientists Think We Don't Have
        It." In Naked Science, ed. by Laura Nader.
        New York: Routledge.

Cole, John Y.
1971    "Of Copyright, Men and a National Library."
        The Quarterly Journal of the Library of
        Congress 28(2):114-136.

1972    "Smithmeyer & Pelz: embattled architects of the
        Library of Congress." Quarterly Journal of the
        Library of Congress 29(4):282-307.

1975    "For Congress & the Nation: The Dual Nature of
        the Library of Congress." The Quarterly
        Journal of the Library of Congress 32(2):
        118-138.

1979    "Storehouses and Workshops: American Libraries
        and the Uses of Knowledge." In The Organization
        of Knowledge in Modern America, 1860-1920.
        Baltimore: Johns Hopkins University Press.

1993    Jefferson's Legacy. Washington, D.C.: Library
        of Congress.

Collins, Samuel Gerald.
1995    "Imagining Gender." In Beyond the Lavender
        Lexicon, ed. by William Leap. New York: Gordon
        and Breach.

Conquergood, Dwight.
1992    "Life in Big Red." In Structuring Diversity,
        ed. by Louise Lamphere, pp.95-144. Chicago:
        University of Chicago Press.

Coombe, Rosemary J.
  1996   "Embodied Trademarks: Mimesis and Alterity on American Commercial Frontiers." Cultural Anthropology 11(2):202-224.

Corbis.
         Corbis Home Page. (http://www.corbis.com).

Coronil, Fernando.
  1996   "Beyond Occidentalism." Cultural Anthropology 11(1):51-87.

Coupland, Douglas.
  1991   Generation X. NY: St. Martin's Press.

Crawley, Laura K. and Joseph C. Hickerson.
  1992   Zora Neale Hurston: Recordings, Manuscripts, and Ephemera in the Archive of Folk Culture and Other Divisions of the Library of Congress. Washington, D.C.: Library of Congress.

Czitrom, Daniel J.
  1982   Media and the American Mind. Chapel Hill: University of North Carolina Press.

Davis, Mike.
  1986   Prisoners of the American Dream. London: Verso.

  1992   City of Quartz. New York: Vintage Books.

de Certeau, Michel.
  1984   The Practice of Everyday Life. Berkeley: University of California Press.

de Lauretis, Teresa.
  1987   Technologies of Gender. Bloomington, Indiana: Indiana University Press.

Demac, Donna.
  1988   "Hearts and Minds Revisited." In The Political Economy of Information, ed. by Vincent Mosco and Janet Wasko. Madison: University of Wisconsin Press.

Denich, Bette.
1994　"Dismembering Yugoslavia." American Ethnologist
21(2):367-390.

Derrida, Jacques.
1981　Dissemination. Chicago: University of Chicago
Press.

Dervin, Brenda and Michael Nilan.
1986　"Information Needs and Uses." Annual Review of
Information Science and Technology 21:3-33.

de Sant'Anna, Affonso Romano.
1996　"Libraries, Social Inequality, and the Challenge
of the Twenty-First Century." Daedalus 125(4):
267-282.

"Development of the Encoded Archival Description Document Type
Definition."
1995　Web document. Library of Congress
(http://lcweb.loc.gov/locstandards/
ead/eadback.html)

Devine, John.
1995　"Can Metal Detectors Replace the Panopticon?"
Cultural Anthropology 10(2):171-195.

De Witt, Karen.
1995　"After Protests, Library of Congress Closes
Exhibition on Slavery." New York Times
12/21/95: A21.

di Leonardo, Micaela.
1994　"White Ethnicities, Identity Politics, and
Baby Bear's Chair." Social Text 41.

1997　"It's the Discourse, Stupid!" The Nation 264(10):
35-37.

Dirks, Nicholas.
1994　"Ritual and Resistance." In Culture/Power/
History, ed. by Nicholas Dirks, Geoff Eley and
Sherry Ortner. Princeton, NJ: Princeton
University Press.

Dosa, Marta, Mona Farid and Pal Vasarhelyi.
　　1988　From Informal Gatekeeper to Information Counselor.
　　　　　 Syracuse, NY: Syracuse University.

Dowler, Lawrence and Laura Farwell.

　　1996　"The Gateway: A Bridge to the Library of the
　　　　　 Future." Reference Services Review, Summer:
　　　　　 7-11.

Downey, Gary Lee, Joseph Dumit and Sarah Williams.
　　1995　"Cyborg Anthropology." Cultural Anthropology
　　　　　 10(2):264-269.

Drucker, Peter F.
　　1993　Post-Capitalist Society. New York: HarperCollins.

Eco, Umberto.
　　1983　The Name of the Rose. New York: Warner Books.

　　1986　Travels in Hyperreality. London: Picador.

Edlund, Paul.
　　1976　"A Monster and a Miracle: the Cataloging
　　　　　 Distribution Service at the Library of Congress,
　　　　　 1901-1976." The Quarterly Journal of the Library
　　　　　 of Congress 33:383-421.

Ellis, David.
　　1993　"Modeling the Information-Seeking Patterns of
　　　　　 Academic Researchers." Library Quarterly 63(4):
　　　　　 469-486.

English-Lueck, Jan.
　　2002　Cultures@SiliconValley. Stanford, CA: Stanford
　　　　　 University Press.

Erkkila, Betsy.
　　1995　"Ethnicity, Literary Theory, and the Grounds of
　　　　　 Resistance." American Quarterly 47(4):563-594.

Evans, Luther.
　　1946　"The Job of the Librarian of Congress." In
　　　　　 Report of the Librarian of Congress for the

_Fiscal Year Ending June 30, 1945_. Washington, D.C.: Library of Congress.

Fabian, Johannes.
1983    _Time and the Other_. New York: Columbia University Press.

Fasana, Paul J.
1980    "Closing the Catalog." In _Closing the Catalog: Proceedings of the 1978 and 1979 Library and Information Technology Association Institutes_. D. Kaye Gapen and Bonnie Juergens, eds. Pp. 6-20. Phoenix, AZ: The Oryx Press.

Fineberg, Gail.
7/26/91
        "LC Pushes Affirmative Action." _The Gazette_ 2(30):1-2,10-11.

5/15/92
        "JHB Asks Staff Help on Security." _The Gazette_ 5/15/92:1,9-10.

10/9/92
        "Cook Class Action Case Began 17 Years Ago with 3-Page Complaint." _The Gazette_ 3(38): 1,10-11.

10/16/92
        "Cook Class Action: The Shaw Case." _The Gazette_ 3(39).

10/23/92
        "Library Reorganizes for Long-Range Plan." _The Gazette_ 3(40):1,10-11.

1995a   "Vision and Technology Revitalize Library." _The Gazette_ 6(14): 3,11.

1995b   "Arrearages Fall by 40 Percent; Goals Intact." _The Gazette_ 6(9):1,9-11.

1995c    "Library Presents Testimony on Capitol
         Visitor Center." The Gazette 6(26):1,
         10-11.

1995d    "JHB Testifies Before Joint Committee." The
         Gazette 6(45):1,11-15.

11/24/95
         "JHB: Staff is Essential to Security."
         The Gazette 6(43):1,7-8.

1996a    "LC Will Base Vision of for 2004 on Broad
         Mission." The Gazette 7(20):3-4,10.

1996b    "Reader Registration System Links Data."
         The Gazette 2/9/96, p.3.

1996c    "Traveling Exhibit Stirs Controversy." The
         Gazette 1/5/96:3.

1997     "Visitors Flock to the Library." The Gazette
         8(26):1,9.

Fischer, Michael M.J.
    1995    "Eye(I)ing the Sciences and Their Signifiers
            (Language, Tropes, Autobiographers)." In
            Technoscientific Imaginaries, George Marcus,
            ed. Chicago: University of Chicago Press.

Fiske, John.
    1989    Understanding Popular Culture. Boston:Unwin
            Hyman.

Flack, James K.
    1968    "The Formation of the Washington Intellectual
            Community, 1870-1898." Ph.D. dissertation,
            Wayne State University.

Foucault, Michel.
    1977    Language, Counter-Memory, Practice. Ithaca, NY:
            Cornell University Press.

1980    "The Eye of Power." In Power/Knowledge, ed. by
        Colin Gordon. New York: Pantheon Books.

1984    "What Is an Author?" In The Foucault Reader, ed.
        by Paul Rabinow. New York: Pantheon Books.

Franklin, Sarah.
1995    "Science as Culture, Cultures of Science." Annual
        Review of Anthropology 24:163-184.

Freeman, Carla.
2000    High Tech and High Heels in the Global Economy.
        Durham, NC: Duke University Press.

Friedland, Lewis A.
1996    "Electronic Democracy and the New Citizenship."
        Media, Culture & Society 18(2):185-212.

Furrie, Betty.
1994    Understanding MARC—Bibliographic. Washington,
        D.C.: Library of Congress cataloging Distribution
        Service.

Gaonkar, Dilip Parameshwar and Robert McCarthy, Jr.
1994    "Panopticism and Publicity." Public Culture

        6: 547-575.

Gawron, Jean Mark.
1993    Dream of Glass. New York: Harcourt, Brace and
        Company.

Geertz, Clifford.
1973    The Interpretation of Cultures. New York: Basic
        Books.

Gellner, Ernest.
1983    Nations and Nationalism. Oxford: Basil Blackwell.

Gibson, William.
1996    Idoru. New York: G.P. Putnam's Sons.

Giddens, Anthony.
1985    The Nation-State and Violence. Cambridge: Polity.

Ginsburg, Faye and Anna L. Tsing, eds.
1990    Uncertain Terms. Boston: Beacon Press.

Ginsburg, Faye and Rayna Rapp, eds.
1996    Conceiving the World Order. Berkeley:
        University of California Press.

Gitlin, Todd.
1987    The Sixties. New York: Bantam Books.

Gleick, Elizabeth.
1995    "She Spoke Volumes." Time 9/25/95:52.

Goffman, Erving.
1961    Asylums. Garden City: Doubleday/Anchor Books.

Goldberg, Carey.
1997    "What's Wrong With This Picture?" New York
        Times Magazine 5/18/97, 6, 32:3.

Goldberg, Stanley.
1986    "Catalog Conundrums: a user's view." In
        Automation at the Library of Congress: inside
        views, ed. by Suzanne Thorin. Washington: Library
        of Congress Professional Association.

Goode, James.
1974    The Outdoor Sculpture of Washington. Washington,
        D.C.: Smithsonian Institution Press.

Goodrum, Charles A.
1974    The Library of Congress. New York: Praeger
        Publishers.

1977    Dewey Decimated. New York: Crown Publishers,
        Inc.

Goonatilake, Susantha.
1991    The Evolution of Information: Lineages in Gene,
        Culture and Artefact. New York: Pinter Publishers.

Gordon, Avery.
1995    "The Work of Corporate Culture." Social Text
        13(3):3-29.

Greenhalgh, Paul.
    1988    Ephemeral Vistas. New York: Manchester University
              Press.

Gregory, Steven and Roger Sanjek (eds).
    1994    Race. New Brunswick, NJ: Rutgers University
              Press.

Grossman, Lawrence K.
    1995    The Electronic Republic. New York: Viking Press.

Gupta, Akhil and James Ferguson (eds.)
    1997    Anthropological Locations. Berkeley:
              University of California.

Gusterson, Hugh.
    1995    Nuclear Rites. Berkeley: University of California
              Press.

Habermas, Jurgen.
    1973    Legitimation Crisis. Boston: Beacon Press.

    1989    The Structural Transformation of the Public
              Sphere. Boston: MIT Press.

Hakken, David and Barbara Andrews.
    1993    Computing Myths and Class Realities. Boulder, CO:

              Westview Press.

Hall, Peter Dobkin.
    1993    "Organization as Artifact." In The Mythmaking
              Frame of Mind, ed. by James Gilbert, Amy Gilman,
              Donald Scott and Joan Scott. Belmont, CA:
              Wadsworth Publishing.

Hall, Stuart.
    1994    "Cultural Studies: Two Paradigms." In
              Culture/Power/History, ed. by Nicholas
              Dirks, Geoff Eley and Sherry Ortner. Princeton,
              NJ: Princeton University Press.

1996    "The Problem of Ideology." In <u>Stuart Hall:
Critical Dialogues in Cultural Studies</u>, ed.
by David Morley and Kuan-Hsing Chen.
New York: Routledge.

Ham, Debra N.
1994    <u>The African-American Mosaic</u>. Washington, D.C.:
Library of Congress.

Hammer, Michael and James Campy.
1993    <u>Reengineering the Corporation</u>. New York:
HarperBusiness.

Handler, Richard.
1988    <u>Nationalism and the Politics of Culture in Quebec</u>.
Madison: University of Wisconsin Press.

Hannerz, Ulf.
1992    <u>Cultural Complexity</u>. New York: Columbia
University Press.

Haraway, Donna.
1989a    <u>Primate Visions</u>. New York: Routledge.

1989b    "A Manifesto for Cyborgs." In <u>Coming to Terms</u>,
ed. by Elizabeth Weed. New York: Routledge
Press.

Harris, Marvin.
1968    <u>The Rise of Anthropological Theory</u>. New York.

Harrison, Taylor (ed.).
1996    <u>Enterprise Zones: critical positions on Star Trek</u>.

Boulder, CO: Westview Press.

Harvey, David.
1989    <u>The Condition of Postmodernity</u>. Cambridge:
Basil Blackwell.

Harvey, Lisa St. Clair.
1995    "Constructions of Person, Self and Identity in
Cyberspace." Paper presented at the American
Anthropological Association Meeting, Washington, D.C.

Hayden, Robert M.
   1996    "imagined communities and real victims."
           American Ethnologist 23(4):783-801.

Heiss, Harry G.
   1993    "Opening Personal Mail." The Gazette 4(39):
           2.

Held, David.
   1982    "Crisis Tendencies, Legitimation and the State."
           In Habermas, ed. by John Thompson and David Held.
           Boston: MIT Press.

Henry, Jules.
   1963    Culture Against Man. New York: Random House.

Henson, Bobby.
   5/15/92
           "LC Police Seek Staff Cooperation." The Gazette
           3(20):3.

Herzfeld, Michael.
   1992    The Social Production of Indifference. Chicago:
           University of Chicago Press.

Hess, David.
   1994    "Comments on Emily Martin's "The Ethnography of
           Natural Selection in the 1990s." Cultural
           Anthropology 9(3):398-401.

   1995    Science and Technology in a Multicultural World.
           New York: Columbia University Press.

Hiam, A.

   1990    The Vest-Pocket CEO. Englewood Cliffs, NJ:
           Prentice-Hall.

   1992    Closing the Quality Gap. Englewood Cliffs, NJ:
           Prentice-Hall.

Hilker, Helen-Anne.
   1972    "Monument to a Civilization." Quarterly Journal
           of the Library of Congress 29(4):234-266.

Himmelfarb, Gertrude.
    1968    Vitorian Minds. New York: Knopf.

Hobsbawm, Eric.
    1984    "Introduction: Inventing Tradition." In The
            Invention of Tradition. New York: Cambridge
            University Press.

Hobsbawm, Eric and Terence Ranger.
    1984    The Invention of Tradition. New York: Cambridge
            University Press.

Holton, Gerald.
    1993    Science and Anti-Science. Cambridge: Harvard
            University Press.

Hughes, T.
    1989    American Genesis. New York: Penguin Books.

Huxtable, Ada Louise.
    1986    Goodbye History, Hello Hamburger. Washington,
            D.C.: Preservation Press.

"Internet Policies of the Library of Congress."
            Memo available online. (gopher://marvel.loc.gov).

Jacob, Kathryn Allamong.
    1994    Capital Elites. Washington, D.C.: Smithsonian
            Institution Press.

Jameson, Fredric.
    1972    The Prison-House of Language. Princeton, NJ:
            Princeton University Press.

    1982    "Progress Versus Utopia." Science Fiction Studies
            9:147-158.

    1984    "Postmodernism, or the Logic of Late Capitalism."
            New Left Review 146: 53-92.
    1991    Postmodernism, Or the Logic of Late Capitalism.
            Durham, NC: Duke University Press.

"JHB Asks Staff to Help Tighten Security."
            9/8/95 The Gazette 6(33):1,4.

Johnson, Ronald M. and Gary D. Libecap.
1994    "Patronage to Merit and Control of the Federal
        Government Labor Force." Explorations in Economic
        History 31(1):91-120.

Jordan, John M.
1994    Machine-Age Ideology, Social Engineering and
        American Liberalism, 1911-1939. Chapel Hill,
        N.C.: University of North Carolina Press.

Keller, Evelyn Fox.
1985    Reflections on Gender and Science. New Haven:
        Yale University Press.

Keeler, Elissa and Robert Miller.
1996    Netscape Virtuoso. New York: MIS Press.

Kellner, Douglas.
1990    Television and the Crisis of Democracy.
        Boulder, CO: Westview Press.

Kennedy, James R. and Gloria Stockton (eds.).
1990    The Great Divide. Chicago: American Library
        Association.

King, Gilbert.
1963    Automation and the Library of Congress.
        Washington, D.C.: Library of Congress.

Kohlstedt, Sally Gregory.
1987    "International Exchange and National Style: A
        View of Natural History Museums in the United
        States, 1850-1900." In Scientific Colonialism,
        ed. by Nathan Reingold and Marc Rothenberg.
        Washington, D.C.: Smithsonian InstitutionPress.

Kolenda, Konstantin.
1987    Cosmic Religion. Prospect Heights, Ill.:
        Waveland Press.

Koster, Martin.
        "World Wide Web Robots, Wanderers, and Spiders."
        [online document]. Http://info.webcrawler.com/mak
        projects/robots/robots.html

Krohn, Roger.
  1981 "Introduction." In <u>The Social Process of</u>
     <u>Scientific Investigation</u>, Karin Knorr, Roger
     Krohn and Richard Whitley, eds. Boston: D.
     Reidel Publishing Company.

Kroker, Arthur and Michael A. Weinstein.
  1994 <u>Data Trash</u>. New York: St. Martin's Press.

Kuhn, Thomas.
  1970 <u>The Structure of Scientific Revolutions</u>.
     Chicago: University of Chicago Press.

Kuklick, Bruce.
  1972 "Myth and Symbol in American Studies." <u>American</u>
     <u>Studies</u> 24.

Kuznick, Peter J.
  1994 "Losing the World of Tomorrow: The Battle
     over the Presentation of Science at the
     1939 New York World's Fair." <u>American</u>
     <u>Quarterly</u> 46(3):341-373.

Ladurie, Emmanuel Le Roy.
  1995 "Introduction." In <u>Creating French Culture</u>,
     ed. by Tesnière and Gifford. New Haven:
     Yale University Press.

Lakoff, George and Mark Johnson.
  1980 <u>Metaphors We Live By</u>. Chicago: University of
     Chicago Press.

La Montagne, Leo.
  1961 <u>American Library Classification</u>. Hamden, CN:
     The Shoestring Press.

Lancaster, Roger.
  1988 <u>Thanks to God and the Revolution</u>. New York:
     Columbia University Press.

Langworthy, Jo Ann.
  1970 "A New Library Building for Congress." <u>Roll</u>
     <u>Call</u>, 3/19/70.

Latour, Bruno.
    1996    Aramis, Or the Love of Technology. Cambridge: Harvard University Press.

Latour, Bruno and Steve Woolgar.
    1979    Laboratory Life. Beverly Hills, CA: Sage Publications.

Lawton, Stephen.
    1991    "Being There: How Well Will Optical Disks Last? What Do Accelerated Ageing Tests Tell Us?" Inform (October): 25-27.

LeFebvre, Henri.
    1991    The Production of Space. New York: Basil Blackwell.

Lehman, Bruce A.
    1995    Intellectual Property and the National Information Infrastructure. Washington, D.C.: Information Infrastructure Task Force.

Leighton, Philip D.
    1986    Planning Academic and Research Libraries. Chicago: American Library Association.

Leone, Mark P.
    1987    "Rule by Ostentation." In History from Things, ed. by Steven Lubar and W. David Kingery. Washington, D.C.: Smithsonian Institution Press.

    1995    "A Historical Archaeology of Capitalism." American Anthropologist 97(2):251-268.

Lessig, Larry, David Post and Eugene Volokh.
    1996    "Cyberspace Law for Non-Lawyers." http://www.counsel.com/cyberspace

Levi-Strauss, Claude.
    1961    Tristes-Tropiques. New York: Atheneum.

"Librarian Requests 8.6% Budget Increase."
    1995    The Gazette 6(8):1,8-11.

Library of Congress.
  1872 Report of the Librarian of Congress Exhibiting
     the Progress of the Library During the Year
     Ended December 1, 1872. Washington, D.C.:
     Library of Congress.

  1898 Report of the Librarian of Congress for the Fiscal
     Year ended June 30, 1898. Washington, D.C.:
     Library of Congress.

  1905 Report of the Librarian of Congress and Report
     of the Superintendent of the Library Building
     and Grounds for the Fiscal Year Ending June 30,
     1905. Washington, D.C.: Library of Congress.

  1906 Report of the Librarian of Congress and Report
     of the Superintendent of the Library Building
     and Grounds for the Fiscal Year Ending June 30,
     1906. Washington, D.C.: Library of Congress.

  1907 Report of the Librarian of Congress and Report
     of the Superintendentr of the Library Building
     and Grounds for the Fiscal Year Ending June 30,
     1907. Washington, D.C.: Library of Congress.

  1910 Report of the Librarian of Congress and Report
     of the Superintendent of the Library Building
     and Grounds for the Fiscal Year Ending June 30,
     1910. Washington, D.C.: Library of Congress.

  1911 Report of the Librarian of Congress and Report
     of the Superintendent of the Library Building
     and Grounds for the Fiscal Year Ending June 30,
     1911. Washington, D.C.: Library of Congress.

  1918 Report of the Librarian of Congress and Report
     of the Superintendent of the Library Building
     and Grounds for the Fiscal Year Ending June 30,
     1918. Washington, D.C.: Library of Congress.

  1923 Report of the Librarian of Congress for the
     Fiscal Year Ending June 30, 1923. Washington,
     D.C.: Library of Congress.

1926    Report of the Librarian of Congress for the Fiscal Year Ending June 30, 1926. Washington, D.C.: Library of Congress.

1935    Report of the Librarian of Congress for the Fiscal Year Ending June 30, 1935. Washington, D.C.: Library of Congress.

1939    Annual Report of the Librarian of Congress for the Fiscal Year Ended June 30, 1938. Washington, D.C.: Library of Congress.

1946    Annual Report of the Librarian of Congress for the Fiscal Year Ending June 30, 1945. Washington, D.C.: Library of Congress.

1947    Annual Report of the Librarian of Congress for the Fiscal Year Ending June 30, 1946. Washington, D.C.: Library of Congress.

1948    Annual Report of the Librarian of Congress for the Fiscal Year Ending June 30, 1947. Washington, D.C.: Library of Congress.

1951    Annual Report of the Librarian of Congress for the Fiscal Year Ending June 30, 1950. Washington, D.C.: Library of Congress.

1952    Annual Report of the Librarian of Congress for the Fiscal Year Ending June 30, 1951. Washington, D.C.: Library of Congress.

1959    Annual Report of the Librarian of Congress for the Fiscal Year Ending June 30, 1958. Washington, D.C.: Library of Congress.

1961    Annual Report of the Librarian of Congress for the Fiscal Year Ending June 30, 1960. Washington, D.C.: Library of Congress.

1962    Annual Report of the Librarian of Congress for the Fiscal Year Ending June 30, 1961. Washington, D.C.: Library of Congress.

1963   Annual Report of the Library of Congress for the Fiscal Year Ending June 30, 1962. Washington, D.C.: Library of Congress.

1965   Annual Report of the Librarian of Congress for the Fiscal Year Ending June 30, 1964. Washington,

D.C.: Library of Congress.

1967   Annual Report of the Librarian of Congress for the Fiscal Year Ending June 30, 1966. Washington, D.C.: Library of Congress.

1968   Annual Report of the Librarian of Congress for the Fiscal Year Ending June 30, 1967. Washington, D.C.: Library of Congress.

1970   Annual Report of the Librarian of Congress for the Fiscal Year Ending June 30, 1969. Washington, D.C.: Library of Congress.

1986   A Tour of the Library of Congress. VHS, 22 min. Distributed by the Library of Congress Information Office.

1987   Annual Report of the Librarian of Congress for the Fiscal Year Ending September 30, 1986. Washington, D.C.: Library of Congress.

1988a   Annual Report of the Librarian of Congress for the Fiscal Year Ending September 30, 1987. Washington, D.C.: Library of Congress.

1988b   "Library's MAP Committee Issues Its Recommendations." Library of Congress Information Bulletin 47(49):485-493.

1991a   Annual Report of the Librarian of Congress for the Fiscal year Ending September 30, 1990. Washington, D.C.: Library of Congress.

1991b   Library of Congress Multi-Year Affirmative Action Plan. Unpublished report.

1992a   Annual Report of the Librarian of Congress for
        the Fiscal Year Ending September 30, 1991.
        Washington, D.C.: Library of Congress.

10/14/92
        "Special Announcement No. 92-19." Unpublished
        memo.

1992b   Library of Congress Strategic Plan, (1993-2000).
        Unpublished report.

1993a   Summary of Conference on Delivering Electronic
        Information in a Knowledge-Based Democracy.
        [Online] Available Gopher: gopher://marvel.loc.
        gov.

1993b   Manuscripts. Washington, D.C.: Library of
        Congress.

1995    Annual Report of the Librarian of Congress for
        the Fiscal Year Ending 30 September 1994.
        Washington, D.C.: Library of Congress.

1996    Annual Report of the Librarian of Congress for
        the fiscal year ending 30 September 1995.
        Washington, D.C.: Library of Congress.

1997    "Report on Core-Level Cataloging." LC Cataloging
        Newsline 5(2) [online].

2005    Annual Report of the Librarian of Congress for
        the fiscal year ending 30 September 2004.


Library of Congress Cataloging Forum.
        1993    Cataloging Quality Is . . . Five Perspectives.
                Washington, D.C.: Library of Congress.

"Library Offers 'Early Out' to Staff."
        10/1/93
                The Gazette 4(37):1,10.
"Library Postpones Freud Exhibition."
        12/8/95
                The Gazette. 6(45):15.

Lipsitz, George.
    1995   "The Possessive Investment in Whiteness."
           American Quarterly 47(3):369-387.

Logan, John R. and Harvey L. Molotch.
    1987   Urban Fortunes. Berkeley: University of
           California Press.

Lovejoy, Arthur O.
    1933   The Great Chain of Being. Harvard University.

Lyotard, Jean-François.
    1984   The Postmodern Condition. Manchester:

           Manchester University Press.

Lyotard, Jean-François and Jean-Loup Thebaud.
    1985   Just Gaming. Minneapolis: University of
           Minnesota Press.

MacLeish, Archibald.
    1945   "The Reorganization of the Library of Congress,
           1939-1944." Reprinted in Annual Report of the
           Librarian of Congress for the Fiscal Year
           Ending June 30, 1944. Washington, D.C.:
           Library of Congress.

Malinowski, Bronislaw.
    1961   Argonauts of the Western Pacific. New York: E.P.
           Dutton and Co.

Mandel, Carol.
    1991   "Cataloging for Access." The Reference Librarian:
           61-68.

Mandel, Ernest.
    1975   Late Capitalism. London.

Manes, Stephen.
    1996   "Science Times." New York Times 2/13/96, C,5:1.

Mann, Thomas.
 1991   "Cataloging Quality, LC Priorities, and Models of
        the Library's Future." Cataloging Forum Opinion
        Papers, No. 1. Washington, D.C.: Library of Congress.
 1993   Library Research Models: A Guide to
        Classification, cataloging, and Computers.
        New York: Oxford University Press.

 2006   "What is Going on at the Library of Congress?"
        Report prepared for AFSCME 2910.
        [www.guild2910.org]

Marcus, George R.
 1995   "Ethnography in/of the World System." Annual
        Review of Anthropology 24:95-117.

Marcus, George E. and Michael M.J. Fischer.
 1986   Anthropology as Cultural Critique. Chicago:
        University of Chicago Press.

Marin, Louis.
 1993   "Frontiers of Utopia: Past and Present." Critical

        Inquiry 19:397-420.

Marine, April, Susan Kirkpatrick, Vivian Neou and Carol Ward.
 1993   Internet: Getting Started. Englewood Cliffs, NJ:
        PTR Prentice-Hall.

Markus, Thomas.
 1993   Knowledge and Power. New York: Routledge Press.

Martin, Emily.
 1994   Flexible Bodies. Boston: Beacon Press.

 1997   "Anthropology and the Cultural Study of Science."
        In Anthropological Locations, ed. by Akhil Gupta
        and James Ferguson. Berkeley: University of
        California Press.

Marx, Leo.
    1964    The Machine in the Garden. New York: Oxford
            University Press.
Maybury-Lewis, David.
    1992    Millenium. New York: Viking.

McCaffery, Larry.
    1991    Storming the Reality Studio. Durham, North
            Carolina: Duke University Press.

McCarthy, Richard C.
    1995    Designing Better Libraries. Fort Atkinson, Wis.:
            Highsmith Press.

McDonald, Maryon.
    1989    "We Are Not French!" New York: Routledge.

McLuhan, Marshall.
    1962    The Gutenberg Galaxy. Toronto: University of
            Toronto Press.

Mead, Margaret.
    1928    Coming of Age in Samoa. New York: Morrow Quill
            Paperbacks.

Mearns, David.
    1947    The Story Up to Now. Washington, D.C.:
            Library of Congress.

Metoyer-Duran, Cheryl.
    1993    "Information Gatekeepers." Annual Review of
            Information Science and Technology 28: 111-150.

Miller, Elizabeth.
    1993a   History and Development of the Library of Congress
            Machine-Assisted Realization of the Virtual
            Electronic Library. Gopher://marvel.loc.gov.

    1993b   What is a Gopher? Gopher://marvel.loc.gov.

Miller, Page Putnam.
    1995    "Hearing Addresses Problems at the Library of
            Congress." NCC Washington Update    1(60)
            [online].

Miska, Francis.
1984    The Development of Classification at the Library
        of Congress. Urbana-Champaign: Occasional Papers,
        No. 164, University of Illinois Graduate School of
        Library and Information Science.

Mitchell, Timothy.
1991    Colonizing Egypt. Berkeley: University of
        California Press.

Nader, Laura.
1996    "The Three-Cornered Constellation." In Naked
        Science, Laura Nader, ed. New York: Routledge
        Press.

National Institute for Occupational Safety and Health.
1991    Indoor Air Quality and Work Environment Study:
        Library of Congress Madison Building.
        Cincinnati, OH: the National Institute for
        Occupational Safety and Health.

Nelson, Diane M.
1996    "Maya Hackers and the Cyberspatialized Nation-
        State." Cultural Anthropology 11(3):287-308.

Nelson, Josephus and Judith Farley.
1991    Full Circle: Ninety Years of Service in the Main
        Reading Room. Washington: Library of Congress.

Ness, Erik.

1994    "BigBrother@cyberspace." The Progressive
        December:22-27.

Noble, David.
1986    Forces of Production: A Social History of
        Industrial Automation. New York: Oxford
        University Press.

Norberg, Arthur L. and Judy E. O'Neill.
1996    Transforming Computer Technology. Baltimore:
        John Hopkins University Press.

NRENNAISSANCE Committee.
1994    Realizing the Information Future: the Internet and
        Beyond. Washington, D.C.: National Academy Press.

Nye, David.
1991    Electrifying America. Cambridge: The MIT Press.

1994    American Technological Sublime. Cambridge: The
        MIT Press.

Oder, Norman.
2004    Black Employees Criticize LC." Library Journal   129(12):
        18.

"Officials See Library Gains in the Past Year."
1995    The Gazette 6(1):1,9-11.

Ohnemus, Edward.
1992    "Rare Book Sleuth Finds Houdini Cases." The
        Gazette 3(22):1,10-11.

1995    "Library Fares Best in House Markup." The Gazette
        6(24):1,8-10.

6/21/96
        "Collections Security Report Released to LC."
        The Gazette 7(24):1,6.

Olaisen, Johan, Erland Munch-Peterson and Patrick Wilson, eds.
1995    Information Science. Olso, Norway: Scandinavian
        University Press.

Oleson, Alexandra.
1976    "Introduction." In The Pursuit of Knowledge in
        Early American Republic, ed. by Alexandra Oleson
        and Sanborn C. Brown. Baltimore: Johns Hopkins
        Press.

Orr, Eric M.
1996    Letter to the Editor. The Gazette 7(1):3.

Orser, Charles E, Jr. (ed.)
1990    "Historical Archaeology on Southern Plantations
        and Farms." Historical Archaeology 24(4).

Palladino, Grace.
1993    "Library of Congress Poses new Threats to
        Scholarship." Chronicle of Higher Education
        6/2/93:A40.

Pettee, Julia.
1946    Subject Headings: The History and Theory of the
        Alphabetical Subject Approach to Books. New York:
        The H.W. Wilson Company.

Pfaffenberger, Bryan.
1988    "The Social Meaning of the Personal Computer:
        Or, Why the Personal Computer Revolution Was
        No Revolution." Anthropological Quarterly 61(1):
        39-47.

1990    Democratizing Information: Online Databases and
        the Rise of End-User Searching. Boston: Hall
        Publishers.

Piore, Michael J.
1993    "Unions." In Labor Economics and Industrial
        Relations, ed. by Clark Kerr and Paul D.
        Staudohar. Boston: Harvard University Press.

Poole, W.F.
1881    "The Construction of Library Buildings." Library
        Journal 6(4):69-77.

Poster, Mark.
1990    The Mode of Information. Chicago: University of
        Chicago Press.

Postrel, Virginia.
1998    "Technocracy R.I.P." Wired 6.01: 52-56.

Pound, Christopher.
1995    "Imagining In-Formation." In Technoscientific
        Imaginaries. George Marcus, ed. Pp. 527-547.

        Chicago: University of Chicago Press.

Price, Richard and Sally Price.
1992    Equatoria. New York: Routledge.

"Psywar at the Library of Congress."
    1994    City Paper 12/9/94:8-9.

Rabinow, Paul.
    1989    French Modern. Cambridge: MIT Press.

    1996    Making PCR. Chicago: University of Chicago
            Press.

Ranganathan, S.R.
    1992    Librarian Looks Back. New Delhi: ABC Publishing
            House.

Redfield, Robert.
    1947    "The Folk Society." American Journal of
            Sociology 52(4):293-308.

Reneker, Maxine H.
    1993    "A Qualitative Study of Information Seeking
            Among Members of an Academic Community." Library
            Quarterly 63(4):487-507.

Rice, Pierce.
    1982    "Introduction: the Library of Congress as a
            Work of Art." In The Library of Congress: Its
            Architecture and Decoration, Herbert Small.
            New York: Norton.

Richard, Paul.
    1967    "Nazi Architecture Thrives on the Hill."
            Washington Post 9/3/67:E6.

Richards, Thomas.
    1993    The Imperial Archive. New York: Verso Press.

Ripley, Dillon.
    1970    The Sacred Grove. London: Victor Gollancz Ltd.

Rosaldo, Michelle Zimbalist.
    1974    "Women, Culture, and Society: A Theoretical
            Overview." In Woman, Culture, and Society,
            pp. 17-42. Stanford, CA: Stanford University
            Press.

Roseberry, William.
 1992    "Multiculturalism and the Challenge of
         Anthropology." Social Research 59(4):
         841-858.

 1996    "The Unbearable Lightness of Anthropology."
         Radical History Review 65:5-25.

Rosen, Brenda.
 1988    "The Age of the Information Broker." In
         Information Brokers and Reference Services, ed.
         by Robin Kinder and Bill Katz. New York: The
         Haworth Press.

Rosenberg, Jane Aikin.
 1993    The Nation's Great Library. Chicago: University
         of Illinois Press.

Rosenberg, Richard S.
 1992    The Social Impact of Computers. Boston: Academic
         Press.

Ross, Andrew.
 1996    "Introduction." Social Text 46/47(1-2):
         1-13.

Rydell, Robert.
 1987    All the World's a Fair. Chicago: University of
         Chicago Press.

Saffady, William.
 1988    Optical Disks vs. Micrographics as Document
         Storage & Retrieval Techniques. Westport,
         Conn.: Meckler.

Said, Edward.
 1979    Orientalism. New York: Vintage Press.

Salamanca, Lucy.
 1942    Fortress of Freedom. NY: J.B. Lippincott Company.

Sandstrom, Alan R. and Pamela Effrein Sandstrom.
 1995    "The Use and Misuse of Anthropological Methods in
         Library and Information Science Research."
         Library Quarterly 65(2):161-199.

Schiller, Dan.
    1988    "How to Think About Information." In
            The Political Economy of Information, ed. by
            Vincent Mosco and Janet Wasko. Madison:
            University of Wisconsin Press.

Schiller, Herbert.
    1981    Who Knows. Norwood, NJ: Ablex.

    1991    "Public Information Goes Corporate." Library
            Journal October: 42-45.

Schrader, A.M.
    1986    "The Domain of Information Science." Information
            Services and Use 6:169-205.

Segal, Howard.
    1994    Future Imperfect. Amherst: University of
            Massachusetts Press.

Sexton, Patricia Cayo.
    1991    The War on Labor and the Left. Boulder: Westview
            Press.

Shenk, David.
    1997    Data Smog. New York:HarperEdge.

Silver, David.
    1997    "Interfacing American Culture." American
            Quarterly 49(4).

Simon, Geoffrey.
    1992    "Closed Stacks: One Staffer's Reaction"
            (op-ed). The Gazette 5/29/92.

Singleton, Theresa (ed.)
    1985    The Archaeology of Slavery and Plantation Life.
            Orlando, FL: Academic Press.

Sloterdijk, Peter.
    1987    Critique of Cynical Reason. Minneapolis:
            University of Minnesota Press.

Small, Herbert.
1901    Handbook of the New Library of Congress.
        Boston: Curtis and Cameron.

Smith, Henry Nash.
1950    Virgin Land. Cambridge: Harvard University
        Press.

Smith, Michael A.
1996    "The Racist Library of Congress and Its Slave
        Exhibit." Afro-American 2/24/96, A, 5:1.

Smith, Rogers M.
1993    "Beyond Tocqueville." American Political Science
        Review 87(3):549-566.

Smithmeyer, John L.
1881    "The National-Library Building—The Proposed
        Plan." Library Journal 6(4):77-81.

Snow, C.P.
1959    The Two Cultures and the Scientific Revolution.
        Cambridge: Cambridge University Press.

Spivak, Gayatri Chakravorty.
1976    "Translator's Preface." In Of Grammatology, by
        Jacques Derrida. Baltimore: Johns Hopkins
        University Press.

"Stacks Crowded; Library Needs More Storage."
1995    The Gazette 6(22): 1,4.

Stephenson, Neal.
1992    Snowcrash. New York: Bantam Books.

Sterling, Bruce.
[online]
        "Cyberpunk in the Nineties." originally appearing
        in Interzone.

Stern, Joel and David Moore.
6/9/95
        "'Being a Library.'" Washington Post:A26.

"Steve Herman Explains Two Types of Stack Passes for Library Employees."
    1992   The Gazette 5/15/92, 3(20):1,10-11.

Stocking, George.
    1992   The Ethnographer's Magic and Other Essays in the

          History of Anthropology. Madison: University of
          Wisconsin Press.

Streitfeld, David.
    1992   "Dealer Held in Library of Congress Theft."
          Washington Post, 3/13/92, F 2:5.

    1995   "Library of Congress Theft Probe Deepens."
          Washington Post 8/17/95:C1,C3.

Studwell, William E.
    1990   Library of Congress Subject Headings: Philosophy,
          Practice, and Prospects. New York: The Haworth
          Press.

"Summary of MAP Committee Recommendations."
    1988   LC Information Bulletin 47(49).

Sutton, Brett.
    1995   "Computer Networking in the Eastern Caribbean."
          Paper presented at the American Anthropological
          Association Meeting, Washington, D.C.

Suvin, Darko.
    1988   Positions and Presuppositions in Science Fiction.
          Kent, Ohio: Kent State University Press.

Tabb, Winston.
    1996   "Rest of the Story." Chicago Tribune 1/22/96:
          1, 14:6.

Taussig, Michael.
    1993   Mimesis and Alterity: A Particular History of the
          Senses. New York: Routledge Press.

    1996   The Magic of the State. New York: Routledge
          Press.

"The Guts of the Digital Library."
    1995    The Gazette 54(12):262-265,279.

Thomas, Hugh.
    1983    The Case for the Round Reading Room. London: Centre for Policy Studies.

"Three Speakers Tout LC's Optical Disk program."
    1992    The Gazette 3(30).

Toffler, Alvin.
    1990    Powershift. New York: Bantam Books.

Trachtenberg, Alan.
    1965    Brooklyn Bridge. New York: Harvard University Press.
Traube, Elizabeth.
    1992    Dreaming Identities. Boulder, CO: Westview Press.

Traweek, Sharon.
    1988    Beamtimes and Lifetimes. Cambridge: Harvard University Press.

    1996    "Unity, Dyads, Triads, Quads, and Complexity." Social Text 46/47(1-2).

Triplett, William.
    1997    "Hurston Plays Discovered." Washington Post, April 24:B2.

Truett, Randall Bond (ed.).
    1968    Washington, D.C. New York: Hastings House.

Tsing, Anna L.
    1993 In the Realm of the Diamond Queen. Princeton, NJ: Princeton University Press.

Turkle, Sherry.
    1984    The Second Self. New York: Simon and Schuster.

Turner, Terence.
    1993    "Anthropology and Multiculturalism." Cultural Anthropology 8(4):411-429.

Turner, Victor.
    1957    Schism and Continuity in an African Society.
              Manchester: University of Manchester Press.

    1967    The Forest of Symbols. Ithaca, NY: Cornell
              University Press.

    1974    Dramas, Fields, and Metaphors. Ithaca: Cornell
              University Press.

Tylor, E.B.
    1871    Primitive Culture. London.

"2477 Bargaining Makes History."
    11/29/91
           The Gazette 2(45):1,11+.

U.S. Congress.
    1964    Legislative Branch Appropriations for 1965.
              88th Cong., 2nd Session. Washington, D.C.:GPO.

    1965    James Madison Memorial Library of Congress
              Building. 89th Cong., 1st Sess. Washington,
              D.C.: GPO.

    1966    Legislative Branch Appropriations for 1967.
              89th Cong., 2nd Sess. Washington, D.C.: GPO.

    1967    Legislative Branch Appropriations for 1968.
              90th Cong., 1st Sess. Washington, D.C.:
              GPO.

    1968    Legislative Branch Appropriations for 1969.
              90th Cong., 2nd Sess. Washington, D.C.: GPO.

    1969    Legislative Branch Appropriations for 1970.
              91st Cong., 1st Sess. Washington, D.C.: GPO.

    1970    Legislative Branch Appropriations for 1971.
              91st Cong., 2nd Sess. Washington, D.C.: GPO.

    1979    Proposed Reorganization of the Library of
              Congress. Washington, D.C.:GPO.

1987    Legislative Branch Appropriations for 1988.
        100th Cong., 1st Sess. Washington, D.C.:
        GPO.

1990    Legislative Branch Appropriations for 1991.
        101st Cong., 2nd Sess. Washington, D.C.:
        GPO.

1994a   Testimony on Library of Congress Security
        Proposals and Policies. 103rd Cong., 1st Sess.
        Washington, D.C.:GPO.

1994b   Slow Progress Toward Workforce Diversity at the
        Library of Congress. 103rd Cong., 2nd Sess.
        Washington, D.C.:GPO.

Vale, Lawrence.
    1992    Architecture, Power, and National Identity.
            New Have, CN: Yale University Press.

Virilio, Paul.
    1996    The Art of the Motor. Minneapolis: University
            of Minnesota Press.

Vlach, John Michael.
    1993    Back of the Big House. Chapel Hill: University
            of North Carolina Press.

Waldinger, Roger, Chris Erickson, Ruth Milkman, Daniel J.B. Mitchell,
Abel Valenzuela, Kent Wong, and Maurice Zeitlin.
    1997    "Justice for Janitors." Dissent winter:37-44.

Weber, Max.
    1946    From Max Weber, ed. by H. Gerth and C. Wright
            Mills. New York: Oxford University Press.

Webster, Frank.
    1995    Theories of Information Society. New York:
            Routledge.

Weeks, Christopher.
    1994    AIA Guide to the Architecture of Washington, D.C.
            Baltimore: Johns Hopkins University Press.
Weeks, Linton.

1995a"The Continuing Hurt of History." <u>Washington Post</u> 12/22/95: C1,5.

1995b"In a Stack of Troubles." <u>Washington Post</u>, 12/27/95:F1,F4.

1996    "Report Throws the Book at the Library of Congress." <u>Washington Post</u>, 4/29/96, B1:5.

Welsch, Erwin K.
1992    "Hypertext, Hypermedia, and the Humanities." <u>Library Trends</u> 40(4): 614-646.

White, Herbert S.
1996    "Do We Want to Be Knowledge Workers?" <u>Library Journal</u> 121:41-42.

Williams, Brett.

1976    "Serving Up Selves and Preserving the Self." <u>Journal of the Steward Anthropological Society</u>.

1992    "Poverty Among African Americans in the Urban United States." <u>Human Organization</u> 51:164-174.

1994    "Babies and Banks." In <u>Race</u>, ed. by Steven Gregory and Roger Sanjek. New Brunswick, NJ: Rutgers University Press.

Wolf, Eric.
1982    <u>Europe and the People Without History</u>. Berkeley: University of California Press.

Wolf, Gary.
1995    "The Curse of Xanadu." <u>Wired</u> 3.06: 137-152,194-202.

Wolf, Milton.
[online document]
    "Cyberpunk: Information as God."
    http://www.ala.org/alayou/publications/
    alaeditions/openstacks/cybrary/cyberpunk

World Bank.
1990    <u>World Development Report 1990: Poverty</u>. New York: Oxford University Press.

Works Progress Administration.
    1983    W.P.A. Guide to Washington, D.C. NY: Pantheon
            Books.

Wurman, Richard Saul.
    1989    Information Anxiety. New York: Doubleday.

Wynar, Bohdan S.
    1972    Introduction to Cataloging and Classification.
            Littleton, CO: Libraries Unlimited, Inc.

Xiang, Biao.
    2005    Global "Body Shopping". Princeton, NJ: Princeton
            University Press.

Young, James Sterling.
    1966    The Washington Community. New York: Harcourt
            Brace Jovanovich.

Zinn, Howard.
    1995    A People's History of the United States.
            New York: HarperPerennial.

Zuboff, Shoshana.
    1988    In the Age of the Smart Machine. New York:
            Basic Books.

Zukin, Sharon.
    1991    Landscapes of Power. Berkeley: University of
            California Press.

# INDEX

# T

Taylorist management, 32, 80, 104
Text, 5, 15-18, 22, 36, 67, 69, 74-
    75, 104-105
Theft, 131-138
THOMAS, 87, 95n, 100, 104
TQM (Total Quality Manage-
    ment), 130, 147
Trolling, 112

# U

Unions, labor, 118, 121, 126-129
User studies, 109-110, 120, 133
Utopia, 9, 23, 26, 31, 34n, 35, 58,
    64-70, 105, 107, 114, 154

# V

Virtual library, 87-144

# X

Xerox (corporation), 94, 148, 151

# W

Washington, D.C., 2, 16, 38, 42,
    79, 80, 140
    Mall, 32, 38, 42
Wikipedia, 99
Wired (magazine), 112
Works Progress Administration,
    63

## ABOUT THE AUTHOR

Samuel Gerald Collins is a cultural anthropologist at Towson University. His research includes cybernetics, information society, globalization and the future. He is the author of *All Tomorrow's Cultures: Anthropological Engagements With the Future* (Berghahn Books, 2008), and the co-editor of *Agent-Based Societies: Social and Cultural Interactions* (IGI Global, 2009). He is a life-long bibliophile, and is raising his two children to love libraries.